Islamic Law Practice and Procedure in Nigerian Courts

Revised Second Edition

Malthouse Law Books

Abdulrazaq, M T, *Revenue Law and Practice in Nigeria*
Adah, C E, The Nigerian Law of Evidence
Akande, I. O., Local go*vernment law and policy in Nigeria: cases and materials*
Asuzu, C., *Fair Hearing in Nigeria*
Bambale, Y Y, *Crimes and Punishments under Islamic Law*
Bambale, Y. Y., *An Outline of Islamic Jurisprudence*
Bambale, Y. Y., *Islamic Law Relating to Property and Commercial Transactions*
Beredugo, A.J., *Nigerian legal system: an introductory text*
Emiri, F, & Deinduomo, G., *Law, Oil and Development Challenges in Nigeria*
Emiri, F. & Deinduomo, G., *Law and Petroleum Industry in Nigeria*
Emiri, F., *The Law of Restitution in Nigeria*
Emiri, F., *Law and Medical Ethics in Nigeria*
Emiri, F., *Equity and Trusts Law in Nigeria*
Fogam, P, *Law of Contract*
Goldface-Irokalibe, I.J., *The Law of Banking in Nigeria*
Gurin, A. M., *An Introduction to Islamic Family Law*
Igweike, K, *Nigerian Commercial Law: Agency*
Igweike, K, *Nigerian Commercial Law: Contract*
Igweike, K, *Nigerian Commercial Law: Hire Purchase*
Ikoni, U.D., *An Introduction to Nigerian Environmental Law*
Ladan, M.T., *Introduction to Jurisprudence: classical and Islamic*
Maidoh, D.C., Oho, F. et al, *Judicial Administration and Other Legal Issues in Nigeria*
Nkum, K.J., *Nigerian legal system: contemporary developments and challenges*
Okoh, Sheriff E. E. *Succession under Islamic Law*
Olong, Adefi M, *Administrative Law in Nigeria: an introduction*
Olong, Adefi M., *The Nigerian Legal System: an introduction*
Omorogbe, Yinka, *Oil and Gas Law in Nigeria*
Omotesho, Aboaba, *The Law of Tort in Nigeria: Selected Themes*
Sagay, I, *Law of Succession and Inheritance*
Sagay, I, *Nigerian Family Law: Principles, Cases, Statutes and Commentaries*
Utuama, A A, *Nigerian Law of Real Property*
Utuama, A A, *The Law of Trusts and their Uses in Nigeria*
Utuama, A. A., *Planning Law in Nigeria*
Uvieghara E E, *Labour Law in Nigeria*
Uvieghara E E, *Sale of Goods (& Hire Purchase) Law in Nigeria*
Yalaju, J.G., *Media law in Nigeria*

Islamic Law Practice and Procedure in Nigerian Courts

Revised Second Edition

Adamu Abubakar Esq.

malthouse *ℳℙ*

Malthouse Press Limited

Lagos, Benin, Ibadan, Jos,Port-Harcourt, Zaria

© Adamu Abubakar Jr 2017
First published 2009
Revised Second Edition 2017
978-978-958-444-4
Published and manufactured in Nigeria by

Published by
Malthouse Press Limited
43 Onitana Street, Off Stadium Hotel Road,
Surulere, Lagos, Lagos State
E-mail: malthouse_press@yahoo.com
malthouselagos@gmail.com
Tel: +234-802 600 3203

Dedication

My Mentor
Sheikh Yusuf Abdullahi Lokoja

My Father
Malam Garba (Muqaddam) Adamu
(Rahmatul Lahi Alaihi)

My Mother
Halima Malam Garba
(Rahmatul Lahi Alaiha)

Acknowledgements

I wish to acknowledge the support, help, encouragement, assistance and advice I received from the followings (and others too numerous to mention) during the research, documentation, writing and compilation of this work.

Hon. Justice A.B. Wali, Justice of the Supreme Court of Nigeria (rtd). Hon. Justice I.T.Muhammad. Justice of the Supreme Court of Nigeria, Hon. Justice Tijjani Abubakar, the Chief Judge & Chairman Jigawa State Judicial Service Commission for proof reading the manuscript & for their encouragement and advice, Barrister Abubakar O. Othman, M. S. Waziri Esq. and Bashir Mohammed Esq. for their encouragement and help in proof reading and with many useful suggestions as to style and contents, Recheal Njoku and Hasana Kehinde for typing the manuscript and Bello S. Tama for typesetting and graphic works. Alkali Mahmoud Sadiq. Ustaz Daudu.

I am also grateful to the publishers of various law reports in Nigeria, authors of Islamic Law books to whose works I have made reference. I am deeply indebted to:

A.A. Ambali, G.K. of the Kwara State Sharia Court of Appeal, to whose judgements and publications I made considerable reference of.

Supreme Court of Nigeria Judgments (SCN) published by Liberty Publishers Ltd.

Nigeria Weekly Law Reports (NWLR) published by the Nigerian Law Publishers Ltd.

All Federation Weekly Law Reports (ALL FWLR) published by New Century Law Books Publishers Ltd.

Sharia Law Reports by Yahaya Mahmoud

Sarauniya Law Reports by Hapsatu Sule Ahman.

Islamic Law Reports (ILR) by Dan Musa M.A. All other Islamic Books too many to mention, and indeed my family for their patience and understanding.

Preface to the First Edition

In the name Allah, Most Gracious, Most Merciful, Peace and blessings of Allah be upon his Messenger and Peace be on his Companions.

This book is a first attempt to bring together classical Islamic law of practice and procedure of Maliki school of thought into direct consort with decisions of superior courts such as the Supreme Court, Court of Appeal, High Court and in some instance decisions of the Sharia courts of Appeal, where relevant.

It is however been difficult venturing into because the whole idea is in my view a novelty as there are no enough English materials except those on Islamic theology (Figh) which are mostly in Arabic and secondly it is challenging because of my inadequacy in Arabic language considering that most of the available materials on the subject are in Arabic. This is not to say that, the rules of procedure and evidence by which Sharia is administered in courts were not well defined in the writings of Muslims jurists of the Maliki School. Indeed they exist and were backed up by the injunctions of the Holy Quran and Sunnah.

Nonetheless, with the little I have of Arabic language which enabled me to consult some of the books on the subject of this book, and plethora of case laws arising from the decisions of our eminent justices, judges and scholars of note, I ventured into the task of putting together this book to be known as *Islamic Law; The Practice And Procedure In Nigerian Courts.*

The book is also an attempt to debunk the notion that Islamic law does not have separate rules of procedure as it exists in English Common law. Contrary to that notion, therefore Islamic law being divine has peculiar features not found in any other law. Every class of its substantive law be it of personal status, property, commercial and criminal such as "Hudud" related, has its corresponding rules of procedure which in itself is not detachable from the rules of evidence thereby making dispensation of Islamic justice far more faster than it is obtained in English law.

What I have tried to do in this book is to extract the rules of procedure and evidence under Maliki school as practically as possible and discuss each with relation to the substantive law, this effort is duly supported and explained with judicial authorities and references to the various texts on Sharia not limited to those texts in Arabic but as discussed by Nigerian scholars, jurists and judicial authorities. I have also employed "Sharia" and "Islamic Law" interchangeably because of my belief that the two represent same thing.

It would be observed that the administrative aspect of Area and Sharia practices are conspicuously left out of this book. It is deliberate as this book is intended only to discuss practice and procedure of the courts as obtained in the court rooms.

In compiling the materials for this book I made adequate comparison between a more recent Sharia Courts (Civil Procedure) Rules as enacted by some Northern States which re-designated the Area Court (Civil Procedure) Rules of 1971 to suit the emerging new approach to the practice of Sharia in the Sharia Courts. The book is a ready practice book on matters before Area or Sharia courts in which Islamic law is to be applied.

It would be appreciated if short comings in this book can be brought to my attention for improvement in the revised edition.

I owe my gratitude to Allah the Most High for giving me the ability to venture into this project and thanks to Hon. Justice Idris Legbo Kutigi, the Chief Justice of Nigeria, for agreeing to write the foreword to this book and for his encouragement.

I still remain solely responsible for any inaccuracy this work may contain.

Adamu Abubakar, ESQ.

Preface to the Second Edition

In the name of Allah, Most Gracious, most merciful, peace and blessing of Allah be upon His massager and His companions.

The first edition of this book was first unveiled to the reading public in the year 2010. The book has since under gone scrutiny from eminent jurists, scholars and general readers. We have in review of this 2nd edition taken the hint and thus made necessary corrections in addition to improvement made to some parts of the book. This we have done believing that no book is ever the product of a single individual.

In this edition, new additional chapter sixteen, which is dedicated to partition of estate of a deceased has been added. The area which forms the bulck of disputes in cases of inheritance.The subject of guarantee has also been added as a part.The need for Sharia Judges to reserve Judgment in inheritance cases until ofter allotment of shares rather than make it secondary issue.

We have, however maintained the character of the book as in the 1st Edition. Once again my gratitude goes to Almighty Allah the most High for giving me the ability to review this book and to those who contributed to the review exercise including those who by way of criticisms offered some advice. I say thank you, may Allah reward you all and particularly to Grand Kadi of Sharia court of Appeal, Kano State. I appreciate your kind advice

Adamu Abubakar Esq.

Foreword to the First Edition

I have had the opportunity of reading in manuscripts the book written and assembled by Adamu Abubakar Esq, Barrister and Solicitor of the Supreme Court of Nigeria and given the title *Islamic Law Practice and Procedure in Nigerian Courts.*

This well researched book, is comprehensive and authoritative on Islamic Rules of Procedure and Evidence, presented uniquely from a variety of judgments, rulings and dicta of judges of superior courts of record in Nigeria as well as quotations from various books of Islamic theology, "*Fiqh*" of Maliki School, writings and opinions of jurists, scholars and authors, local and international. The author has divided the book into seventeen chapters, with a number of parts and paragraphs numbered consecutively and succinctly to make for easy reading and reference.

The book so lucidly written is essentially a Practitioner's working tool on the practice and procedure of Islamic Law in our various courts in the country. It will also serve as a handy reference book for use by Judges, Jurists as well as legal practitioners, Muslims and non-Muslims a like, when faced with cases before Sharia Courts, Area Courts and Sharia Courts of Appeal. Islamic law teachers as well as law students, will find the work handy and a useful tool in their research works. Administrator of Area and Sharia Courts would as well find the book a useful guide in their day to day administration of these Courts.

The book is the best of its kind written and produced in English language on the subject matter. Undoubtedly the book has enriched an area of scarce authorship on Islamic law and practice. I recommend it to the Bar, the Bench and all and sundry.

Hon. Justice Idris L. Kutigi, GCON
Chief Justice of Nigeria
Supreme Court of Nigeria, Three Arms Zone, Abuja.   *1 March 2008*

Foreword to the Second Edition

Bismillahi Al-Rahmani Al-Rahimi. It is a great honour and privilege to be asked to write the Foreword to the Second Edition to the book, *Islamic Law Practice and Procedure in Nigerian Courts* authored by Adamu Abubakar Esq.

The First Edtion of this book came on stream in the year 2010, when it was formally unveiled to the reading public. Even then, I was privileged to be part of the event marking its presentation having been assigned to review the book at the occasion in my capacity as a Kadi of the Sharia Court of Appeal, Kano.

Once again, I have been called upon to write the foreward to a book which was earlier described by his lordship, Honourable Justice Idris L. Kutigi GCON the Chief Justice of Nigeria as "….essentially a practitioner's working tool on the practice and procedure of Islamic Law in our various courts in the country."

His lordship's description is apt, cogent and indeed unimpeachable. As Grand Kadi of the Sharia Court of Appeal, I with utmost responsibility adopt this description for this 2nd Edition without hesitation.

The book which I may also describe as "practice of Shaira made simple" enhances, undoubtely the knowledge of sharia and its practice in sharia courts in Nigeria. This is a rare effort and achievement by the author who to my understanding is identified and associated more with the practice of sharia in our sharia courts.

The book, in addition to being essentially a practitioner's working tool is a reference for use by judges, Jurists, Legal Practitioners and students of Sharia as well.

The author has indeed succeeded in producing a handy reference book that provides a useful Sharia Practice in Courts. I congratulate him for achieving this enviable feat.

Alh. Abdullahi Wayya
The Grand Kadi
*   Sharia Court of Appeal,* Ka

Table of Cases

Ayanda *v* Akanji (2002) LRNN 209; 39
Awoyele *v.* Ogunbiyi (1986) 2 NWLR (Pt. 24) 626 at 636; 117
Baba *v.* Baba (1991) 9 NWLR 248; 79
Babayo *v.* Diddi (1997) 1 NWLR (pt.488)
Balarabe *v.* Audu (1997) 10 NWLR (pt. 524) ; 144
Balarabe *v.* Balarabe (2006) 3 SLR (pt. 1) 248 ; 173
Balarabe D/Zungura *v.* Dano D/Zungura (1973) NSNLR 160 ; 76
Balarabe Mazada *v* Sule A. Garba & 5 ors. (2006) SLR (pt.21) ; 174
Balan Ayye & 1 or. Vs. Musa Yar'Adua (1991) 8 NWLR (pt.210); 171
Beli *v.* Umar (2005) ALL FWLR (pt.920)1512; 65, 193
Ben Ikpang *v.* Chief Sam Edoho & 1 or. (1978) 67 & SC 221; 193
Biri *v.* Mairuwa (1996) 8 NWLR (pt.467) 425; 52, 183
Boyi Umar *v.* Aisha Bakashi (2006) 3 SLR (pt.1)
Bulunkutu *v.* Zangina Lior CA/J/37/5/95
Chamberlain *v.* Abdullahi Danfulani K/57A/75 ; 164
Danbaba *v.* Sale (2004) ALL FWLR (pt.226) 1915; 64
Dandume *v.* Adamu (1997)10 NWLR (pt. 525) 452 CA 119; 66
Dauda *v.* Asabe (1998)1 NWLR (pt. 532) 102; 146
Dutsi & 6 Ors *v.* Tofa & 4 ors. (2000) LRNN 406; 35, 36
Emmanuel *v.* Gomez (2003)2 NWLR (pt. 803)
Ezekiel Hart *v.* Ezekiel Hart (1990) 1 NWLR 279; 45
Fatayinbo *v.* Osadeyi (2002) FwLR (pt.110) 1770; 177
First Bank Nig, v, Tsakwa 2003 FWLR pt. 153 205; 23
Garba Maina *v.* Hajia Falta & Ali Abana BOS/SCA/CV/73/2003; 93
Gulma *v.* Bahago (1993)1 NWLR (pt.272) 766; 146
Gunbi *v.* Doro (1992) 3 NWLR (pt.228) 190 CA; 112
Govt. of Oyo State *v.* Akinyemi (2003) 1 NWLR (pt.800) 1; 177
Hada *v.* Malumfashi (1993)7 SCNJ (pt.11); 18, 79, 144
Hajiya Talle *v.* Bagobiri Bakori (1989) ILR ; 123
Hakimin Boyi v. Bakoshi 2006 3 SLR; 165
Hako *v.* Adamawa NA (1957) NRNLR 113
Haruna *v.* Nana (1996) 1 SCNJ 135; 77, 143
Husain *v.* Bagade CA/K/798/89; 14
Ibani *v.* Kano Native Authority (1958) NRNLR 61; 91, 135
Ibodo *v.* Enarofi (1980) 5-7 SC 92; 191
Ige *v.* Dobi (1999) 3 NWLR (pt.550) 550 CA ; 187
Jatau *v.* Mailafiya (1998) SCNJ 48 ; 66
Jindun *v.* Abuna (2000) 10 SCNJ 14 ; 64
Jushi *v.* Jushi (2006) 3 SLR (pt.1) 153 ; 79
Kabara *v.* Kabara (2006)3 SLR (pt.1) 115 ; 120, 134

Table of Statutes

Table of Contents

Chapter 13 - Hearsay Evidence

Chapter 14 - Oath

Chapter 1

Rules of Procedure

PART I
Introduction

Islamic law was prior to the 1979 Constitution of the Federal Republic of Nigeria a Regional law, christened by British colonisers simply and wrongly too as "Native Law and Custom". Section 1(2) of the High Court Law, Cap. 49 Laws of the Northern Nigeria defined native law and custom to include "Moslem Law". Islamic law was also under the Law subjected to all sorts of validity test including repugnancy test.

When however the 1979 Constitution came into effect its regional base was replaced by the Constitution which for the first time accorded the law a national status and recognition pursuant to Section 242(2). In the same regard Section 6(5)(e) of the 1999 Constitution of the Federal Republic of Nigeria created and accorded Sharia Court of Appeal a status of superior court of record in Nigeria.

It was to this end that the Supreme Court of Nigeria in *Alkamawa* v. *Bello & 1 Or.* (1998) 6 SCNJ 127, concluded that "Islamic law is not the same as customary law as it does not belong to any particular tribe. It is a complete system of universal law, more certain and permanent and more universal than English Common Law. The Court further went on "…on the principles of notoriety the law has gained acceptance and recognition by both the inferior and the superior courts in Nigeria that judicial notice of it can be taken…"

The Sharia Judicial System has before now undergone significant transformations, ranging from the functions of the courts to the changes in their nomenclature i.e. rising from its pre-colonial status of Alkali courts, to native courts, then to area courts and now to sharia courts in some states of the North. The Sharia Courts, came into being soon after the Zamfara State of the North in 1999, introduced a full sharia legal system and following the adoption of same in other States of the North, notably, Bauchi, Borno, Gombe, Jigawa, Kaduna, Kano, Katsina, Niger and Yobe states, Area Courts in these states were renamed Sharia Courts. Other States such as Adamawa, Benue, Kogi, Kwara, Nasarawa, Plateau, Taraba, and Abuja the Federal Capital Territory retained the existing Area Courts structure.

In place of Area Courts Law 1967 and Area Courts (Civil Procedure) Rules 1971, Sharia Courts Laws and Sharia Courts (Civil Procedure) Rules, Sharia Penal Codes and Sharia Criminal Procedure Codes, came into being. It is significant to note that, apart from Order II and change in nomenclature, all other provisions of the rules remained materially the same with the old Area Court Rules and procedure. The process of adjudication of civil cases and indeed criminal cases based on the principles of Islamic law in Area Courts and Sharia Courts remained the same, except for few amendments to the CPC. The other difference being that the Sharia states enacted separate Sharia Penal Code for Muslims only, while Penal Code continued to apply to Muslims and non-Muslims in other courts.

Traditionally, law is classified between substantive and adjectival laws.[1] While the former defines the right and liabilities of person, the latter consists of rules of procedure which regulate the way and manner in which those rights and liabilities may be given effect to, implemented and enforced in proceedings before the court. In other words, rules of procedure lay down the methods by which proceedings are commenced, determined and executed.

Procedure

The adjectival law which is the subject matter of this book is in turn divided into the law of procedure and the law of evidence. Broadly speaking the law of procedure regulates the steps which must be taken by parties in litigation from the time that the plaintiff commences his proceedings to the time when judgment is given and when it is to be enforced against the unsuccessful party, while the law of evidence concern the proof of facts in court. Under the English law, the rules of procedure and evidence are distinct that one could apply in a given case without reference to the other. Contrary however, to the position of English law, the Islamic law rules of procedure and law of evidence "*Murafat*", though ultimately serve the same objective are so intimately mixed up, that they are inseparable in both interpretation and application in court. Further, there is no difference between what exist distinctly, in English law as civil and criminal procedures. The processes in Islamic law have no dividing line; it is the same rules of procedure that are applicable in both civil "*Huquq Al-Adamiyyi*" and criminal "*Hudud* Offences". These rules however find their application more in Area and Sharia Courts[2] in Nigeria.

Evidence

Evidence is about the rules and use of evidence in the proof of civil or criminal right, duty and or liability before a court of law or judicial tribunal. It is accepted

---

[1] *Civil Procedure* by P. St. S. Langan & D. G. Lawrence 2nd Edition S/Maxwell 1976
[2] See Sharia Penal Code Laws of Kano, Zamfara, and Sokoto, etc.

both in Islamic law and English law that evidence is the surest means by which facts are proved before a court of law either in civil or criminal proceedings. It is therefore a necessary component of the rules of procedure. This suggests that any breach of the rules of evidence is tantamount to a breach of rules of natural justice and as such may render a judgment obtained therefrom void and can be set aside on appeal. In Islamic law therefore, fairness and justice in any given case is determined by the process through which they are attained. This is because Islamic law places emphasis upon the process of trial much as it does on the attainment of justice. Further, rules of court are for faster dispensation of justice, they are meant to guide the practice and procedure of the court, and that includes application of evidence.

The primary source of Nigerian Law of Evidence is the Evidence Act. It is pursuant to item 23 of the Second Schedule to the 1999 Constitution of the Federal Republic of Nigeria, an Act of the National Assembly. On the other hand, the primary source of Islamic Law of evidence is from divine texts of the Holy Qur'an and the Tradition of the Holy Prophet (SAW). While the Evidence Act applies or is administered in all courts it however excluded its application in or before Area Courts and Sharia Courts. Section 256(2)(c) of the Evidence Act, Laws of the Federation of Nigeria 2011, made the Evidence Act inapplicable in any civil cause or matter in or before any Sharia Courts of Appeal and Area Courts. It provides thus:

> "This Act shall apply to all judicial proceedings in or before any court established in the Federal Republic of Nigeria but it shall not apply:
> a) x x x x x
> b) x x x x x
> c) To judicial proceedings in any civil cause or matter in or before any Sharia Court of Appeal...Area Court...or...unless the President, or the Governor of a State by order published in the Gazette, confers upon any or all Sharia Courts of Appeal...or Area Court...or...n the Federal Capital Territory Abuja or a State as the case may be have powers to enforce any or all the provisions of this Act."

Area Courts and by extension Sharia Courts are to be guided by the rules of Evidence Act, in criminal cases and to be bound by Sections 135, 136, 137, 138, 139, and 140 of the Act. What this suggests therefore, is that Islamic rules of procedure and evidence are fully applicable in the Area and Sharia Courts in Nigeria and there exist no basis for any reference to the Evidence Act in any proceeding before Sharia Court. The Supreme Court in *Nuhu* v. *Ogele*[3], held:

---

[3] (2003) 18 NWLR (pt.852) 251

"The provision of section 1(2)(c) (now 256 (2) (c) of the Evidence Act does not apply in Area Courts in any civil proceedings but the provisions of the Constitution that have procedural and evidential flavour are applicable in the Area Courts."

Consequently, Islamic law of evidence is the applicable law of evidence in any civil proceedings before Area and Sharia Courts except where it contravenes the provisions of the Constitution on fair hearing, that is to say that any part of Evidence Act which emphasizes on fair hearing is applicable in Area and Sharia Courts in civil proceeding notwithstanding the provisions of Section 256(2) and (c). It also shows that Islamic law of evidence as applicable in matters of personal status is not contrary to the rules of natural justice and indeed recognized by the Evidence Act.

The application of Islamic Law

Order 11 Part 1 of the Area Court (Civil Procedure) Rules 1971, enjoined application of Moslem practice and procedure where a matter before the court involves a Muslim and subject of dispute is of Muslim nature. It provides:

Part 1:   Moslem cases: "After the provisions of Order 10 (presentation of case to defendant) have been complied with, then if the case is one in which Moslem law is to be administered or applied, the court shall continue the hearing in accordance with Moslem practice and procedure."

Part 11:   Non-Moslem cases; after the provisions of Order 10 have been complied with, then if the case is not one in which Moslem law is to be administered or applied, the court shall continue the hearing in accordance with the following rules of this part.

It is on the bases of Part 1 thereof, that it was held in *Ochoko Marmara* v. *Ibrahim Yaye*,[4] Per Uwais, J (as he then was), that "whenever the law to be applied in a case or matter is Islamic law, the court is bound to follow Islamic law procedure." To this requirement, Ambali G.K postulated that once the subject matter before the court is one to which Islamic Law will apply, the procedure and evidence applicable must be Islamic law as according to him,

"It is no justice to cannibalize our legal system in the Area Courts by using one law to bring the defendants to courts and resorting to another to decide the substantive matters involved in the litigation. All matters that fall

---

[4] (1974) NSNLR 131

within the jurisdiction of Islamic law should be processed from the beginning to the end through the applicable law, which is Sharia."[5]

Order 11 of the Sharia Court (Civil Procedure) Rules as applicable in the Northern States Sharia Judicial System made separate civil rules for sharia courts for the first time in the history of Sharia law in Nigeria. It is produced in a form of legislation and in consonance with the procedures envisaged by Order 11 Part 1 of the Area Court Civil (Procedure Rules) of 1971 to wit: "*Moslem practice and procedure*".

Right to Courts
It is the indisputable right of every citizen to seek justice by recourse to competent courts including the Sharia Courts. "All citizens have right of access to such courts to which he has a legal right of recourse."[6] On the other hand, the defendant as the person claimed against has no right to avoid litigation as he is compellable to respond to the claims against him. While the plaintiff exercises his right to court freely, to institute or lay his claim, if he relinquished such right no body questions him. In contrast the defendant can be punished if he refuses to appear when called upon to do so.

Claim
Claim is attribution or assertion to oneself of a right or maturity of a thing in the hand of other than him or in his custody.[7] The person attributing or asserting such right is simply referred to as *"Al-Muddai"* claimant or plaintiff and the person against whom the assertion is made is *Mudda'a Alaihi,* the defendant or respondent and the subject matter of the claim is *"Mudda'a Fihi".* In other words a claimant is one whose assertion is that something is and the defendant is one whose assertion is in the negative.[8]

PART II
Constituents of Claim
In any claim there must be the claimant, the defendant respondent and the subject matter of claim.
i) The Claimant or plaintiff is the person who personally or through personal representatives lodges the complaint before a Judge on his own free will,

---

[5] *Sule* v. *Abike* KWS/SCA/CV/AP/17/2001(unreported)
[6] Section 35(4) of the Constitution 1999
[7] Fiqh Al-Sunnah p. 361 v. iv Translation
[8] Tuhfa of Ibn Asimi

voluntarily in a claim of right, if he voluntarily abandons his claim he cannot be questioned. The nature of his claim could alter his status.

ii)   The Defendant Respondent is a person against whom claim is made with rights to admit or deny the claim. He is not permitted to avoid litigation and may be compelled to sustain it, even in his absence and his whereabouts must be clearly shown. In some instances, his response to a claim could alter his status.

iii)   The Subject Matter is the subject of litigation or a thing which is subject of dispute; it must be something probable and reasonable and discernible to common knowledge and custom, describable, distinguishable and explainable.

The law is thus that for any claim to be sustainable in court it must have reference to the claimant, the defendant and the subject matter otherwise the claim may be rejected.

Generally claims are of two types claimable and not claimable. Not claimable are such as from father to son and those between suitors to their fiancлes.[9] The law is that all gifts and charities are recoverable or refundable if it has been made to a spouse.[10] The claim must be such that if proved shall be enforceable against whom it is obtained. A claim by a son for the enforcement of gift against his father for instance is not a proper claim as same may be withdrawn by the donor.

Commencement of Civil and Criminal Claims

An action or claim is commenced by a claimant personally or through his authorized representative, orally or in writing before a Judge in the Area or Sharia court. He files his claim and offers explanation or reason for such claim and the Area or Sharia Judge shall listen to or study the claim carefully to determine whether the claim makes sense or not, or whether *prima facie* case is disclosed or not. If the Judge satisfies himself that one is disclosed he shall direct for the registration of the complaint in the *Diwanul-Qadai* (court register book) and fix a return date and orders for the letter of invitation or summons to be issued to the person claimed against.

Order 2 Rule 2 Area Courts (Civil Procedure) Rules 1971, provides that every civil case shall be commenced by a complaint made in person or the authorized representatives of the person making the complaint. Rule 3 provides that the court shall cause the clerk to enter the substance of such a matter in books to be kept for the purposes as prescribed in Order 27. The court shall under Rule 4

9 Ihkam AL-Ahkam P.8
10 Dalil Al-Salik P.132

refuse to entertain a matter which fails to disclose any cause of action which must be stated. If the judge ascertains the detail of the complaint he shall issue summons to the defendant whose address must be supplied by the plaintiff.[11] This order is in *pari materia* with the requirements of Order 2 of the Sharia Court (Civil Procedure) Rules of Sharia Judicial System.

Under the Islamic Criminal Law of Procedure, any individual can initiate a criminal prosecution, whether or not he has suffered any special harm over and above other members of the public. This is because every human being is a vicegerent of Allah on the earth and it is his first and foremost duty to safeguard the rights of Allah. The most common practice now however, is that in all crimes liable to *Hudud* and *Ta'azir* punishments prosecution is carried out by the police or other public officers who have no personal interest therein. For example, under the Sharia Criminal Procedure Code (Amendment) Law 2000, by Section 385, a criminal action is commenced by the means of a written complaint made by the Attorney General or by a complainant of fact of an act which constitute an offence by a victim of crime or his representative when the Attorney General's consent is sought for and obtained.

The consent of the Attorney General is required in view of the provisions of Section 211(1)(a) of the 1999 Constitution of the Federal Republic of Nigeria, and the provisions of the Police Act, 1990 (which is a federal legislation) particularly at section 19 which empowers the police to prosecute in courts.[12] The procedure envisaged by Section 385 of the Sharia Criminal Procedure Code is by means of submission of *First Information Report* pursuant to Section 118 of the Criminal Procedure Code of the Northern States of Nigeria, which provides that, "after complying with the provisions of Section 117, the officer in charge of a police station shall act as follows: "He shall send to the appropriate court in the manner set out in Section 119 the First Information Report." By Section 386 of Sharia CPC Amendment law every such complaint shall disclose a cause of action and shall have sufficient statement of complaint, with date, place and when material, the value of the property in respect of which the offence has been committed. The consequence is that any criminal complaint which did not comply with Section 385 and 386 of the Sharia Criminal Procedure Code (Amendment) Law and Section 118 of the Criminal Procedure Code could be rejected by the court.

Competence of Parties
A valid claim is one which is commenced by a free person, not a slave, the rational, not insane or idiot, the mature, not immature, the reasonable, not lad

---

[11] Order 2 R.5

[12] The Sharia CPC of some states (however, not Kano State) did not make provision for the consent of the Attorney General. This creates a conflict with both the FRN 1999 Constitution and the Police Act.

and lewd. The claimant with all the negative attributes would have his claim rejected, as having no legal capacity. These requirements apply to the defendant in the same manner as it applies to the claimant.[13]

The legal capacity arises from any of the following causes: infancy, lunacy, prodigality, slavery, bankruptcy, sickness, it relates much to the disposal of one's property as it does to one's ability to institute an action in court or be claimed against. The law is therefore that parties (Plaintiff and Defendant) and their legal representatives must have *"Al-Ahliyyah"* meaning; legal capacity, which presupposes the parties' ability to sustain an action before a court of law.

In *Alhassan B. Hassan* v. *Estate of Late B. Hassan*[14] preliminary objection was taken bordering on the competence of "the Estate of Late B. Hassan" as a party in a case of inheritance. *Kadi Nagogo* (as he then was) held that an action cannot be maintained in the name of "Estate of Late B. Hassan" it being neither human nor a creation of law. He therefore struck out the case. Only a natural or juristic person can sue in law. The general rule therefore, requires that the Plaintiff and the Defendant should be natural persons or juristic persons living or existing at the time the action is instituted.[15]

A claim to be sustainable in court therefore must have been filed by a person or persons with legal capacity to do so. In *Maersk Line* v. *Addide Invest. Ltd*, the Supreme Court has held; Per Ayoola JSC, that: "A person who is made a party to an action either as a plaintiff or as a defendant must be a legal person or, if not, a body vested by law with power to sue or be sued."[16]

Claims by Non-Muslim in Sharia Courts

As a general rule, a claim by a Non-Muslim before a Sharia Judge in an area predominantly Islamic, may be heard, and judgment shall be given on bases of the requirement of Sharia much as it will be given among Muslims. This is in accordance with Allah's saying in the Qur'an:

> "If they cometh to thee, either judge between them or decline to interfere. If thou decline, they cannot hurt thee in the least. If thou judge, judge in equity between them, for Allah loveth those who judge in equity,"[17]

A judge however should preserve the most absolute impartiality as between the contending parties and this should be the case even in suits between a Muslim

---

[13] Fiqh Sunnah vol. III P.327
[14] Suit NO PLS/SCA/ CV.71A/96
[15] *The Administrators/Executors of the Estate of Gen. Sani Abacha (Deceased)* v. *Samuel David Eke-Spiff & 3 Ors* (2009) 2SCNJ 119
[16] (2002) FWLR (pt. 125) 608 at 655.
[17] Quran Cap. V Verse 42

and a non-Muslim.[18] Religious belief should not be a disadvantage to litigants before Sharia Court.[19]

Under the Nigeria legal system however, the principles of Islamic laws are not applicable to non-Muslims.[20] Section 3 of the Sharia Penal Code Law No. 10 of 2000 of Zamfara, Sokoto and Kano States, etc., made application of Sharia specifically applicable to Muslims as against non-Muslims in criminal offences. The situation is the same in respect of personal law, as Section 277(2)(e) of the 1999 Constitution of the Federal Republic of Nigeria provides:

> "where all the parties to the proceedings being Muslims have requested the court that hears the case in the first instance to determine the case in accordance with Islamic personal law..."

It follows that in Nigeria, in determination of any question of Islamic personal law as recognized by the Constitution, the parties involved must give their respective consents. This might appear to be a deviation from the Islamic general rule but painfully in tandem with the fact that Nigeria is not an Islamic state.

Further, the state might be predominantly Muslim yet may not be able to enforce absolute Sharia law in view of the competing rights of the Muslims and non-Muslims in the state in view of the collective rights Muslims and non-Muslims share as provided for in the Constitution of the Federal Republic of Nigeria 1999. Ordinarily, non-Muslims who live in an Islamic state are to enjoy some limited rights which are twofold: i) right of protection from all external threats; and ii) right of protection from all internal tyranny and persecution.

The non-Muslims who enjoy these rights are called *"Ahlil-Dhimmah"* or *"Dhimmis."* In Sharia they are the covenanted people. Non-Muslims in Nigeria do not seem to fit into this requirement, by the nature of their rights as enshrined in Section 42(1) of the 1999 Constitution of the Federal Republic of Nigeria. This is fundamentally because Nigerian Constitution is multi-religious, the rights enshrined therein are individual and interdependent and transcend regional and religious divide.

PART III
Sources of the Rules of Procedure

The primary sources of Islamic law are *The Holy Qur'an* and the *Sunnah*, which are collectively referred to as *"Al-Nass"* (*Command*). The Qur'an is the original

---

[18] *Maliki Law* by Ruxton p.281
[19] *Ango* v. *Aruwa* (1998) 1 NWLR (pt.532) 146
[20] *Wali* v. *Ibrahim* (1997) 9 NWLR (pt.519) 160

and substantive source of Islamic law. It is the final authority for both religion and the laws governing all Muslims in their individual and social behaviours. The second main source of Islamic law is the *Sunnah*. *Sunnah* in ordinary language means the "way," custom or in jurisprudence, what has emanated from the Prophet, either with respect to his actions, his words or his tacit approval. The secondary sources of Sharia include:

(a) *Al-Ijima*, which means the consensus of the Islamic jurists, i.e. the *Fuqahah* in a particular age or a particular question of law. It is resorted to only when *An-Nass* the Holy Quran and the *Sunnah* are silent on a particular issue;

(b) *Al-Qiyas* is an opinion a jurist arrives at on the basis of the principle of analogy. In other words, *Al-Qiyas* is analogical deduction based on the similarity between a matter in which there is *"Nass"* and another one in which *"Nass"* is silent.[21]

Al-Sheik Muhammad El-Kafi, in his short commentary on Tuhfa postulated that:

> "The ingredients which are indispensable for valid decision and which the absence of any of them renders it invalid are six in numbers; the judge, the plaintiff, the defendant, the subject matter in dispute and the applicable laws leading to the decision (Qur'an or Sunnah text or the consensus) and lastly the procedure.[22]

Then in more practical terms, the first instrument of judicial appointment issued by the second Caliph, Calipha Umar Bin Alkhatab, on the occasion of the appointment of Abu Musa Al-Asha'iri as a *Kadi* which instrument could best be described as the bases of Sharia Rules of Procedure when viewed as a warrant of a court. The instrument provides thus:

> "The office of the judge is a definite religious obligation and followed up tradition/practice. Do understand the decisions that are made before you for it is useless to consider a plea that is not valid. Maintain equality of all the peoples that appear before your court so that the noble will not expect favour and the humble will not despair of justice from you. The claimant must produce evidence and from the defendant, an oath is apparent. Compromise is permissible among Muslims, but not agreement through which something forbidden would be permitted, or something permitted forbidden. If you give judgment yesterday and after such reconsideration

---

[21] *Wali* v *Ibrahim* (1997) 9 NWLR (PT.519) 160
[22] Ihkam Al-Ahkam P.8

you come to the correct opinion, you should not feel prevented by your first judgment from doing what is worthwhile. It is better to review the judgment than to persist in worthlessness. Use your brain about matters that perplex you and which neither Qur'an nor Sunnah seem to cover, study similar cases and evaluate the situation through analogy with those similar cases. If a person brings a claim, which he may not be able to prove set a time limit for him. If he brings proof within the time limit allow his claim otherwise you are permitted to give judgment against him. This is the best way to forestall or clear up any possible doubt. All Muslims are acceptable as witnesses against each other, except such as having received a punishment provided for by religion/Sharia such as are proved to have given false evidence, and such as suspected of partiality on account of litigants' status or relationship, for Allah the Exalted had entrusted of you intentions and defence , evidence and faith. I warn you against fatigue and weariness and annoyance at the litigant and denial at the dispute. Allah extols with it the recompense and improves with it the supply that whose intention is righteous and he comes to himself, Allah makes sufficient what is between him and the people. And that who shows the people what is contrary to his intention with what Allah knows. For establishing justice in the courts of law God will grant you a rich reward and give you a rich reputation."[23]

This important instrument laid what could be called today in Islamic point of view, as an adjectival law, in that it establishes for the Islamic Judicial System Practical Rules of Procedure and Rules of Evidence which together make up Sharia Civil and Criminal Procedure Rules. What therefore flows from this all important instrument are:

a) the position of a judge;
b) the jurisdiction;
c) the service of process of court;
d) the parties (plaintiff and defendant);
e) the statement of claim;
f) judicial means of proof;
g) judgment and all its attendant consequences;
h) Appeal.

---

[23] Fiqh Sunnah v. 4 p. 321

Chapter 2

Judicial Position and Powers

PART I
The Judge

Islam attaches great importance to justice which must be done at all cost and the process by which justice is to be administered; thus those who perform the functions of the "Kadis" Judges or "*Kadi Al-Quddat*" Chief Justice or what is referred to in Nigeria Legal System as Grand Kadi must be men with deep insight and profound knowledge of the Sharia, they must also be Allah fearing, forth right, honest and sincere and men of integrity. The Prophet (*S.A.W.*) is reported to have said of a Judge:

> "There are three categories of judges; two will go to Hell, while one will enter paradise. The person who knew the truth and did not pass judgment accordingly, and oppressed people in his judgment shall go to Hell. The person who did not know the truth and passed judgment over people based on ignorance shall go to Hell. The person who knew the truth and passed judgment accordingly will go to paradise."[1]

A judge as a representative of the Muslim Ruler is preferred that he should be courageous in his proceedings and judgment and should also satisfy the condition of being responsible and man of integrity. He should also be a free man and free from loss of sight, hearing and speech. It is also required that he should be a man of learning and piety. He must know the principles of Islamic jurisprudence. He should sit whenever it is suitable for him to hold court.

Appointment of Judges

The universal principles guiding the appointment of judges under Islamic law are summed up in the following attributes. For a man to be appointed a judge, he should be a Muslim, free person, male and "*Mukallaf*" that is accountable for all his deeds. He should posses the capacities to hear and see. He should be literate, intelligent, conscious, scrupulous, upright, and should be capable of making independent research and interpretation of the Holy Quran and the "*Sunnah*" or

---

[1] Reported by Abu Daud and Ibn Majah

at least possess the capacity to re-interpret on the bases of the Holy Quran and *"Sunnah"*.[2]

Okunola, JCA, in *Husain* v. *Bagade* held that it can be seen that by its nature Islamic law abhors a Judge not learned in its proceedings toiling with the sacred law. This is why it is mandatory under the Islamic Legal System that only a man well versed in the science of Islamic jurisprudence should be made a Judge... From the foregoing, it is clear that if a person or judge is ignorant of Islamic law his decision on Islamic law is a nullity.[3]

Under the Nigeria Legal System, a person shall be deemed to be learned in Islamic law if he has attended and has obtained a recognized qualification in Islamic Personal Law from an institution approved by the Federal Judicial Service Commission, Judicial Service Committee of the Federal Capital Territory, or State Judicial Service Commission and has held the qualification for a period of not less than seven years; in respect of Area or Sharia Court Judges of a State and not less than 10 years in respect of Kadis of Sharia Court of Appeal and if in the opinion of the National Judicial Council or State Judicial, Service Commission as the case may be he has considerable experience in the practice of Islamic Personal Law or he is a distinguished scholar of Islamic Personal Law.[4]

Area Court in some states in the North, though courts of first instance are constituted to sit with member or members depending on the subject matter of dispute. Where the subject matter of dispute is a matter to which Islamic law is applicable, a single Judge learned in Islamic law or Sharia presides. Where however, the subject matter has elements of custom the judge sits with an assessor or member. This arrangement is much prevalent in the states where Muslims are in minority or where the non-Muslims are of significant proportion, for example, Benue, Plateau, Kogi, etc. Kaduna State, for instance, in the year 2001, created separate courts, one for the Muslims and the other for the trial of customary cases. It was then the customary court of Appeal was established in the state for the first time.

The Duties of Judge

The duty of judge had been during the period of Khalifas merely to settle disputes between two or more contending parties, later the function expanded to include general concern and supervision of all matters concerning Muslim Community, specifically supervision of the well being of the insane, orphans, bankrupts, missing persons, conduct of marriages of the women without guardians, wills, donations, *waqf,* etc. were brought under the functions of the judge.[5]

---

[2] Ashalul Madarik v.III P.196
[3] CA/K/798/89 (Unreported)
[4] S.276 (3) (b) (i) & (ii) of 1999 Constitution
[5] Al Qawaneen Al FIQHI P. 321

Office of a Judge

The office of a judge is a definite religious duty in Islam though not obligatory but of the features of "*Fard Kifaya*" being of the same category with leading prayers on the dead. If the duty is undertaken by one, others are relieved; but where there is only one person suitable for appointment he may be compelled to take the appointment.[6]

Ethics of a Judicial Officer in Islam

A judge of Sharia Court is primarily required to observe the most absolute impartiality between the contending parties. There shall be transparent neutrality of the court to the parties in the way the judge listen and speaks to the litigants. Equal treatment is due to all parties without consideration for creed, age, status and sex. This should be the case even in suit between a Muslim and non Muslim. The litigants should be placed on equal footing in terms of sitting or standing arrangement before the court. The judge should not frown at a party and smile at the other. No person is entitled to any special treatment in the process of justice as there is no consideration for a highly placed litigant over his lowly opponent before an Area, or Sharia court.

A judge is obliged to treat the litigants before him equally in their appearance before him; their sitting in his court; their reception in the court; attention to them and in his judgment. A judge shall not only do justice to parties but must be seen to do so in his actions and conduct in court. He must not show inclination to one against the other, guide one to succeed against the other, or teach one a better argument or guide a witness in his testimony or guide a claimant as to how to present his claim or the process of oath, or advise the defendant and the need for denial and admission nor shall he teach witness how to testify and how not and shall not accord one party a special recognition against the other as will break the heart of the other, shall not extend hospitality on either of them or both of them as long as they are litigants before him.

He shall not accept gift from the litigant, because accepting a gift from one who was not accustomed to offering him gift is bribery. This is because the Holy Prophet (*PBUH*) said "Allah's curse is on the briber and the one who takes the bribe at will." A Judge is enjoined to exhibit impartiality in his sittings, conduct and word in court, all his proceedings must be in public and oral.

A judge must not seek for guidance or offer assistance to either of the parties in anything connected to the case before him and shall hold no opinion on same.[7]

It is forbidden for a judge to take bribes in any form. The law is very strict about bribery and in an attempt to prevent it a judge is not expected to take a gift

---

[6] Imam Malik rept. In Tabsirat Hukkam v.1 p.12
[7] Bahjah p. Tuhfa r. 4

from people who had not been familiar with him before his appointment. "He whom we employ to discharge a duty and we provide remuneration for him, whatever he takes after that in the course of the job is abnormal."[8]

Judges are advised to avoid holding sessions while they are in the state of anger, hunger, thirst, feeling too hot, cold or tired. The reasons are to ensure that he takes decisions under normal state of mind, thus no judge should adjudicate between two persons when he is in the state of anger.[9]

PART II
Appearance of Litigants in Court

A judge is enjoined to dispense justice according to the dictates and nature of the case as well as the parties involved in the case before him. Thus hearing or trial in the Sharia Court is required to follow the order of the dates the case are filed to determine the order of attending to them. At any sitting of the Sharia court a judge shall commence hearing on the principles of first come first serve. Unless there are cases which involve parties who are travellers or perishable subject matter or disposable in such cases the travellers or perishable matter may be taken first. Circumstances however, may demand that certain cases should be given priority over others, which were filed before them in view of their special characteristics:

a. A case involving a person who is not resident in the town where the court operates and has to travel from outside the town to attend the court should be attended to before a case whose parties are resident within the jurisdiction of the court;

b. A case whose subject matter of dispute is perishable or could become valueless or obsolete if the case has to take its ordinary order should be given priority over other cases;

c. A case that involves the detention of person whose guilty or innocence is not yet determined is given priority over others;

d. The cases of Will "*Wasiyyah*" and those concerning orphans are also deserving of prompt attention;

e. Legal practitioners could, by virtue of the privilege they have, mention their cases before others. That however, is to the discretion and determination of the presiding judge.

---

[8] Minhajul Muslim 8th Edition p.463

[9] Fiqh *Sunnah* v.iii p. 317

Under Islamic law, the rule is that a plaintiff or a claimant cannot be compelled to pursue his interest. Thus where a party who files a suit is called upon and he/she is absent, the call shall be repeated thrice and if he does not show up, the court shall proceed to the next suit. If the former shows up before the beginning of the latter, he is attended to but if the court has started it does not stop the proceedings. Accordingly, Order 9(2) of the Area Court Civil Procedure Rules 1971 provides that on the day when a case is called for hearing or at any adjournment of such hearing, if the plaintiff does not appear, the court shall strike out the case unless the court sees good reason to the contrary.

This Order has the same content with Sharia Court Civil Procedure Rules 2000, only that it required that the reason for striking out must be recorded in the civil cause record book. It is also same by virtue of Order viii (1) (i) Sharia Court of Appeal Rules Cap.122 laws of Northern Nigeria 1963. It is required that the judge must treat the parties on equal terms in sitting, talking, hearing and in paying attention to the parties. The judge should not show any discrimination.

The plaintiff starts by stating his case and the defendant shall maintain silence until the plaintiff concludes. If the claim has merit, the judge shall request the defendant to respond where appropriate. If however the plaintiff could not explain his claim with the required reasons or the case lacked substance, the judge shall strike out the claim and send the plaintiff away particularly where he had identified who the plaintiff is and who the defendant is.

In the terms of Order 2 Rule 4, a court shall refuse to entertain a case or matter, if the said case or matter fails to disclose any cause of action.

If neither the plaintiff nor the defendant is able to ascertain his claim or where both maintain silence before the judge while he the judge is unable to ascertain between the plaintiff and the defendant he shall send them away from his court.

Where two people appear before a judge and each presents himself as plaintiff, the judge shall ask them to be out, and whoever firstly returns to the judge between them shall be considered as the plaintiff.[10]

PART III
Jurisdiction and Power

Basically, jurisdiction is crucial, foundational, fundamental, radical and pivotal to adjudication. If it is missing, then everything in the adjudicatory process would be equal to nothing be it good or bad. Jurisdiction is not conferred on courts by mere orders of trial courts, agreement of the parties it is either that a court, constitutionally or statutorily has jurisdiction vested on it or not. The issue of

---

[10] Tuhfa R. 29

jurisdiction whether limited or not is not novel to Islamic law. It has long been acknowledged as a valid functional aspect of Islamic law jurisprudence, and therefore is crucial, basic and fundamental to the adjudicatory process under Islamic law. Under Islamic law jurisdiction of court is created under three heads namely:

a) the Imam
b) the litigant; and,
c) the subject matter.

The Imam

By the 'Imam' (the Sovereign), he limits the jurisdiction of the courts as it pleases him. No court therefore has right to adjudicate outside the powers donated to it by the Imam. In Islamic Law, limitations placed on jurisdiction of courts are matters within the discretion of the Imam - leader, authority or government. Jurisdiction can either be limited or unlimited.

Limitations can be with regards to:

a) Applicable law
b) Subject matter
c) Territory
d) Venue.

F. H. Ruxton's Maliki Law, states:

"Every *kadi* must have a separate jurisdiction but the Imam or sovereign can limit their jurisdiction in any way he pleases, either as to the district over which their power extends, or as to their powers of entertaining any judicial proceeding..."

The Litigant

A litigant creates into a court a jurisdiction in exercise of his right of choice as to which court he files his claim and that is of cause subject to the powers and limitation placed on the court by the legislations.

The subject matter

The subject matter of dispute confers jurisdiction as well, as it is not permissible for a judge to entertain any dispute in a claim the subject of which is based on illegality. No claim of money earned out of any prohibited thing can be entertained by Sharia court. In other words the claim of the plaintiff determines jurisdiction of the court and not either the defence or counter-claim of the defendant.[11]

---

[11] *Hada* v. *Malumfashi* (1993) 7 SCNJ 504

Thus, Islamic law provides for jurisdiction over person's territory and subject matter in the manner as most other legal systems. But in the case of jurisdiction over subject matter, it provides for classification of jurisdiction into criminal and civil. It further breaks the former into '*Al-hudud*', with fixed punishment; '*Al-qisas*', retaliation, etc. In the same vein, the jurisdiction such as family law, contract and commercial causes, juvenile causes, specific/periodic causes and so on, this division is primarily to allow for specialization of courts and enhance speedy dispensation of justice. One of the pre-requisites of a court in the exercise of its jurisdiction is that the subject matter of the action must be within its jurisdiction and there should be no feature in the case which prevents the court from exercising jurisdiction. Where therefore, the subject matter is not within the jurisdiction of the court, then there is nothing to adjudicate and the decision reached in the absence of jurisdiction is a nullity. Similarly all other proceedings are nullity.[12] No court shall entertain a case or matter which it considers that it has no jurisdiction or not sufficient power to try, but shall transfer or obtain the transfer of the case or matter to a court of appropriate and competent jurisdiction or power.[13]

Jurisdiction of Area & Sharia Courts

In Nigeria, Area and Sharia Courts owe their jurisdiction to the state laws establishing them. For instance, by Section 2 of the Area Courts Edict 1967 as applicable in the North, every Area court shall exercise the jurisdiction conferred upon it by or under this law within such area and to such extent as may be specified in its warrant. Section 14 (2) provides that any person who institutes or prosecutes any cause or matter in an area court shall in that cause or matter be subject to the jurisdiction of that Area court. Section 15(1) made distinctions as to person who are subject of the jurisdiction of Area Court between Native, Africans and non Africans and those person(s) who freely gave their consent to the exercise of the jurisdiction of the area court. Section 17 created three grades of Area Courts, grade I, II and III of the court with different sets of subject matter jurisdiction in addition to Upper Area Court of Appeal.

On the other hand, the Sharia Court Laws of the Northern States Sharia judicial system conferred original jurisdiction in all civil and criminal matters on Sharia courts. So also is the jurisdiction to hear and determine civil matters and causes where all the parties are Muslims. Where one party is a non Muslim no jurisdiction is to be exercised unless he gives a written consent, likewise in criminal cases where the accused are jointly Muslims and non Muslims the

---

[12] *Matari* v. *Dan Galadima & Ors* (1993) NWLR (PT. 287) 266
[13] O. R. Sharia Courts C.P.R. Kano State

jurisdiction of the court is limited to Muslims only. See Section 5 of the Sharia Courts Law.

Upper Area Court

Upper Area Courts and Upper Sharia Courts have dual jurisdiction, first as courts of first instance and secondly as appellate courts with powers to entertain appeals arising from the decisions of the Area and Sharia Courts on all civil matters, personal and commercial where the subject matter is founded on Islamic law and parties are Muslims other than those commercial matters covered by Federal Legislation (except where the presiding judge is himself, by his training a qualified legal practitioner).[14]

By Section 54 of Area Courts Law 1967, appeals lie from the decisions of Upper Area Courts to Sharia Court of Appeal. The section provides:

> "Any party aggrieved by a decision of or order of an Upper Area Court may appeal to:
> (a) The Sharia Court of Appeal in cases involving questions regarding Muslims personal law; and,
> (b) The High Court in all other cases."

Jurisdiction of the Sharia Court of Appeal

Sharia Courts of Appeal is a creation of the 1999 Constitution by virtue of Sections 6(4) (f) and (g) of the Constitution. These sections confer on the courts jurisdiction pursuant to Sections 262(2) in respect of Federal Capital Territory and 277(2) of other states.

More explicitly, sub-section 2 provides:

> "a) Any question of Islamic personal law regarding a   marriage conducted in accordance with that law, including a question relating to the validity or dissolution of such a marriage or a question that depends on such a marriage and relating to family relationship or the guardianship of an infant;

> b) Where all the parties to the proceedings are Muslims, any question of Islamic personal law regarding a marriage including the validity or dissolution of that marriage, or regarding family relationship. A foundling or the guardianship of an infant;

> c) Any question of Islamic personal law regarding a *wakf*, gift, will or succession where the endowed, donor, testator or deceased person is a Muslim;

---

[14] Section 286 (2) of the Constitution 1999

d) Any question of Islamic personal law regarding an infant, prodigal or person of unsound mind who is a Muslim or the maintenance or the guardianship of a Muslim who is physically or mentally infirm; or,

e) Where all parties to the proceeding, being Muslims, requests the court at first instance to determine that case in accordance with Islamic personal law, any other question."

The jurisdiction of the Sharia Court of Appeal is thus limited to issues relating to Islamic personal law namely; marriage, divorce, inheritance including matters concerning *waqf*, gift, will or succession; custody and guardianship of children.[15] Therefore where the subject matter of the claim of the plaintiff at the trial court is simply and purely a matter of declaration of title to land or sale of landed property quite unconnected with Islamic personal law matters as contained under Section 242 (2) of the 1979 Constitution (now S. 277 (2) of the 1999 Constitution of the Federal Republic of Nigeria), the Sharia court of Appeal will not have jurisdiction to entertain any appeal emanating therefrom.

Further, the Sharia court of Appeal does not have jurisdiction to entertain a claim involving ownership of cow *simplicita* without more, per Coomassie, JCA.[16]

The jurisdiction of Sharia Court of Appeal as prescribed in the relevant provisions of the Constitution does not include enforcement of contracts. Further, Islamic law of contract of sale is not one of the items categorized as Islamic personal law in Section 277 of the 1999 Constitution of the Federal Republic of Nigeria.[17] Land dispute or action for recovery of premises can only be heard by Sharia court of Appeal if it involves issues of Islamic personal law such as *waqf*, gift), will or succession.[18]

It is the rule of interpretation of statutes, that where general provision as in subsection (1) of Section 277 of the Constitution precedes specific provision as in sub-section (2) (a-e) the specific provision prevails.[19] The consequence is that any state legislation that is contrary to the items listed is null and void.

Jurisdiction of the Court of Appeal
Section 244 of the 1999 Constitution conferred jurisdiction on the Court of Appeal to entertain appeals on any civil proceeding from the Sharia Court of Appeal with respect to any question of Islamic personal law. And the appeal to the Court of Appeal shall be of right. The section provides:

---

[15] (2002) 1 NWLR (PT.748) 453 CA
[16] *Ado* v. *Dije* (1983) SLR P.11 CA
[17] *Alkali* v. *Alkali* (ibid); *Maina* v. *Falmata Alhaji Lamu* CA/J/65/9(Unreported)
[18] *Ado* v. *Dije* (1983) SLR P.11 CA
[19] *Magaji* v. *Matari* (2000)5 SC 45

1) "An appeal shall lie from decision of Sharia Court of Appeal to the Court of Appeal as of right in civil proceedings before the Sharia Court of Appeal with respect to any question of Islamic personal law which the Sharia Court of Appeal is competent to decide.

2) Any right of appeal to the Court of Appeal from the decisions of Sharia Court of Appeal conferred by this section shall be:
(a) "Exercised at the instance of a party thereto or with the leave of the Sharia Court of Appeal or of the Court of Appeal, at the instance of any other person having an interest in the matter; and,
(b) Exercised in accordance with any Act of the National Assembly and rules of court, for the time being in force regulating the powers, practice and procedure of the Court of Appeal."

The Court of Appeal has the jurisdiction to the exclusion of any other court of law in Nigeria, to hear and determine appeals from the Sharia Court of Appeal.[20] When the Court of Appeal is to exercise jurisdiction on matters of Islamic law it shall sit with judges learned in Islamic law.[21] In the same vain the Supreme Court exercises exclusive jurisdiction to hear and determine appeals from the Court of Appeal in all matters concerning Islamic laws.[22]

Territorial Jurisdiction of Sharia Courts

Conferment of jurisdiction on the judge is in order...specific mention must be made of the territorial limit of jurisdiction assigned in order to differentiate it from those exercised by others. If his jurisdiction is over a specified territory, his judgment will be enforced on those who are domiciled within (the territory) both indigenes and foreigners. If his judgment is confined to a particular locality, his judgment will not be enforced outside the specified area.[23]

While the territorial jurisdiction of the Area Courts and Sharia Courts are at all levels limited within such areas as may be specified in the warrant establishing them, the Sharia Courts of Appeal have their territorial jurisdiction limited to respective states by S. 275 (1) of the Constitution of the FRN 1999, which enjoins any state which requires to establish it and in the case of the FCT by Section 260 (1). Only Benue and Plateau States have desired to maintain one court with jurisdiction over the two states.

Decisions of a court with requisite jurisdiction will be enforced and it will not be enforced, where the court lacks jurisdiction.[24]

---

[20] *Oruba* v. *NEC* (1988) 5NWLR Pt.94 at 323
[21] S. 240 of the Constitution 1999
[22] S. 237 of the 1999 Constitution
[23] S. 233 of the 1999 Constitution
[24] Al-Raudul Murabbai f Imam Bohuti p.434-435

In *First Bank of Nigeria* v. *Tsokwa*,[25] a case belonging to one particular state should not be taken to another and tried in that other state. Where such is done, the jurisdiction of the court in that wrong state is non-existent and as such, any decision handed down by that incompetent court is a nullity.

The subject matter of claim whether immovable or movable such as cloth or money and where the parties to the case reside in different places, the judge residing in the same jurisdiction with the defendant shall have jurisdiction to hear the claim/case. If the subject matter is landed property or any other immovable type, such as house or farm the plaintiff shall institute/commence the action at the place where the subject matter is situated.

In cases of recovery of money owed, the venue shall be at any place where the creditor meets the debtor (defendant) should he be a traveller or resident.

Ibn Asimi says:

"The judgment according to dominant opinion is to take place where the defendant happens to be in respect of immovable and money as well, wherever a person meets a man indebted to him, he seeks payment in the court in that area, but in the case of immovable property (like farms. Houses and trees), the litigation must take place wherever they happened to be located. The defendant is either resident or traveller, if he is resident, then according to the majority opinion, he cannot be sued except at his place of domicile whether or not the cause of action is or arose at his place of domicile".[26]

والمدعى عليه إما ان يكون مقيما اومسا فرا فإن كن مقيما فلاتقام عليه دعوى إلاافى محل اقامتة على المشهور. سواء كان المدعى فيه فى محل اقامته أم لا.

While under Area Courts Edict or Law Territorial jurisdiction of Area court is conferred by the warrant establishing the Courts. Section 22 of the Sharia Court Law 2000 places emphasis more on the parties who are subject to the jurisdiction of the Sharia Courts (O. 2 R.1).[27]

When statutes set forth limits of jurisdiction of courts; "It is in order that the jurisdiction of a judge is confined and limited to specific matter of disputes and parties, so it is out of order for the judge to adjudicate on matters which are outside these issues."[28]

Supervisory Jurisdiction

Section 43(1) of Area Courts' Edict or Law says: "all Area Courts shall be subject to the general supervision of the Chief Judge," while S. 9 of the Sharia Courts' Law

---

[25] (2003) FWLR (pt 153) 205
[26] Tabsiratul Hukkam vol.1 p. 19
[27] Tuhfa R. 26-27
[28] S. (5) & (2)

2000 provides that "the courts shall be under the general supervision of the Grandi Kadi." In contradiction to this provision, the Constitution of the Federal Republic of Nigeria 1999 by Section 277 (1) states that:

> "The Sharia Court of Appeal of a State shall in addition to such other jurisdiction as may be conferred upon it by the law of the state, exercise such appellate and supervisory jurisdiction in civil proceedings involving questions of Islamic personal law which the court is competent to decide in accordance with the provisions of subsection (2) of this section."

What this suggests therefore is that the supervisory powers of the Sharia Court of Appeal on Area and Sharia Courts are limited if not confined to question of Islamic personal law only which it has the competence to decide in accordance with the provisions of subsection (2) of Section 277 of the 1999 Constitution of Federal Republic of Nigeria. This implies that the general supervisory jurisdiction of the courts rests with the Chief Judge of the State who is constitutionally the Chairman of the State Judicial Service Commission by virtue of the third Schedule to the Constitution and subject to the general jurisdiction of the State High Court as enunciated by Section 272 providing thus:

> (i) Subject to the provisions of S.251 and other provisions of this Constitution, the High Court of a State shall have jurisdiction to hear and determine any civil proceedings in which the existence or extent of a legal right, power, duty, liability, privilege, interest, obligation or claim is in issue or to hear and determine any criminal proceedings involving or relating to any penalty, forfeiture, punishment or other liability in respect of an offence committed by any person.

> (ii) "The reference to civil or criminal proceedings in this section includes a reference to the proceedings which originate in the High Court of a State and those which are brought before the High Court to be dealt with by a court in the exercise of its appellate or supervisory jurisdiction."

Chapter 3

Processes of Courts

PART I
Presence of Defendant in Court

Presence of parties in a case in court before commencement of hearing is a fundamental requirement for the proper adjudication of dispute between litigants. "Maliki School" is of the view that entry of judgment in a case in absence of the other litigant (defendant) is a deprivation of right as he shall be heard and his arguments taken even if such should lead to set aside the judgment. This is in accordance with the saying of Shuraih, Umar ben Abdul-Aziz and the son of Abu laila, and Abu Hanifa reported in *Fiqh Sunnah* vol. III p.323 that:

> "The judge shall not proceed to judgment on an absent litigant except he is present or has his proxy, guardian in attendance as he may have an argument with him which may refute the claim of the claimant and because the Messenger S.W.A. said to Ali in the Hadith, Oh, Ali, if two of the litigants are before you do not give judgment between them until you hear of the other, as you hear of the first. That if you do that, judgment shall be manifestly clear to you."[1]

Service of Process

To secure the attendance of a Defendant to court the court must invite him and such shall be by process of court duly served on him. Under the sharia rules of procedure, service of process of court is issued under the following circumstances:

1) Where the defendant is resident within the jurisdiction of the court and the Plaintiff has offered cogent and satisfactory explanation to his claim or made a *prima facie* case, the Judge shall issue a process inviting the defendant to court.

---

[1] Tuhfatu Hukkami R. 31-35

2) Where the Defendant is resident in a different location whose distance is about 12 miles a letter shall be sent to him inviting him to court or a Messenger may be sent where the road is safe.

3) Where the residence of the Defendant is a far away distance and the road thereto is unsafe the Judge shall transfer the complaint and case to the Judge under whose jurisdiction the Defendant is resident with a request that the Judge shall look into the case and do what is judicially right, whether for or against either party.   But if the receiving Judge could not appreciate the complaint he shall request the trial Judge to direct the Defendant to appear at a certain place and time and day to hear the complaint against him.

Payment of Service Fees

The Plaintiff is to bear the travelling expenses incurred in the course of inviting the defendant to attend the court where the Defendant was not stubborn in paying his debt. But where he was he shall be made to refund the expenses to the Plaintiff. This is however applicable if the authority does not make provision for such expenses. Ibn Asimi concluded that:

> "On knowing the signs of truthfulness in the claim of the Plaintiff, the Defendant whose whereabouts are known should be sent for. If the person lives a few miles away a letter (Summons) will be quiet sufficient if the road happens to be safe. If the distance is great or there is some fear (along the road) a letter should be written to the chief of that area to do whatever seems to be appropriate. Either he should settle the dispute or he should ask the defendant to pay what he owes or he should send for the Plaintiff to come and face litigation The person who disobeyed the court order and refuses to present himself due to his business, his shop should be locked so that he comes along."[2]

> "The fee of the Plaintiff to be paid by the Plaintiff but the Defendant pays it if he obstinately refuses to come to the court each time he is commanded."[3]

3.04 Service of process shall be effected by any person authorized under the provisions of section 12 of the Area Courts law. Service as is herewith provided shall be effected by handing the duplicate copy of the document to the person to be served. On the other hand Order III rule 6 of the Sharia Court of Appeal Rules provides that when appeal has been duly entered and necessary orders made in

---

[2] O. 3 r. 1&2 Area Courts (civil proc.) Rules 1971
[3] Tuhfa R. 36

compliance with rule 5, the registrar shall (a) cause notice of appeal, time and date fixed for the hearing of the appeal to be served on the appellant and to the respondent and to all other persons if any.

The Concept of Substituted Service

It is the principle of Islamic law that *"the Complainant is he that will be left alone if he or she decided to keep mute on his/her complaint."*[4] But Defendant must either respond to the claim willingly or be compelled to appear in court by all means possible. Islamic law recognizes the concept of substituted services, thus, whoever the Judge or his agent orders to appear in a court and such person refuses to come and hide in his house or somewhere else, the Judge or his agent may paste the summons at a conspicuous place where he lives. He shall do that by using candle, a sticker or anything similar to it, which is good to be used to imprint the invitation indelibly. The essence of that is to compel him to come to court. The modern day practice could be to paste a notice on the premises of the defendant or public place or at worst, publish same in the newspapers as would bring the notice of the case to the attention of the defendant. If after such efforts to bring the defendant to court, he still refuses to attend and continuously, hide himself in his house; the Judge shall seal any property which is dear to him. For instance, his shop or a house on which he collects rent from. The sealing shall be in such a way that he can only be accessible to the property if it is unsealed by the judge.[5]

ومن أعصى الامر ولم يحضر   طبع عليه مايهمه كى يرتفع.

Whenever the defendant blatantly refuses to admit or deny the claim against him by defiantly maintaining silence, the Judge shall compel him to either admit or deny the claim. This could be done by flogging or imprisoning him as may be appropriate. If despite the imprisonment the Defendant maintains his defiant conduct the Judge shall hear the Plaintiff and proceed to enter judgment against him.[6] Tuhfa further provides "if a Defendant should refuse to either admit or deny the claims of the Plaintiff, he should be compelled to either admit or deny."[7] If he should remain obdurate, then judgment shall be given in favour of the Plaintiff, with or without an oath by the plaintiff to buttress his claim.[8]

---

[4] *Mohammad Ndako* v. *Aishatu Muhammad* KWS/SCA/CV/M/28/98 (UNREPORTED)
[5] Ihkam A-AHKAM P.12 & O. 3 R. 6 ACCPR 1971
[6] Ar Court (Civil Procedure Rules 1071)
[7] Ihkam Al-AHKAM P. 12
[8] Order 3 R. 8, 9, Area Court (CIVIL PROCEDURE) RULES 1971

PART II
Judgment in Default

The rule requiring presence of the Defendant in court does not preclude judgment in his absence, where his presence may not be secured with ease and early. This is because Sharia also recognizes and applies the concept of judgment in default. However, unlike the common law, Sharia classified judgment by default into three categories as per the teaching of the school of Imam Malik:

1. the nearby absent party (Defendant) who lives a distance of one, two or three days journey from the court is the first one, summons will be issued to him to come to court and the effects and consequences of his absence shall be explained to him. This is done in respect of all matters. He either appoints a representative or come before judgment is entered against him (provided the claim against him is proved).This is the procedure in the recovery of debts, claims of animals, consanguinity and all kinds of claims such as divorce (*talaq*) emancipation of slave and so on. He is not allowed thereafter to put of claims such as divorce (*talaq*) emancipation of slave and so on. He is not allowed thereafter to put up any defence in any of all these because he has no reason to do that;

2. the second category is a Defendant who is away from the town where the court is based, to a distant place of ten days journey. Besides the distance is whether life and property of the traveller is safe, to and from the place where the court is based. Such Defendant is treated in similar manner to the Defendant who lives in the territorial jurisdiction of the court and those who live close to it. Claim and proof against him shall be listened to and decision taken on all matters except those having to, do with disputes over land and property. However, he is allowed in law to come to court thereafter to put his defence with a view to set aside the judgment by default;

3. the third category of the absent Defendant is he who lives very far away from the base of the court. The distance is more than ten days journey. In this regard, the plaintiff's case is heard and determined on the basis of its merit. In addition, the plaintiff is subjected to an oath called *Yaminal Qadai*, which is the oath of having the judgment entered in his favour despite the fact that his opponent is absent.[9]

Similarly, Order vii Rule 3 of the Sharia Court of Appeal 1960 provides that

---

[9] Ibid.

"if the respondent and his representative in a question of maintenance or divorce is absent and their where about are unknown or they are in a place where a summons cannot be served on either of them the court, after satisfying itself as to the above facts shall hear the suit and give judgment accordingly."

If the litigant who has concluded his case before a judge absconds from judgment after "*Al-Izar*", to which he replied that he no longer had anything more to add to the facts of the case, the judge shall enter judgment in the case as if the parties are present. At that stage the defendant may not be entertained to offer additional facts or complain if he resurfaces[10]. But if he was to abscond before presenting his conclusive grounds "*Izar*" or stayed away from the court for long period and all attempt to reach him proved impossible, the judge may proceed to judgment. This however cannot foreclose his right to be heard if he resurfaces.

PART III
Adjournment of Sittings

Adjournments

Adjournment of sitting of court to a time and dates within which a certain act or acts shall be carried out is within or left to the discretion of the judge. A court is not duty bound to grant an adjournment in a matter before it. The question of whether or not to grant an adjournment is a matter of discretion and depends on the facts and circumstances of each case, Per Coomassie JCA.[11]

Exception to the General Rule

Any dispute between two contending parties which inevitably had to lead to an adjournment to another day and time either to enable one of the contending parties time to produce witness or money or any reason which will necessitate an adjournment of the sitting of the court or judge is left at the discretion of the judge, he is possessed of the power to adjourn and fix any day and time as suits his convenience. A judge is however not permitted to exercise such discretion in case where Sharia had stipulated time or date for the performance of an act, of such as a sick one "*Mu'utarili*" or one who has sworn never to cohabit with his wife until after four (4) months. "*Illa'a or Muli*" A judge is obliged to stipulate three (3) days for the performance of an obligation imposed by his judgment or order in the following instances:

---

[10] Tuhfa R. 50 & 51
[11] *Bulunkutu* v. *Zangina Lior* CA:J:37:5:95

a) Person who has right of pre-emption *"Shufu'a"* is to be given three (3) days to pay for the portion of property due for sale on which he has such right. He shall lose his right of pre-emption if he fails to pay within three days.

A debtor who before a judge, claims he is not certain of the total amount of his indebtedness or that he has forgotten the amount, is entitled to three days adjournment to enable him reflect or think on the amount of the loan outstanding against him.

b)   A person adjudged to subscribe to an Oath, if he seeks for an adjournment to enable him consult on the said Oath, is entitled to the grant of three (3) days adjournment.

c)   A person who alleges that his debtor has some money he lend to another third party which money will be enough to settle his debt should his debtor collect his loan from the third party while the debtor refutes the allegation, the person alleging shall be given three (3) days adjournment to confirm and inform the court of the existence of such loan or not.

d)   A person who lost a claim of the house in which he lives to another who has proof or better title to the house shall be given three (3) days adjournment before (*Izar*) to evacuate his belongings out of the house.

Adjournment Sought for by Judgment Debtor
Any adjournment other than as provided for in the exceptions thereon such as adjournments sought for by a judgment debtor to enable him pay for judgment sum shall be granted by a judge in the following manner:

(i)   twenty-one (21) days to pay the judgment sum, if he fails to do so within time, he shall be entitled to additional;
(ii) eight (8) days if he is unable to meet up he shall be entitled to additional;
(iii) six (6) days further adjournment, if he fails to pay he shall be given additional;
(iv) four (4) days if he also fails he shall lastly be entitled to;
(v)   three (3) days to liquidate the sum.

If at the end of the last three days however the judgment debtor shall be exhaustively examined by the court to ascertain whether his claim of inability to pay is genuine or not, this shall be done before any further action could be taken by the court against him.

Adjournment Regarding Immovable Properties
Adjournment (stipulation) regarding immovable properties such as house, farmland is statutorily thirty (30) days to any person who wishes or seeks to establish before a judge whether or not a house or farmland is subject of inheritance or that the house or farmland is his share of inheritance. A claimant

under this thirty (30) days stipulation is entitled to adjournments to proffer proof to his claim under the following procedure:

   i. the first adjournment of 15 days, and where he fails or is unable to furnish proof within that period, he shall have additional;

   ii. eight (8) days afterwards another;

   iii. four (4) days and finally;

   iv. three (3) days after which the judge shall enter judgment in the case.

Where a claimant claims from the defendant a house or farm which he alleged to have inherited from his father or he alleges that he lent his house or farm to the defendant which allegation/claim the defendant denies. But when asked for proof he claims that his witnesses are not within the jurisdiction of the court, the judge shall at his instance adjourn the hearing for three (3) months to enable him call his witnesses to court.

Where a person has lived in a house for unspecified number of years or leased a house to another person for unspecified number of years, suddenly another person surfaces and claims that the house belongs to him and called witnesses who testified that the house is his/belongs to him while in the same vein the person in possession of the house also claims that he has witnesses to establish the fact that the house belongs to him or that he leased out his own, and seeks for adjournment to call such witnesses, he shall be given three (3) months adjournment within which to produce his witnesses.

If at the end of the stipulated period he is not able to produce his witnesses the judge shall place him under close observation to ascertain his seriousness or otherwise. If he is serious with his claim, the judge may in his discretion give him further adjournment otherwise he shall exhaust (*Izar*) him towards entering judgment.

Where a person obtains judgment against another judgment debtor for say, the sum of ₦30,000.00 and the judgment debtor claims that he has no money to pay the judgment sum except that he has a house or farm. In the circumstances the judge shall give him adjournment for one to two months within which he should either sell or pay the judgment sum; or,

Where a person (seller) sells a house to another (Buyer) and due to some unforeseen judicial reasons the sale was invalidated the seller shall be given one month adjournment within which to refund the consideration paid to the buyer.

Judge is required to give a judgment debtor thirty (30) days to pay the judgment sum, he is however required appropriately to stagger; the payment into; first fifteen (15) days then eight (8) days then four (4) days and lastly three (3) days enjoyable days before acting towards execution of his judgment.[12]

---

[12] Bahjah Fi-Sharhil Tuhfa p

Adjournment/Extension is granted by the court in favour of one or both parties in order to bring forth any evidence in his support...In a circumstance where it is applied it is left to the discretion of the judge, subject to their conviction in respect of the application and issue in dispute, that is, by extension of time or otherwise, merging or separating the matters accordingly (such as instances involving appeal and cross appeal).[13]

A party who has exhausted the right of adjournment shall be listened to after the expiration of the time except in the followings: endowment, release from marital bond, claim of genealogy, murder and emancipation.[14]

---

[13] Bahjah Fi Sharhil Tuhfa vol. 1 p.56
[14] Bahjah Fi Sharhil Tuhfa vol. 1 p. 82-84

Chapter 4

Settlement out of Court

PART I
Introduction

A judge is not permitted to proceed to hearing without satisfying himself that he ascertained and distinguished the litigants as to who is the plaintiff and who is the defendant. Appreciates the wishes of the litigants and facts of the claim and that the subject matter of claim is not tainted with illegality. If however he is unable to ascertain the case because of its complexity he shall turn the litigants away for a while, until he consults with specialists or experts including the jurists on the subject matter and on the claim or in alternative suggest reconciliation or settlement out of court to the parties. Indeed,

> "a Judge should do so by first referring the matter to another wiser and more intelligent (arbitrator) jurist than himself for directions as to the exact texts to consult, but if he remains in doubt he should make effort to reconcile the parties through out of court settlement."[1]

Quran Chapter IV: 10 say thus:

> "The Believers are but a single brotherhood so make peace and reconciliation between your two (contending) brothers, and fear Allah; that yee may receive mercy."

Prophet (S.W.A.) said:

> "Reconciliation is permissible among the Muslims except reconciliation that makes unlawful what is lawful and lawful what is unlawful."

---

[1] Tuhfa R.38 note 23

A judge is however not allowed to urge settlement in those cases where he sees from the proof or avowals that one of the parties is entirely in the right.

> "Generally speaking, there is in reconciliation that which humiliates or brings into discredit, at times also a reconciliation is injurious to certain right."[2]

4.03 Where the parties are honourable persons enjoying certain amount of consideration or are well known on account of their high character or who give themselves up to the study of religion or are united by close family ties, it will be the judge's duty to recommend that they settle their difference out of court.[3] Order 11, Rule 12 enjoins that where the parties to an action are related to each other or where they are important personalities, the judge may first request them to agree to arbitration or reconciliation rather than litigation. If they refuse to accept a reconciliation or arbitration the judge shall proceed to hear the matter in accordance with Islamic law.

Grounds for Settlement

A judge is enjoined to suggest settlement out of court under the following circumstances:

a.   if he cannot appreciate what law is applicable to solve the matter before him;
b.   if he cannot decide the matter because of the contradictory evidence given by witnesses on either side and of equal legal witnessing capacity;
c.   if there is immense fear that the judgment may lead to the eruption of strife afterwards on the part of the losing party;
d.   if there is fear that the judgment will create enmity among the most revered leaders of the community; or,
e.   if enmity among the families or family members or relations will be perpetuated by the judgment.[4]

Conciliation

Sulh, (conciliation) in the common usage, means the cutting-off of a dispute. By judicial or jurisprudential definition it means: a contract that ends the dispute between the litigants.[5]

In Islamic law it signifies a contract by means of which dispute (litigation) is avoided, set aside or settled:

---

[2] *Maliki Law* by Ruxton p.285
[3] *Maliki Law* by Ruxton p.286
[4] Ihkam Al- Ahkam p.
[5] Fiqh Sunnah p. 336

"Settlement or Conciliation means transfer that is leaving a certain right or suit by way of receiving something or giving it in order to avoid dispute or for the fear of its occurrence."[6]

IHKAM AL-AHKAM provides:

"If dispute becomes too intricate or there appears a (hitch) the litigants are called upon to agree to conciliation (compromise). But if it is a straightforward case, that shall not be so as long as one does not fear any trouble through passing judgment on the people who are blood relations."[7]

The essentials of conciliation are declaration and acceptance and its conditions are that the subject matter of the contract must be defined and clear to the judge.[8] In *Dutsi & 6 Ors* v. *Tofa & 4 Ors* (*supra*) it was held, that "conciliation in respect of receiving something in particular in place of the subject in dispute becomes contract."

الصلح على اخذ شىء غير المدعى اى به مع بيع لذات أو بالمأخوذ

Reference to Arbitration

Order 12 of the Sharia Court Civil Procedure Rules made provision for reference to arbitration:

(1) "A court may with the consent of the   parties to any proceedings order the proceedings to be referred for arbitration to such person or persons and or such terms as it deems reasonable."

(2) On observation of the report or award of arbitration the court may:
a- Confirm any award of arbitration and enter it as the judgment of the court, or
b- Set aside the award and fix a date for the hearing of the case accordingly.

Islamic law accepts a reference to arbitrators, that is to say that "*Tahkim*" appointment of arbitrator is in consonance with the principles of Islamic law, this is where the warring parties agree to place their dispute before a jurist, and agree to abide by whatever he decides.

It is noteworthy that Arbitration is in certain issues governed by certain regulations under Maliki School, *Duraid*, in "*Aqrab Masalik*" said:

---

[6] Marafa, GK in *Dutsi* v. *Tofa* (2001) LRNN 406
[7] Tuhfa R. 38-39
[8] (2000) LRNN 406 Per Marafa G.K.

"It is in order to appoint an Arbitrator a learned and neutral person in matter of property and injury; it shall not be to settle "*Hadd*" murder, "*Lian*" dispute on consanguinity, *talaq*, "Fuskh" emancipation, disputes of attainment of the status of adulthood, endowment or contract."

Mudawwanah, on the other hand provides: "If two parties seek that a man adjudicates in a dispute between them and he does that, the court endorsed it, the court shall not revoke or reject the verdict unless it contains fundamental injustice."[9] In principle therefore, it is in order that two disputing parties make one person their arbitrator.[10]

Fundamentally, where reconciliation is freely reached by the parties it becomes an enforceable contract, none of the parties to the reconciliation shall be permitted to set it aside unilaterally. In *Dutsi* v. *Tofa* (*supra*) it was held that it is not permissible that either of the parties to a reconciliation/settlement to set it aside only to continue disputing. This is based on *Haddabu*, the explanatory work to the book of '*Mukhyasar*, vol.v, page 84 where it provides;

"Where a valid reconciliation/ settlement on the face of Sharia law is effected, a party to a dispute is not allowed to subsequently set it aside in order to continue disputing as doing so will amount to a deviation from what is known (settlement/reconciliation) to what is unknown".
(*Wama iza waqa'al sulhu ala wajhil jaiz wa arada naqdihi, warrujuhi ilal khusuma lam yajzi zalika lima fihi minittiqal minal maalumi ilal majhool*).

و ما إذا وقع الصلح على وجه جائز وأراد نقضه والرجوع الى الخصومة لم يحز ذالك لما فيه من الانتقال من المعلوم الى المجهول.

Further more,

"It is not permissible to set aside the reconciliation /settlement that is in accordance with the sharia even if the parties thereto subsequently agreed to set it aside between them. Such parties are compelled to be bound by the reconciliation/settlement earlier reached. It is not permissible to set it aside to pave way for the continuing dispute between them."

("*Wala Yajuzu naqdi sulhu abrama, wain taradaya wa Khabara Alzama*.")

9 Ashalul Madarik vol. III P. 209-210
10 Tabsiratul Hukkam vol. p.55

ولايجوز نقضى يعنى ان الصلح على انكار إذا ابرم ونقد على الوجه الجائز لايجوز نقضه والرجوع
للحصام ولو ترا ضيا على ذالك

No person who has played a role in the reconciliation or settlement of dispute between two persons shall be permitted to give evidence in favour of either of them as doing so amounts to giving evidence about oneself.[11]

إذا اصلح إنسان بين شخصين لايجوز ان يشهد عليهما
الصلح ولا بما وقع به لأنها تشبه الشهادة على فعل نفسه

PART II
Representation

The law is that the Judge is not hindered from assisting a party to frame and present his case with clarity and he may ask him questions which will make him alert to protect his interest.[12] But such assistance is not permitted where doing so will lead to wrongful insinuation and accusation of bias or partiality. It is therefore only logical that where a party in litigation is unable to express himself due to some genuine or bona fide reasons, the party should be at liberty to appoint a representative who will assist him in the case, who will either appear on his behalf or along with the party represented. If he is representing the plaintiff to present the plaintiff's case with sufficient clarity and help him adduce evidence to prove it. If he is representing the defendant, he will have the opportunity to cross examine and challenge the evidence presented by the plaintiff and to discredit the witness.

Wakil (Agent)
Agency (representation) is known as "*Wakalah*" and the person so appointed to represent another is the "*Wakil*" or agent. Agency in Islamic law is permitted in all transactions and in litigation. "It is permitted for a person who has free control over his wealth while being an adult, sane and not bankrupt to appoint another as his agent, to represent him in all situations that accept representation."[13]

In litigation however, Islamic law allows a person to delegate someone to represent him or her in a case provided the agent is one not more, where they are more than one the other party should have to agree. If he agrees that more than one agent face him in the dispute such will be allowed. This position was upheld Per Marafa, GK. in *Alhaji Sa'idi Umar* v. *Maidawa Isa*, Sharia Court of Appeal

---

[11] Hashiyyat Dasuki vol.iv p.179
[12] Tuhfa R. 4
[13] Ihkam Al-Ahkam p. 69

decision[14] wherein he held; the appellant, Sa'idi Umar is represented by two counsels, A. A. Jibril and Muhammadu Malidi: the court asked (2) Maidawa, (the respondent) whether he accepted that two counsels should represent the appellant, the respondent replied that he agreed. The court therefore allowed the two counsels learned (sic) to represent the appellant as allowed in Ihkamul Ahkam, the explanatory work on the book of Tuhfa at page 65 regarding representation of agent in dispute, quoting from the book thus:- *"Wama minal Taukil Li-ithnaini, famazada, Minal Mamnu'I Indal Ulama'a"*

وما من التوكيل لاثنين ممـا   زاد من الممنوع عند العلماء

"Meaning Scholars have   forbidden two or more than two persons to represent a party in a case before a judge without the consent of other party in the case: But if the case involved in buying or selling of something then two representatives of a party are allowed."

ليس لرجل ولامرأة ان يوكل فى الحصام أكثر من واحد إلا برضا خصمه واما فى البيع والشراء وغير ذالك فله ذالك.

Ambali, G.K. also in his book[15] came to a similar conclusion saying; In Islamic law system a lawyer is in the shoes of a *wakil* (*"Wakili"*) and appointed agent. He does not merit more than what his principal qualifies for under the law (Islamic Law of agency)."

The Arabic word *"Al-muhami"* means lawyer. It can be described as a person who represents and conducts cases for litigants before a judge for on behalf his client. *"Al-muhamah"* on the other hand, means the "legal profession". The appellations were embraced by the Muslim world and adopted into the Islamic judicial system from their European counter-parts after the collapse of the Ottoman Empire in 1923. This does not however, suggest that the legal assistance and services were alien to the Islamic judicial system. Far from that, it is only that no effort was made to distinguish the words *"Al-muhamah"* and *"AL-Wakalah"*. While the latter (*Wakalah*) is permissible in anything that accepts representation as in an agency, its scope not only covers worldly affairs, but extends to the performance of religious duties such as *"Zakat"* and *"Hajj"*. No fee is charged. *"Al-muhamah"* on the other hand does not permit of any other role except that of defending litigants in court or offering advice upon payment of fees, save where legislation enjoins more. Furthermore wakil is by the provisions of Ihkam Al-Ahkam page 67 permitted to switch over to the side of his former adversary upon

---

[14] (2002) LRNN 365-367
[15] *The Practice of Islamic Law in Nigeria*, cap 6

disagreement with his principal even when he opposes same but that could amount to misconduct if he were a lawyer.

Another condition for allowing an agent to represent one is that such representation should be from the beginning of the case or matter. Where a principal was to have undertaken the proceedings himself for at least, three or more sittings no more representation will be allowed because it will involve repetition, recapitulation and cause delay, it will also involve repetition of matters already dealt with which will entail changes in the address and waste of time in dispensing with the case, per Orire, GK in *Ayanda* v. *Akanji.* [16]

Legal Practitioner

Prior to the 1979 Constitution of the Federal Republic of Nigeria the judgment of Marafa, GK of the Zamfara State Sharia Court of Appeal, would have been valid, because the duo of the Area Courts Edict 1967, and Sharia Court of Appeal Law of 1963 Laws of the Northern Nigeria, by SS. 28(1) and 20(1) respectively, representation by a legal practitioner in or before Area Courts and Sharia Court of Appeal was not permitted or allowed.

The exclusion of legal practitioners in or before the courts did not however include personal representation in a form of agency as person with authority continued to represent litigants in the court. Those laws though recognize agency *"Wakalah"* never considered legal practitioner as an agent and at best did not accord him any such status. This remained the position of law until 1979 Constitution came into force and following the landmark decision in *Karimatu Yakubu & 1 other* v. *Yakubu Paiko & 1 other).*[17] The Court of Appeal held Per A.B. Wali JCA (as he then was):

> "Islamic law is not a static law; it is a living law subject to interpretation, like any other law to suit all times and circumstances."

On legal representation by a legal practitioner before Sharia Court of Appeal, the learned jurist held:

> "Once a Lawyer has been enrolled in the Supreme Court to practice in Nigeria, no court shall put an additional qualification on him as a prerequisite to his appearance before it. And any number of lawyers can appear and represent a litigant in any court or tribunal established under the Constitution or any other law."

---

[16] (2002) LRNN 209
[17] (1961- 1989) SLRN vol. I p. 126

It follows then that a lawyer known as "*Muhami*" in the Islamic world does not measure as "*Wakil*" or agent, in so far as he is qualified so to function in accordance with the relevant legislation. And in case of Nigeria, pursuant to Legal Practitioners Act, 2004, Laws of the Federation of Nigeria, and having the privileges accorded him by S. 33 (6) (b) (c) of the 1979 Constitution which is *in pari materia* with S. 36 of the 1999 Constitution. Their lordships further held:

> "It is clear direction that whenever a court is dealing with civil as well as criminal matters. It cannot exclude from its proceedings parties or their legal representatives. It is party's right to be represented by a legal practitioner of his choice and who has satisfied the requirements of Legal Practitioners Act 1990."

Following the decision, all subsequent legislations hitherto excluding legal practitioners from proceedings ensured that Lawyers are no longer excluded. For instance S. 8(1) (2) of the Sharia Court Law 2000 of Kano State allows legal representation in both *criminal* and *civil* cases before the Sharia Courts.

Representation by a "*Wakil*" or agent of the defendant does not preclude the defendant's appearance before the court because if oath becomes apparent the "*Wakil*" or agent cannot take his place. It is not necessary, however, for a party to a suit to be present in court if he is legally represented, and if his counsel can conduct his case in his absence. Appearance of the party's counsel amounts to an appearance of the party itself.[18] Furthermore, any legal practitioner appearing before a Sharia Judge should ideally be learned in the rudiment of Sharia law and practice because his appearance is not only for his client, but he has a duty to assist and guide the court in the quest for justice, hence he cannot offer assistance on what he knows nothing about. Bahjah,[19] states:

ولا تقبل الوكالة إلا ان يحضر الموكل مع وكيله فى وقت الحكم ليقر بما يوقف عليه حصمه أويكون قريبا من مجلس القاضى.

Meaning: "Representation is not accepted except with presence of the principal at the time of judgment or oath taking or he be within reach so that he shall answer charges against him."

Representation by Agent "Wakil"
Representation, other than that of a legal practitioner, is however not of right. Further, the person representing is no more than *a "wakili"* or an appointed agent, whose appointment must come along with prerequisite proof.

---

[18] *Alake* v. *Afejuku* (1994) 9 NWLR (pt 368) 379 at 408
[19] Vol. 1 p. 207

There must be proof in court which suggests that the person is appointed to represent a litigant in court. For, under Islamic law one cannot say he is suing in representative capacity unless the principal confirms this to the court or the agent (representative) establishes his agency by calling two unimpeachable witnesses to testify that he has been appointed as agent, or he produces one witness and supports his evidence by taking a complementary oath, per Uthman Mohmmed, JCA.[20]

On the other hand, there is a presumption, which is a mark of honour to the legal profession that a counsel who announces representation for a client has the instruction and authority of that client to so do. The courts will normally not inquire into such authority. The courts do not require the counsel to tender written evidence to prove that he has so been briefed.[21]

Section 28(2) of the Area Court Law says, an Area Court may permit the husband, wife, brother, sister, son, daughter, guardian, servant, master or any inmate of the household of any party, who shall give satisfactory proof that he or she has authority in that behalf...to appear for any party before an Area court.

Order 2(2) Area Courts (Civil Procedure) Rules 1971 and Sharia Courts (Civil Procedure) Rules 2000, provide:

"Every civil cause shall be commenced by a complaint made in person or by the authorized representative of the person."

It is thus in order to appoint a representative "*Wakili*" to discharge a duty which a person can do by himself such as sale or purchase of goods, hiring, recovery of debt, its payment, marriage contract or repudiation of a wife.

An agent can only bring action before the court on the following grounds:

a. if he has a personal interest in the goods of his principal;
b. if he has hired goods from his principal; or
c. has borrowed goods;
d. if he has received goods in pawn from his principal; or
e. if his guaranty is concerned.

Where the case, which is the subject of representation, is distribution of estate of a deceased and there is more than one heir to the estate, one can represent the others in the matter. Also where one of such heirs is not available, consent of such none available heir is not mandatory. In a situation that other

---

[20] *Ahmed* v. *Jibrin & Ors* FCA/K/36/S/89, relying on Mukhtasar Al-Khlil, Vol. 5 p 182
[21] *Salim* v. *Ifenkwe* (1996) 5 NWLR (pt 450) 564; *Tukur* v. *Gov. of Gongola State* (1988) 1 NWLR (pt 409) 537

heirs are available but show no interest, the court may proceed to hear the heirs who are before the court.[22]

PART III
Guarantee

Guarantee is a promise or pledge to fulfil another person's obligation in case that other person defaults upon that obligation.

The guarantor, on the other hand, is a person who is secondarily liable for another's obligation or debt. It is permissible under Sharia and could be judicial or extra-judicial. The Prophet (PBUH) said of it thus:

الزعيم غريم (*Al-Zaeem Garimun*) meaning *"Liability is on the Guarantor."* The guarantor is responsible.

Islamic law recognizes three (3) types of guarantee and they are as follows:

i.   Guarantee to produce a person guaranteed to make a payment or to fulfil an obligation when the time is due. This is known as: ضا من الوجه
      And it is akin to bail under the criminal justice system. It is a pledge to produce a person on any agreed or appointed date;

ii.   Guarantee to find a person or supply his address of residence, or give information of the whereabouts of a person who defaults to fulfil an obligation. Usually, when the guarantor is unable to do so, he becomes liable;

iii. Guarantee to pay the amount guaranteed upon the time of such a payment being due. In this case, the creditor shall be free to receive payments either from the guarantor or from the person guaranteed on any specific date after default, whether he be present or not. ضا من الما ل

Terms of a Guarantee

The terms of a guarantee are worded as follows:

> "I pledge to pay the money or perform the obligation upon the person guaranteed;" or, "I promise to bring and produce the person guaranteed before this court at the lapse of the time so appointed;" or, "if the person guaranteed is unable to pay his debt as at when due, I shall be liable to pay it."

---

[22] *Sa'idi Umar* v. *Maiwada Isa* (2002) LRNN 365

A guarantee is an act of kindness and no fee or reward is permitted to be charged. In other words, payment of a fee cannot be used as a condition. A guarantee cannot be exchanged between two people - there must be three (3) parties to a guarantee who are the debtor, the creditor and the guarantor. Furthermore, a guarantee cannot be used to legalize an illegality.

The consent of the person in whose favour a guarantee is given is immaterial for people do not pay the debts of others without their permission.

The nature of a guarantee is dependent on the expression employed by the guarantor. If he is specific as to the type of guarantee or security he is offering, he is bound by it. If he did not specify, the judge could infer from the term the payment of debts. Tuhfat al hukkam, provides:

وهو بما عين للمعين   وهو بما ل حيث لم يعين

If his expressions refer to the production of the person guaranteed and did not specifically absolve himself of any obligation to redeem money against him, he will be bound to pay whatever is against him.

It is not incumbent upon the guarantor to pay the debt he guaranteed, if the person in favour of whom the guarantee was given dies before the time for payment is due. A guarantor shall not be liable to redeem the guaranteed money if the guaranteed dies before the expiration of the date of redemption .Tuhfa; further provides:

وما على الحميل غرم ما حمل   ا ن مات مضمون ولم يحن اجل

If a guarantor discharges his pledge at the expiration of the due date, he is entitled to recover his money from the person guaranteed.

Where a claim is established against a person with one witness and the Claimant seeks an adjournment to call the second witness, the Defendant must be ordered to bring a surety to bail him until the adjournment date.

The guarantor shall be discharged of liability if at the adjournment date he produces the person guaranteed, dead or alive. This is only applicable in the case of "Laminu Al-Wajhid". The person who guarantees to bring to court a debtor whenever he is wanted shall be free from liability to make payment, if he brings the person for whom he gave the guarantee at the appointed time even if the latter were dead.

The Defendant is to be given a grace of one day when the court gives judgment against him on that amount. A guarantor, who fails to discharge his obligations when due shall, on application being granted, have a reprieve of one day; and only if he still fails, shall he be sent to jail.

If the Defendant did not find anyone to provide a guarantee for him, it shall be said to the Plaintiff "keep an eye on him". But he shall not be imprisoned. However, Ash-hab; has opined that in such a situation, it shall be necessary for the Defendant to provide the court with someone who will guarantee bringing him to court whenever he is required. And, it is upon this view that judges base their judgment.

PART IV
Contempt of Court

Any conduct which defies the authority or dignity of a court is contemptuous and punishable because it interferes with the administration of justice. Under Islamic law, it is preferable to discipline anybody who, in the open court, misbehaves to a judge, a witness, mufti or the opposing party, rather than to over look it especially if the misconduct is direct. But when it is indirect the court may or may not discipline him.[23]

Contempt Facie Curiae

The powers of the judge to deal so decisively and justifiably with such conduct are derived from both Islamic law and English law as well as in statutory laws. Under Islamic law, a judge in whose face contempt is committed is not inhibited from punishing the contemnor. The law recognizes the judge's power to act promptly in an offence which is committed in *facie curiae*, i.e. in the presence of the court or outside the court, such as the English law provides for sanction in the similar situation. Islamic law provides that:

---

[23] Jawahirul Ikhlil vol. II P. 202

"It is preferable to discipline the fellow who is rude to the judge; it is also desirable that anyone who insults a witness, in court should also be disciplined."[24]

Contempt in Islamic sense therefore encompasses any act that prejudices any court official and even the witnesses. Islamic law does not contemplate any conduct outside the court but it is certainly inferred that it is punishable depending on its effect on the administration of justice. Generally obedience to orders of court is fundamental to the good order, peace and stability of the Nigerian nation. A. B. Wali, JSC in *Ezekiel Hart* v. *Ezekiel Hart*,[25] stated, *inter alia*:

"...To allow orders to be disobeyed would be to tread the road toward anarchy. If orders of the court can be treated with disrespect, the whole administration of justice is brought unto scorn..."

If the remedies that the courts grant to correct wrongs can be ignored, then there will be nothing left for each person but to take the law into his own hands. Loss of respect for the courts will quickly result into the destruction of our society.

Punishing the Contemnor

Whosoever acts in contempt of a Judge or his proceeding, *Mufti*, witness or litigants in open court and before the judge shall be punished. But where the contemnor's conduct is not in open or before the judge such may be pardoned. Also pardonable after warning the contemnor is that which is based on genuine mistake committed by a reputable person against the judge, witness, *Mufti* or litigant.[26]

"Any person who slanders in court either against the other litigants or a witness or is contemptuous towards the judge commits a misdemeanour and shall be punished accordingly. But where the person merely says to a witness that his evidence is false or tells the other party that he is, or they are, in error, such a person has committed no misdemeanour and may be pardoned."[27]

---

[24] Tuhfa R.
[25] (1990) 1 NWLR (Pt.) 279
[26] Ihkam Al-Ahkam p. 14
[27] Tuhfa R. 28

The punishment for contempt or slander would usually be a few strokes with a lash, the number of lashing may vary with the rank of the accused and that of the slandered witness.[28] But where person committing slander or in contempt is a man of outstanding character he should usually be pardoned if his conduct was in error.

PART V
Custody of a Minor

Custodyship may be regarded as vesting of legal custody of a minor or lunatic in a person so as to have his lawful charge, care and responsibility.

Custodyship is distinct from adoption. While custodyship is islamically recognized adoption is not. It entails care for an infant as regards his sleeping place, feeding, clothing, beddings and cleanness of his body.[29]

4.30 A minor who is yet to attain puberty, his natural guardian under Islamic law is his father and upon his death his executor takes his position. Mother on the other hand shall generally be entitled to the custody of her minor child up to certain age according to the sex of the child. She, among all persons is most entitled to the custody of her minor during marriage and after separation from her husband upon failure of marriage Ruxton states:

> "If the mother remarries or is excused from taking care of her children, this duty becomes incumbent upon the children's relatives in the following order:- the children's maternal grandmother, the mother's maternal or paternal grandmother. The children's paternal grandmother; the children's father, the children's sister, the children's paternal aunt or great-aunt, the father's maternal aunt or great aunt.

The circumstances by which mother could lose her right to custody of her child are:
a. if she remarries a stranger; or
b. where not remarried but leaves the town where the father of her child resides;[30]
c. if she is sick of leprosy or transmittable disease;
d. insanity or madness;
e. *Fasiq* transgressor – in which case Muslim leaders are approached to keep watch on the child's development.

---

[28] Ibid.
[29] Ihkan Al-Ahkan –Page 141
[30] Bahjah vol II page 411 the journey must be such that could expose the guardian to hardship and danger and of 6 miles and beyond.

Loss of right of custody arising out of reason of   sickness which appeared on the mother cannot disentitle a mother of custody if the reason disappears or she gets cured of the sickness, she can claim back her right, even if she had given consent to the loss due to such reason.

Where however, a mother who is entitled to custody due to death of her husband or separation but choose to abandons such right for another marriage, she loses her night to custody and will not lay claim to custody even after separation from her husband.

Where a mother has right to custody knowing fully that such right exist in her favour but abandons such right for up to one year she will not be considered on demand for custody.

So also where a person says or gives up his right to custody and did not bother until after one year he will not be permitted to seek for the right afterwards.[31]

So is a guardian of a child who decides to travel with a child to a place where he is going to stay permanently with the child he will take custody and the mother would lose her right.[32]

PART VI
Maintenance of Wife

The responsibility for feeding and clothing of a wife is on her husband. If he is unable to discharge that burden a judge before whom the matter is reported is required to consider setting for him a time limit of two months or more as the circumstances may require for him to provide his wife with feeding or clothing.

If after the periods of time given to him he is still unable to discharge that burden, the judge shall either direct him to divorce his wife or do so himself or direct the wife to divorce her husband by way of *khule* and the judge shall record the same.

Setting a period of two months or more is subject to the discretion of the judge who is enjoined to exercise with diligence after taking into consideration the economic situation of the society and that of the husband in particular.

PART VII
Absentee Husband

Whosoever, after marriage with his wife set out for a long journey, a journey which could keep him away from his wife for upward of ten days or more Whether his where about is known or not shall be given a reprieve of one month

---

[31] Ihkam Al-Ahkam page 144
[32] Ihkam Al- Ahkam page 145

(whether before the journey he consummated the marriage or not). If the wife complains to a judge, that he left and did not provide for her feeding or clothing and did not live for her anything that could translate into money or whatever she could sell to take care of her feedings and clothing and in her complaint seeks for divorce the trial judge shall give him one month period upon expiration of which, she will call two witnesses who will establish:

i.   that she is the wife of the absentee;
ii. that in fact the absentee is not around;
iii. that before his absence he did not consummate the marriage;
iv. that presently he is residing in certain place or that they don't know where he lives;
v.   that to the best of their knowledge they are unaware that he provided her with feeding or clothing or made provision for any;
vi. that they are unaware that he came back to her after his departure or sent her any massage since he left till this date.

If the judge is satisfied with the evidence he shall set a one month time limit or more months as the circumstances may require. At the expiration of such time the judge shall administer an oath on the wife that all she alleged and what the witnesses stated are nothing but the truth. If she swears, the judge shall order her to divorce her husband afterwards he shall decree the divorce. If it is established that there was no consummation of marriage between then, the divorce shall be "*Dalaq ba'in*" which will accord her absolute freedom. If at any time the husband reappears she will have the option to restore the marriage or declined.

Chapter 5

Statement of Claim

PART I
Oral Presentation of Claim

Claims, i.e. *"Al-Da'awa or Al-Dalab"* (الدعوى او الطلب), and statement of claim, pleadings or written complaint, i.e *"Al-Tauqif or Maqal"* (التوقيف او المقال), are two respective means or ways by which proceedings are commenced before Area and Sharia Courts. The adoption of either of the ways will depend on the nature of the claim and the subject matter of the claim. In *Aremu* v. *Akanni & others,* while referring to Al-Fawakihid Dawaniy, commentary on Risalah, Abdullahi Al-Qairawaniy volume 11 pages 301, Grand Kadi Ambali, reproduced the procedure thus:

> "The procedure of filling a claim is that the judge orders the plaintiff to first speak. He then makes his claim precise and definite. If he fails to give the bases of his claim, the judge shall demand for them. It is when he lands that the judge asks the defendant to respond..."

Order 2 Rules 4 of both Area and Sharia Courts civil procedure rules respectively provide that a court shall refuse to entertain a cause or matter made if the said cause or matter fails to disclose any cause of action. Also referring to the Aqrabul Masalik[1] the learned jurist in the same case explained further:

> "The plaintiff makes the statement of claim in respect of definite matter such as amount of money or anything else; He offers the basis of the claim. If he cannot, the claim will not be entertained..."

Written Statement of Claim

Claim could also be by means of written statement on which a plaintiff lists his claims against the defendant and seeks his reply to it. This procedure is referred to in Tuhfa as "Tauqif", it is also referred to as *"Maqal"* meaning *"Pleadings".*

---

[1] Vol. IV P. 18-19

If claim is presented by the means of *Tauqif,* the defendant is required to respond promptly; otherwise he should be compelled to do so. The defendant shall be entitled to a copy of the statement of claim if he demands for one as that will assist him to respond or prepare his response appropriately. The defendant is however at liberty to respond or reply in like manner with a written statement of defence or orally. Whichever method he adopts, the same rule which applies to the oral claim is applicable to written claim. Order 1 Rule 1 of the Sharia Courts (Civil Procedure) Rules as applicable in the Northern states sharia judicial system provides that:

> "After the parties have appeared in the Court the judge shall ask the plaintiff to make a statement of his claim. The statement shall be a definite, clear averment which must clearly state the subject matter of the claim..."

The rule did not make provision, however for a written statement, perhaps, because *Ibn Asimi,* is of the view that "for many a time, a verbal statement is clearer than a written document." This position is not without exception for where a claim has complexity with various attachments its presentation by means of written statement such as will give a clear and vivid picture and details of the attachment will be most appropriate.[2]

Claim of Large Sum of Money

Where also the claim is of large sums of money the source of which are diverse, a presentation by a written complaint is mandatory because only then the detailed explanation of each source and the attachments thereof will be accepted. Where however the claim can better be explained orally than in writing oral explanation can be adhered to.[3] Where a written statement is presented on a complex claim over a huge amount of money it is necessary for the statement of claim to be recorded, for this makes judgment more precise and prevents dispute from arising later on.[4] The judicial proof in both oral statement and written statement of claim is however the same.

Right of Defendant to Reply to Written Statement

It is significant that reply to the statement of claim, be it written as well as oral, must be prompt except under some special circumstances. A defendant who receives a written claim and afterwards request, for time or adjournment to enable him study the claim so as to appreciate its import or to enable him appoint a

---

[2] Ihkam Al-Ahkam p. 16
[3] *Shitu* v. *Ibrahim* (*supra*)
[4] Tuhfa R. 58-59

representative or an expert, to sort out the claim for him, the judge should oblige him such adjournment, for grant of adjournment is at the discretion of the Judge. There will be no adjournment in cases where the claim is simple to comprehend or in cases where the adjournment is merely sought by the defendant just to waste the time of the court. In such a situation the Judge shall compel the defendant to respond immediately. Tuhfa, put it thus:

> "But if the document needs some consideration; the thing to do is to copy it and ask for time to study it. But if the defendant should ask for a deferment (adjournment) over something which is clear and easy, such a request should be turned down. According to some authority, however another view is that the request be granted."

PART II
Ingredients of Complaint

For claim to mature for hearing before a judge, it must have the following ingredients:

a. The claim must be known, positive and definite; if the subject matter of claim is uncertain, the claim may not qualify for hearing.

b. The claim shall be such that if proved shall be executable and binding upon the respondent. A claim for the enforcement of gift is not proper claim as same mighty be withdrawn by the maker

c. The claim shall not be founded on what the custom and tradition considers as false. Where a person is known to reside in a house for several years while everyone in the society sees him manage the property and the claimant did not complain.

d. The claim if it is for land, house or farm must specify the boundaries.

e. The claim if it is for moveable, must explain the species, quality, value, measurement and weight of the thing claimed.

f. The claim must explain the reasons why the claimant has such thing he is claiming with the respondent, otherwise his claim may be rejected.

Claim to be Specific, Definite and Clear

Generally, the person who complains is ordinarily referred to as the Plaintiff or "*Al-Muddai*" (المدعى). He states his claim(s) while the Judge and the Defendant or "*Al-Mudd'a Alaihi*" (المدعى عليه) listens with rapt attention. The requirement of Sharia is that the claim must be specific and it shall have full explanation. *Tuhfa* provides that 'the matter in dispute must satisfy two conditions: the claim must be specific and that it should have full explanation."[5]

المدعى فيه له شرطان   تحقق الدعوى مع البيان

Thus, the necessity to make a clear, distinct and unambiguous claim has been the basis upon which the principle of Islamic procedural law rests. *Mukhtasar Al-Khalil* provides:

"A claimant ought to claim (before a judge) something known and defined in number, amount, kind and structure not something unknown, assumed, doubted or conjectured. Any claim which does not measure up to the above qualifications should not be entertained."

This principle of law has received judicial applications by the Superior Courts in Nigeria. For instance, in *Biri* v. *Mairuwa*,[6] the Court of Appeal held, Per A.B. Wali,

"Under Islamic Law, the subject matter of a dispute has two conditions, namely;-ascertainment of the claim and explanation of the claim through evidence. The first circumscribes the scope of the claim whereas the second establishes the claim."

Maidama, JCA, in *Mafolatu* v. *Usain Akanbi Ita Alamu*,[7] explained the principle further when he held that "two conditions are essential to the subject matter in dispute. There should be clear statement of the complaint followed by a proper description of the subject matter."

A. B. Wali, on landed property claim further expatiated that "it is fundamental in Islamic law that every claim must be stated in clear terms or clear statements and in the case of land, its clear boundaries and locations must be stated."

Following this, Order 2 Rule 1, provides:

"If the subject matter is land or landed interest the statement of claim shall give a full address of the land and its boundaries."[8]

5.07 What these requirements go to show is that it is the pre-requisite, that a claim to meet the degree of clarity required by Sharia and to qualify for hearing, it

---

[5] Tuhfa R. 23
[6] (1996) 8 NWLR (Pt. 467) 425
[7] CV/K/81s/84
[8] Sharia Civil Proceduer Rules

must be realistic, unambiguous, definite, precise, apt, succinct, full and complete and must not be evasive, vague and bogus. It is improper for a plaintiff to say; I think the defendant owes me money; or the defendant owes me *about* ₦100.00, thus, if the subject matter of claim is land, the plaintiff must mention or state the boundaries and its location, if it is money, he must state the amount, if it involves animals he must mention them numerically and by description by their species, if it is moveable he must explain the species, qualities, quantity, value, measurement or weight of the subject matter, thus it is not enough to make a claim of an amount of money without stating the exact amount involved, it is not valid for a plaintiff to make a claim of undefined parcel of land or unknown property because such do not help the course of justice. A claim, however, such as 'I have a share in the house or land in dispute' which goes on to state the level or extent of the share, should be listened to.

Adducing Reasons for Claims

The claim must explain the reasons why the plaintiff has such thing he is claiming with the defendant otherwise the claim may be struck out or rejected. This formed the bases of the Court of Appeal and the Sharia Court of Appeal of Kwara State decisions in *Maisingba* v. *Opobiyi*[9] *and Okino* v. *Bello*[10] where it was respectively held thus:

> "Sharia therefore demands that claim (at *talab* or *al-da'awa*) should be precise. No claim is considered unless it is exact, defined and specific. It is not enough to make a claim of an amount of money without stating the exact amount involved. Similarly, it is not valid for a plaintiff (*Al-Muddaee*) to make a claim of an unidentified parcel of land or unknown property because such claim does not help the course of justice. A valid claim should, therefore indicate the exact amount of money which the plaintiff intends to claim from the defendant, the size, location and boundaries of the parcel of land he wished to claim as well as full description of any property the plaintiff intends to claim. *A valid statement of claim also needs to show the basis of the claim,* if it is a loan which price of the defendant has defaulted to pay back, sold goods to the defendant by the plaintiff or any other cause such as entitlement on the basis of inheritance."

Judicial Reasons for Detail Explanation

The purposes of the required details is not far-fetched, it is to enable the plaintiff explain the bases of his claim and his reasons thereof, for the defendant to determine whether to admit liability or deny it, i.e. put up defence and above all

---

[9] (1982) FCA/K/7/82

[10] KWS/SCA/CV/17/81 (Unreported)

enable the judge distinguish between the plaintiff and the defendant, identify the subject matter in dispute, the applicable law and the procedure to follow in deciding the case.

For instance Part 1 of Order 11 of the Area Courts (Civil Procedure) Rules 1971 unlike Sharia Civil Procedure Rules 2000 confers dual jurisdiction on Area Court over cases involving Muslims and non Muslims. In its wording..."if the case is one in which Moslem Law is to be administered or applied, the court shall continue the hearing in accordance with Moslem practice and procedure but if the case is not one in which Moslem law is to be administered or applied, the court shall continue the hearing in accordance with the following rules of this Part, meaning; applying the practice and procedure other than that of the Islamic law.

Interrogation of the Plaintiff

In order to obtain classification and precision in a claim the law also enjoins that both defendant and the court should interrogate the plaintiff who fails to furnish a vivid picture of his claim and its basis. If the claim pertains to land, the plaintiff has to explain where it is situated and defines its extent and boundary. It may also require a visit to *locus in-quo*. This is in line with the requirement which provides "otherwise, i.e. if the plaintiff did not give the bases of his claims, the judge and the defendant shall demand the explanation from him" "*Wailla Fliyasalhu Al-Hakim Annin Sabbab Summa Almudai Alahi.*"

وإلا فليسأله الحاكم عن السبب ثم المدعى عليه

The required explanation will also expose the legality or otherwise of the subject matter to validity test i.e. whether the article in dispute is the type which in the eyes of Sharia is illegal or prohibited which cannot be subject of the jurisdiction of the Sharia court. A dispute arising out of or connected with the sale or ownership of intoxicants, pigs, pork and thing whose ownership is prohibited for Muslims by Sharia cannot confer jurisdiction on Sharia court as such complaint or claim of it cannot be entertained *ab initio* as transaction on it are considered in Sharia as invalid.

Defendant's Reply

As soon as the judge satisfies himself with the explanation provided by the plaintiff and is satisfied that the plaintiff has by his claim and the explanation thereof made a *prima facie* case, the judge shall ask the defendant to reply to the plaintiff's statement of claim.[11] The defendant in his reply may admit liability in

---

[11] O. II R. 2 Sh. Civil Proc. Rules

respect of the whole claim or part of the claim made by the plaintiff or he may totally deny liability or remain silent.[12] Where the defendant admits liability and he is a person whose admission is acceptable in law, i.e. he is an adult and sane, upon satisfying some conditions precedent to admission of liability or guilt in Sharia then the judge shall enter judgment in favour of the plaintiff after administering the procedure of 'Izar[13] (both admission and Izar are fully discussed in coming chapters).

Where the defendant has denied the plaintiff's claim the judge shall scrutinize and examine the statement of claim before him and decide as to who among the parties shall be the (Muddai) the plaintiff and who shall be (mudda'a alaihi), the defendant, the judge shall then call upon the plaintiff to bring evidence to prove his case.[14] The essence of the scrutiny and careful examination of the statement of claim is among others to distinguish between the parties and to ascertain upon whom among the parties should the burden of proof lies and who should be asked to call witnesses or tender documents if any. The judge shall also examine the claim before him and see whether it pertains to wealth such as land, farmland or house, or dispute as to whether there is consummation or not between spouse which may finally lead to payment of full dowry or claims different from these, like claims of divorce or dispute over paternity which does not involve inheritance. The examination is also to ascertain the claim which shall entail oath taking.

PART III
Distinguishing Between Plaintiff and Defendant

The law regarding distinguishing between the plaintiff and the defendant is of necessity such that "a judge who fails to identify who is who among the litigants is said to have missed the path of justice" this is because he would not know who to saddle with the onus of proof. To this Sayyadi Saeed Bin Al-Musayyib said "Man Arafa Al-farq baina Muddai wal Mudda Alaihi fa Qad arafa wajhul Qadai") (meaning, "Anybody who has the knowledge to distinguish the plaintiff from the defendant has discovered the gate to just decision.")[15]

من عرف بين المدعى والمدعى عليه فقد عرف وجه القضاء

Identification of Plaintiff and Defendant therefore constitute daunting task for a trial judge. It does not follow in Islamic law that whosoever goes to lodge a complaint in court automatically becomes the Plaintiff "Al-Muddai" (المدعى) while

---

[12] O. II R.2
[13] O. II R. 4
[14] O. II R. 5
[15] Ihkam Al-Ahkam p. 8

the person against whom complaint is lodged is automatically Defendant *"Al-Mudda'a alihi"* (عليه المدعى). This principle of Islamic procedure has been emphasized by Sheik Muhammad Bin Yusuf El-Kafi, in his Ihkam Al-Ahkam, commentary on Tuhfa where he said, "Distinguishing the circumstances and positions of the plaintiff and defendant is certainly the pivot (milestone) upon which the substructure or substratum of litigation lies." In *Danbaba* v. *Sale,*[16] it was held that "under Islamic law and procedure, a litigant can file a claim as a plaintiff and, after a thorough examination which a judge is mandated to do, the plaintiff may turn out to be a defendant. Also, in *Shatache* v. *Balarabe,*[17] it was observed that:

> "Under Islamic law and procedure, the trial court is empowered to alter the status of the parties to an action. Thus once a case has been accepted by a trial judge, it is the duty of the judge to conduct preliminary investigation in order to determine who are the claimant/plaintiff and the defendant. It is not a matter of course to say that whosoever initiates or institutes action becomes the plaintiff and the other party a defendant as obtained in the common law system. Under Islamic law it is possible that "A" appears in court as the complainant/plaintiff and "B" as the defendant after preliminary investigations by the trial judge of the matter "B" the defendant may become the claimant and the initial claimant "A" becomes the defendant. Consequently the person who appeared as the defendant may be asked to prove his case as the plaintiff. Determining the nature of the plaintiff and the defendant enhances the judgment of the court."

The Supreme Court, in *Jundun* v. *Abuna*[18] A.B. Wali, JSC put the principle more succinctly when he concluded, *inter alia*, viz:

> "Under the Sharia procedural law, it is not always necessary that a litigant who complains first   before the court shall always be the plaintiff, it is the judge, based on the dictates of the facts of the case, that decides who is to be the plaintiff. The judge has to determine, from what is most reasonable and in conforming to the normal state of things, which of the two parties is to be cited as the defendant."

Achike, JSC. (as he then was)[19] in his judgment decided that "under Sharia, it is the nature of the complaint before the court and not necessarily the party who initiates the action that may be designed Plaintiff by the court."

---

[16] (2004) All FWLR (Pt.226) 1915
[17] (2002) 10 NWLR (Pt.775) 227
[18] (2000) 10 SCNJ 14 at 20

This shows a fundamental difference between Islamic law and common law. In *Mandara* v. *Amin*,[20] the difference between the two laws was made vivid, when his lordship, Coomasie JCA rightly concluded that:

"The proceedings in English law are at variance with that of Islamic law, for instance, under Islamic law procedure, it is the Judge, based on the dictates of Sharia that decides who is to be the plaintiff and which of the two parties is to be called the defendant."

The *Tuhfa of IBN ASIM*, on distinguishing plaintiff and defendant, states as follows:

"The plaintiff is the person whose statement is contrary to the original state of affairs or custom and yet he claims what he says to be true, the defendant is the person whose statement is reinforced by custom and the original state of affairs bear witness in support of him. Conversely, the person who claims that such and such a case has taken place is the plaintiff, while the person who argues that it has not taken place is the defendant.^"

Bahjah fi sharhi al-Tuhfa, also provides (though with exception) that:

"He whose claim is in affirmative form is the plaintiff. He whose claim is in negative is the defendant, the only exception is in the case of a woman who complains that her husband under whom she lives is not maintaining her to which claim he says, I did. In this situation such a woman shall become the plaintiff and the onus of proof shifts to her."[21]

On the other hand Ruxton defines plaintiff and defendant thus:

"Plaintiff is he in favour of whom the normal, state of things entails no presumption. The defendant on the contrary, is he whose pleadings are the outcome of presumptions resulting from the normal state of things."[22]

The author went on to explain that "the normal state of things" is described in text in two words *"Asl"* and *"Urf"*. He explained that the word *"Asl"* is applied in personal matters and it means ordinary state of relations between any two

---

[19] Achike Justice, SC. At p. 221
[20] (2004) All FWLR (pt. 239) 1022
[21] Bahjah Fi Sharhi Tuhfa, Vol. I p. 26
[22] *Maliki Law* by F.H. Ruxton p

persons between whom ordinarily no obligation exists. If any one of them pleads that he is a creditor, he has the presumption of originality *"Asl"* on him in that respect he will be the plaintiff and will have the burden of proving his claim on him, that is proof of the existence of an obligation and if the other one pleads extinction of such obligation then the burden will shift on him to prove it. For example "A" pleads that he gave a loan to "B" the burden shall ordinary rest on "A" to prove his claim. But if "B" claims that he has paid up the loan then he becomes the plaintiff and "A" becomes the defendant.

The author further explained that the word *"Urf"* (custom) applies to chattels, thus "A" and "B" each plead that a certain chattel belongs to him; if one of them alone is in possession he will be the defendant and the other the plaintiff, the presumption will therefore be that he has *"Urf"* from the fact that ordinarily possession and ownership go together. Thus if a man and his wife both lay claim to a mirror, it is more reasonable to suppose that the mirror belongs to the wife and thus she becomes the defendant and the defendant plaintiff for he has against him the presumption resulting from *"Urf"*.

The erudite, Ambali, GK[23] provided for six type formulae designed by Islamic jurists to guide and assist courts of first instance on the task of identifying on whom to place the burden of proof between plaintiff and defendant as follows:

i.   **Right of Withdrawal:** A Complainant is the party who demands certain rights due to him from the Defendant. It is he, whose silence means withdrawal and the suit automatically terminates. But the Defendant is he, whose silence does not terminate the suit. Rather the force of law shall be invoked to make him reply;

ii.   **The Application of the Principles of "Asl":** The term refers to normal state of things or presumption of regularity. The concept of *"Asl"* is applied in personal matters and it means ordinary state of relation between any two persons taken at random between whom, as a general rule, there exists no obligation. A Plaintiff then is he, who claims that something derogatory to the normal state has occurred. For instance "A" claims that "B" is his slave. The *"Asl"*, i.e. the normal state of things, is that "B" is a free citizen. The claim of "A" is contrary to the ordinary state of affairs *"Asl"* and "A" as Plaintiff has the burden of proving the circumstances that made "B" lose his (birth right) freedom to him;

iii. **The Application of the Principle of "Urf":** The concept of *"Urf"* is also a presumption of regularity but it applies to chattels. In the case of the claim of a parcel of land for instance, *"Urf"* is that the possession and ownership

---

23 *The Practice of Muslim Family Law in Nigeria,* p. 104

go together. Hence he who enjoys possession has the advantage and the person who does not have it but claims title over a parcel of land is the Plaintiff. This is because his claim is not in conformity with the normal state of affairs that the possession goes with the ownership. As such Shariah demands proof from him to show that the situation at hand is not the normal practice. He owes the duty to explain the circumstance that changed the normal situation;

iv. **The Nature of the Party in Relation to the Bone of Contention:-** A woman who disputes the ownership of sword, or say a gun with a man, or soldier preferably is the Plaintiff because her claim runs counter to *"Urf"* while the man/soldier enjoys the support of the normal state of affairs. On the other hand, a man who disputes the ownership of cooking utensils, earrings or, say bangles with a woman is Plaintiff because his claim runs counter to the ordinary state of affairs. The woman who challenges him is favoured by *"Urf"*—the presumption of regularity. She does not need to be saddled with task of proof. The onus of proof is on him while hers is to defend the status quo because the *"Urf"* is on her side. Who sues in this situation is irrelevant to determine Plaintiff on whom the onus of proof should normally be placed;

v. **The Seeker of Rights is the Plaintiff:** Another key to distinguish the Plaintiff from the Defendant is for the court to ask itself which of the parties is seeking rights or redress, and from whom are the rights being sought. The former is the Plaintiff he moves and urges the court to exercise the power in his favour to secure for him his rights from the Defendant. He should therefore convince the court by putting up cogent reasons why he is entitled to the judgment. The latter is the Defendant. He is at an advantage because the rights are in his possession. However, there is an exception to this general rule. For instance, an orphan demanding the return of his property from the trustee is not considered as Plaintiff on whom the onus of proof lies. He is a Defendant, if the trustee asserts that he had returned the property to the orphan. Although the orphan is seeking his rights from the trustee; the latter is to prove that he has handed over the property to the orphan because basically, the law requires him to call witnesses when ever he wants to hand over the entrusted property of the orphan to him. See Qur'an 4:7. "And test the understanding of orphans until they attain the age of marriage then if you perceive in them mature judgment, deliver to them their property; when the you deliver to them their property then call witnesses in their presence." It is therefore assumed that the property is in the care of the trustee till he satisfied the requirement of the law.

vi.   **Affirmative Claims:** The theory of a jurist called *Al-Mussayab* is that he whose claim is in the affirmative form should be taken as the Plaintiff. His argument is that proofs are brought to establish what is positive, that is he who assets must prove. It is illogical to demand proof for what does not exist, i.e. negative. For instance "A" claims that "B" owed him a sum of money and "B" denied it. The onus of proof lies on "A" and not on "B" However, this general principle has an exception. "A", a woman who alleges that her husband "B" with whom she resides, fails to maintain her is a Plaintiff even though her claim is not in the affirmative form. The man "B", who denies such allegation is a Defendant even though his claim is in an affirmative form. The reasons is clear, the law assumes that a wife under roof of her husband is maintained by him. So the *"Urf"* favours him. It is her claim that runs counter to the presumption of regularity. She is therefore saddled with the onus of proof. But if they live in different towns or she resides outside the house in which he lives he is the Plaintiff who has the burden to establish that he maintains her, irrespective of who initiate the action.

The big challenge of the trial court is to know which of these formulae of law is applicable in any given claim. It has to fully understand the claim. Its basis is for the determination of the relationship between the two contending parties with respect to the subject of claims and to determine on whom to place the burden of proof and who is at the receiving end.

PART IV
Criminal Complaint

The trial of "*Hudud*" and "*Qisas*" (criminal) offences is commenced when the accused appears or is brought before the court, the particular details of the offence of which he is being accused is read over to him by the court in a language he understands. The emphases are that the information read over to the accused must be clear so that he understands it.

Upon the courts satisfaction that the accused understood the accusation against him he shall be asked to make a plea.[24] If the accused confesses before the court to the commission of an offence of which he is accused of, in the words used by him, the court may convict and sentence him accordingly.[25] If he however denies the accusation against him or he refuses to admit or deny, the court shall

[24] S.388 Sharia Criminal Procedure (Amend.) Code Kano
[25] S.389 Sharia Criminal Procedure (Amend.) Code Kano

proceed to hear the accusation against him.[26] In other words the burden shall be on the accuser or the complaint to prove the accusation. The accusation may range from the offences of *Zina*, rape, sodomy, false accusation, theft, alcoholism, robbery, homicide, causing miscarriage, injuries to unborn children, exposure of infants, cruelty to children, concealment of birth, and hurt, among others.[27]

---

[26] S.390 Sharia Criminal Procedure (Amend.) Code Kano
[27] Cap. V111- x SPC Law

Chapter 6

Trial Procedure

PART I
Burden of Proof under Islamic Law

In every dispute, there are at least two litigating parties: the Plaintiff and the Defendant. The former claims what is contrary to the apparent facts and the Defendant denies such claims. The burden of proof lies on the Plaintiff because what is apparent is presumed to be the original state.[1]

Burden or standard of proof generally connotes a party's duty to prove or establish a fact in dispute in civil or criminal cases. It is fundamental in both civil and criminal trials to just dispensation of justice. As soon as a sharia judge is in no doubt as regarding the party upon whom to place the burden of proof, having distinguished the plaintiff from the defendant. He shall begin from the person so identified as the plaintiff call upon him to prove his claim on the maxim which enjoins "Evidence or proof is on he who claims and oath is on he who denies."

البينة على المدعى واليمين على من انكر

Ibn Asimi, put it lucidly when he stated:

"The plaintiff is required to bring witnesses to testify for him; and this rule has a general application. The defendant is required to take an oath in the event of failure of the plaintiff to bring forth witnesses."[2]

Proof in Islamic law is known as "*Bayyinah*" while evidence is referred to as "*Shahadah*." Burden of proof on the other hand is known as "*Al-Bayyinat alal Muddai*" (البينة على المدعى). Burden of proof becomes apparent when the Defendant denies the claim, complaint, or allegation against him. In both English Law and Islamic law procedure the burden of proof is the same namely, he who asserts must prove but the manner in which that burden is discharged *is*

---

[1] *Islamic Law of Evidence*, by Prof. Dr. Anwarullah
[2] Tuhfa R. 24-25 & *Hada* v. *Malumfashi* (*supra*)

fundamentally different.[3] Whereas under English Law the burden required in any civil or criminal trial is a proof beyond reasonable doubt, the standard under Islamic Law covers not just the right or material type of evidence, but also a specific number and type of witnesses required in a given case. This is in addition to the burden placed on sharia judge in criminal trial to observe the provisions of sections 135, 136, 137, 138, 139 and 140 of the Evidence Act. In *Danbaba* v. *Sale,*[4] Amiru Sanusi, JCA, while elaborating on the difference decided:

> "It is a cardinal principle of Islamic law as in English common law too that he who asserts must prove. Under Islamic law however, there is a required number and quality of witnesses whose testimony could be acted on as proof in a claim. For example in Islamic law, the party asserting must prove his case by calling a minimum of two unimpeachable witnesses to testify on all the facts."

In *Abdullahi* v. *Batagarawa*[5] the Court of Appeal held that "the burden of proof under Islamic law is on the plaintiff and failure to discharge, the defendant is called upon to take an oath of rebuttal." Also in *Aishatu Kausani* v. *Wada Kausani & 3 Ors,*[6] A.B. Wali, JCA (as he then was) stated that "the plaintiff is required to produce witnesses to testify for him in almost all situations. The defendant is required to take an oath where the plaintiff fails to establish his claim." A.B. Wali, JSC. Had also held, that; "In Islamic law or Sharia where a person who is declared by the court to be the plaintiff fails to prove his case in a claim for money or something which can be estimated in money's worth, the defendant shall be called upon to take oath rebutting the plaintiff's claim."

In *Jindun* v. *Abuna,* Achike, JSC, while following the principle as stated in the Maliki Law, by F.H. Ruxton held that "under Sharia Law, where a plaintiff, who was so designated failed to establish his allegation, the defendant would be invited to subscribe to oath of rebuttal to enable him succeed in the case. Should he decline to so subscribe, the plaintiff would be asked to do so."[7]

A person who has taken evidence from among some people and was later required to testify before a court and he so did whether by means of oral testimony or written testimony he cannot be invited later to the same court for repetition of the testimony or to another different court. This is so because of the Quranic verse which says: "Do not over bear a writer or witness." Tuhfa, also at page 31, provides:

---

[3] *Shitu* v. *Biu* (1973) NSNLR 40
[4] (2004) All FWLR (Pt.225) 1915
[5] (1997) 5 NWLR (Pt.506) 650
[6] CA/K/119/S/94
[7] *Jindun* v. *Abuna* (2000) FWLR (Pt.24) 1405 at 1418

ومابه قدوقعت شهادة   وطلب العود فلا إعادة

If the plaintiff is unable to produce witnesses while the defendant denies the claim, the plaintiff should begin by establishing the fact (by the evidence of a witness) that he has had, if only on one single occasion, business relations with the defendant. He must do this in order to establish the origin of the matter in dispute and be in a position to extract an oath from the defendant.

When a defendant denies the whole of the fact alleged against him saying there has never been any transaction whatever between us, it is for the plaintiff to produce his proof. If these are accepted, the defendant can advance no further answer to the charge, for since he has denied the very origin of the fact of the allegation, he cannot be allowed to bring forward any proof with reference to the claim contained within the allegation/charge; although, he must be required to swear to an oath.

وان انكر مطلوب بحق المعاملة من اصلها بان قال بان لامعاملة بينى وبينه والبينة على المدعى تشهد بالحق على المطلوب ثم بعد اقامتها لاتقبل من المطلوب بينة بالقضاء بحلاف قوله لاحق اولا دين لك.

If both of them decline to do so, the plaintiff's case would be dismissed by the court. This is based on the principle which says: " *Waiza Nakalal Muda'a Alaihi Lam Yuqla lil Dalib Khatta yahlifa fima Yaddai fihi ma'arifat.*"

وإذا نكل المدعى عليه لم يقض للطالب حتى يحلف فيما يدعى فيه معرفة.

In criminal cases punishable with *Hadd*, *Qisas*, or *Tazir*, Maliki School, does not permit of such a reversion of oath to the plaintiff if the accused declines the oath. Thus, if the plaintiff fails to furnish proof while the accused when demanded to take oath declines, the oath cannot revert to the plaintiff, according to *Tabsirat Hukkam.*

Plaintiff not being a Witness

A Plaintiff under Sharia is not a competent witness in his own case. His statement of claim before the court does not qualify as evidence.[8]

The plaintiff is not allowed to testify in his case unlike the position in English law where the plaintiff can testify in proof of his claim and in some cases the court can rely on his evidence if such evidence can establish his case on the balance of

---

[8] *Belli* v. *Umar* (2005) All FWLR (Pt.290) 1512

probability. In Islamic law, the plaintiff can not do that. He is only required to call witnesses to come to court and testify in favour of him.[9]

A. B. Wali, JSC, also concluded in a matter where the issue of trust over a disputed farmland was raised by the defendant before Area Court which heard the complaint, the learned jurist stated:

> "the statement by the respondent alleging the existence of any trust in respect of the disputed farmland is not, *per se*, evidence of such a trust, this was part of, if not the thrust of the respondent's complaint which he had to prove."

Furthermore, under Moslem law and unlike the English law, parties are not competent witnesses in court in their respective cases. Hence their statement in court would not be regarded as evidence but something akin to statement of claim and defence in the District and High Courts.[10]

This manner of discharging the burden of proof in Islamic Law Procedure is not repugnant to natural justice.

PART III
Plaintiff's Witnesses

If the Plaintiff "*muddai*" brings witnesses then the judge shall admit them into court one by one. As a general rule, any witness who shall give evidence in court must do so personally and his evidence shall be rendered orally in open court. "Islamic law prefers and lays emphasis on personally given oral evidence."

Under Islamic law, it is not permissible to admit in evidence a statement reduced into writing when a maker is physically available to testify because in that situation the written statement is weak and less credible as evidence and is not permissible for the judge to base his decision on it when oral evidence is available.[11]

A witness shall not be required to subscribe to an oath or be subjected to an affirmation before he testifies, the court may however, require any witness to argument his evidence by taking oath to confirm the truth of what he has said. "Some jurists opined that it is no longer tenable to assume that every Muslim is "*Adil*" (Just). That some Muslims and non Muslims may not necessarily want to tell the truth in that regard therefore, affirmation or oath may be administered to

---

[9] *Dandume* v. *Adamu* (1997) 10 NWLR (pt.525) 452
[10] *Jatau* v. *Mailafiya* (1998) 1 SCNJ 48 at 57
[11] *Usman* v. *Kareem* (1995) 2 SCNJ 158

a witness before he offers his evidence, despite that he could as well be subjected to test of his credibility," per Maidama.

If a witness testifies and his testimony agrees with the statement of claim the judge shall give the defendant "*mudda'a alaihi*". The opportunity to cross examines him. This he will do after he must have put to either of the parties such questions as "what do you say about the evidence of the witness, is his evidence true? Is his evidence correct? *("Wa La budda Lil Kadi an yaqula Lil hasamaini, ma taqul fi shahadatul Fulani, hal annahu sadiq? Hal shahadatuhu sahih?")* Bahjah, at page 20 provides:

ولابد للقاضى ان يقول للمتحاصمين ما تقول فى شهادة فلان, هل انه صادق؟ هل شهادته صحيحة؟

The judge will also ask him what he knows about the dispute between the parties, if he does not testify anything, the judge may discharge him, if the witness gives evidence in support of the plaintiff's claim the defendant shall be allowed to cross examine him. Any judgment obtained in which a witness's evidence is not subjected to cross examination shall be void except that a witness called to discredit evidence given by other witnesses shall not be subjected to cross examination. During cross-examination, a party has the right to challenge the competence of the witness to give evidence on a number of grounds, e.g. bias or prejudice. When the evidence of a witness is challenged on any competence ground the judge shall allow the witness to defend himself against the challenge by means of re-examination.[12]

If a party succeeds in discrediting the evidence given by a witness, the evidence shall be discarded. But if he fails to succeed in discrediting the evidence, that evidence shall stand. All witnesses called by the parties shall be treated in the same manner; and in each case, the judge shall allow witnesses to be cross examined.[13] Where a party fails to challenge the competence of a witness to give evidence, the court should accept the evidence. It is the duty of a party to object to the competency of a witness.[14] The plaintiff shall also be allowed to examine his own witness and the judge shall allow every witness to defend himself in reply to the cross examination.

Grounds for Impeachment of a Witness

Where a witness is previously declared "*Fasiq*" a transferor, or transferors or who was known as a liar or an adulterer or an alcoholic, then his testimony/evidence

---

[12] *Mafolaku* v. *A Lmu* (*supra*)
[13] Ihkam Al- Ahkam p. 26-30
[14] Ibid.

can be impeached on such ground. If he had already testified, his evidence is inadmissible and should be expunged from the record of the court.

A witness can also be impeached on the ground of his moral standing if he is one that commits great sins and minor sins alike. He has to be a just, fair, equitable and independent person who could not be influenced by anything. If therefore he is not fair or upright person or that he is a person of low moral values he can be impeached. A witness can also be impeached on the ground of enmity or that the witness is an in-law.[15] Section 233 of the Evidence Act, is relevant.

In case of impeachment of a witness, two male witnesses are required to confirm the impeachment before the court can approve it.[16]

Evidence as to Character

Evidence as to the soundness of character is known as "*Al-Ta'adil* "while that of discrediting a witness is known as "*Al-Tajrih*" the two play great role in Islamic judicial process. The former is employed where it is desired to bring as witness someone who is not personally known to the judge, without such knowledge or what is equivalent thereto no witness can be admitted. The equivalent is *Ta'adil,* i.e. the bringing of two honourable persons known to the judge to testify to the good character of a witness whose evidence the court is to admit.

" *Tajrih*" is therefore the converse process, when a witness is brought on one side, it is the duty of the judge to invite the opposing party to show cause why their testimony should be rejected and this is successfully done, e.g. impiety, waywardness, bribing, etc. Such evidence will be treated as incompetent and therefore inadmissible.

Decision on Credibility of Witnesses

On all the trial procedures, in sharia court a trial judge plays no significant role on the testimony of the witnesses and their credibility. In *S.A. Shittu* v. *Ibrahim*, the High Court of the north-eastern States stated the law thus:

1) In English procedure, the judge in the exercise of his judicial discretion, decides the credibility of witnesses, it is therefore repugnant to natural justice if he exercises that discretion unless and until he has heard all the witnesses of both parties to the dispute.

2) In Islamic law procedure, the defendant has the right to challenge any witness called by the party asserting, and the judge exercises a judicial discretion in deciding whether or not he should reject the witness.

---

[15] Section 210, Evidence Act, LFN 2004
[16] *Ahmadu* v. *Usman* (1997) 5 NWLR (Pt.503 103

3) In Islamic Law Procedure, if a judge finds that a witness is unimpeachable he has no discretion in deciding the credibility of the witness; his evidence is accepted as proof of the facts to which he testifies.

Admission of Documents in Evidence

Where the plaintiff tenders any document in evidence the judge shall admit it in evidence and may require the proof of authenticity of each document.

When a document or thing is exhibited to the court and admitted in evidence, the court shall allot to it a distinctive letter of number and shall record the same in the record book; and the clerk shall mark it with the letter or number allotted and the titled and number of the case. If the document is admitted to be marked "admitted" otherwise it shall be marked "rejected".

Under Islamic Law, however, relevance among others determines admissibility. Once a document is found to be relevant, then it is admissible the evidential or probative value or not of the document is determined upon its admission in evidence.

PART III
Defence by the Defendant

Where the plaintiff "*muddai*" fails to produce any witnesses or where he tells the court of his inability to bring any witness to testify in favour of his claim or where he produces witnesses who did not meet the standard required by the law, in terms of the quality or quantity or where the witnesses were discredited or impeached, the judge shall request the defendant where nexus is established to swear the oath of denial or rebuttal to free himself from liability and the claim against him shall be dismissed, if he takes the oath. In terms of F. H. Ruxton; "after the plaintiff has stated his case and the circumstances connected with it, the Kadi (judge) orders the defendant to make an answer to confess or deny. The plaintiff's statement of the case will not necessarily be accepted."[17]

Under Islamic law of procedure, the defendant shall not be required to call witnesses in rebuttal.[18] Mohammed Bello J. (as he then was) concluded that:

> "Islamic law of procedure which does not permit the defendant to adduce evidence after the plaintiff has proved his claim in accordance with that procedure is not repugnant to natural justice, equity and good conscience."

In *Aishatu Kausani* v. *Kausani* (*supra*) A.B. Wali, JCA (as he then was) held:

---

[17] Ruxton's *Maliki Law*, p.281-282
[18] *Abdu Biye* v. *Dan Asabe Macitta* (1974) NSNLR 70

"the plaintiff is required to produce witnesses to testify for him in almost all situations. The defendant is required to take an oath where the plaintiff fails to establish his claim.

Oath taking, however, is only applicable in claims against which oath is permissible such as claims for money or money worth, chattel, moveable immovable. But if the claim is the type in respect of which only two credible unimpeachable witnesses are required such as marriage divorce, revocation of divorce, menstrual period, maturity, credibility of a witness, impeachment of a witness, homicide, injury, apostasy, emancipation, relationship, death, theft, robbery or guardianship oath is not administered automatically upon denial of claim.[19]

If the defendant declines or refuses to swear then the oath shall be returned to the plaintiff (*mudda'i*) who shall be required to swear in support of his claim, if he swears or takes the oath, judgment shall be entered for him or else the claim is dismissed based on the maxim which states:

"Al-Nukul ba'adal Nukul Tasdiqil Nakilil Awwal"

النكول بعد النكول تصديق للناكل الاول

This principle of law is better defined thus: "Refusal of the plaintiff to swear when the defendant had declined to do so is a justification of the position of the defendant."[20] The consequence therefore is that if he the plaintiff declines or refuses as did the defendant his claim fails and it shall be dismissed.

In a mixed cause (criminal and civil) but where the case has more civil element than criminal element the consequence of which will be civil judgment, the judge shall where the defendant is known to be either vexatious or frivolous litigant or a notorious criminal the court shall request him to swear an oath that he is innocent. If he swears he shall be absolved from liability. If he refuses to swear he shall be liable for civil aspect of the claim, in such a case the oath shall not be directed to the plaintiff in the event of the defendant refusing to swear.

Unlike in civil cases, the procedure in "*Hudud*" and "*Qisas*"(criminal) trials, a case does not terminate upon oath by the defendants. The law allows an accused to call witnesses in his own defence if *prima facie* case is made against him. For instance, section 397 of the Kano State Criminal Procedure Code (Amendment) Law 2000, provides that the accused is at liberty to call as many witnesses as he can in his defence. This of course is in line with the requirements of section 135(3) of the Evidence Act, and 36(6) of the Constitution of the Federal Republic of

---

[19] Ihkam Al-Ahkam p. 10

[20] *Maigari* v. *Bida* (2002) FWLR (Pt. 88) 917 at 927

Nigeria, 1999. While the Evidence Act provides: "If the prosecution proves the commission of a crime beyond reasonable doubt, the burden of proving beyond reasonable doubt is shifted on to the defendant." The Constitution on the other hand enjoins that: (6)" Every person who is charged with a criminal offence shall be entitled to (a) x x x x x, (b) be given adequate time and facilities for the preparation of his defence, (c) defend himself or by legal practitioner of his own choice. Where however, after exhausting all witnesses for the prosecution or complainant, the court comes to the conclusion that *a prima facie* case is not established against the accused or the evidence against him is not sufficient to justify continuation of the trial for any other offence the court shall discharge the accused after administering an oath of denial on him. This discharge is however, not a bar to further proceeding against the accused for the same offence.[19]

Chapter 7

Conflicting Claims of Title

PART I
Introduction

Where there are two conflicting claims each party is treated as a plaintiff in respect of his claim. Both parties are to be given the opportunity of knowing the claim of the other and be given the opportunity of inviting witnesses to prove their claims or counter claim as the case may be. It is simply justice to both sides.

The practice is that the two parties to a claim would both qualify as plaintiffs in view of the nature of the claim before the court, i.e. each of the two called "*Mudda'i*". This could occur where every one of them is claiming the property as his own.

The property could be house, farmland, plot of land, animals, cloths, utensil which could be ascribed to both male and female, the judge shall first find out in whose hand is the disputed article. Is it in the possession of one of them or held by both of them, or is it in the hand of a third party or not in anybody's hand? The judge shall demand for proof from them. He who among the two is able to prove his ownership shall be so declared and the case is terminated.

This practice is summed up under the following notes as produced in *Tuhfat Alhukkam* page 47:

والشىء يدعيه شخصان معا   ولايـــــــدولاشـهـيديد عـــــــــــــــى يقسم مـابينهما

بعـــد القسـم   وذاك حكم فالتساوى ملتزم فـــــــــى بينات او نكول اويـــد   والقول قول ذى

يــــــد منفرد

وهو لمن أقـــام فـــــــيه البينة   وحالة الأعـــدل منهـــا بينة

These principles of law could manifest in any of the following nine (9) forms:

a. the subject matter of dispute is not in possession of either of the claimants and none has proof of ownership in his claim;

b. the subject matter of dispute is not in possession of either of the claimants but each has proof of ownership in his claim;

c.   the subject matter of dispute is not in possession of either of the claimants and each refused to swear when required to do so;

d.   the subject matter of dispute is in each possession and each agreed to swear or swore;

e.   the subject matter of dispute is in possession of one of them and none of them has proof (witnesses to call);

f.   the subject matter of dispute is in possession of one but he has no proof of ownership but the other claimant who is not in possession has proof of ownership;

g.   the subject matter of dispute is in possession of all the claimants and all of them produced proof, i.e. credible witnesses but the court rated some witnesses above others;

h.   the subject matter of dispute is in possession of all the claimants and all produced credible witnesses and the court is unable to rate the witnesses accordingly;

i.   the subject matter is in possession of one of the claimant and the other claimant produces credible witnesses but court could not rate any witness above the other.

Where the two parties were able to procure witnesses to prove their cases while the article is not in possession of either of them, in this regard the judge shall weigh the evidence of both of them to see which of the two is more reliable and from whom should oath be extracted in addition, which if he does, judgment shall be entered in his favour and the other claim of the other party shall be dismissed. If he declines to take the oath his opponent shall be offered the oath.

However, consideration of weight of evidence is only applicable in cases involving money or things which have monetary value. Number of witnesses could not be used to determine weight of evidence as to entitle a party to judgment. Evidence of long established traditional evidence and evidence of whose ownership pre dates the others could be another means that could give weight to evidence.

وقدم التاريخ ترجيح قبل   لا مع يد والعكس عن بعض نقل

If separate evidence of both parties before the court equal the same in weight, the two evidence shall be discarded as if no one among them has proffered evidence in his support from the onset. In these two circumstances, that is, when parties have no evidence to support their respective cases and when their evidence are of equal weight, the judge shall enquire in whose hand is the article and give such party preference over the other and request him to swear to an oath. This is because the possession of the article is equated with one witness in Sharia. If he declines to take the oath, the court shall request the other party who hold no possession to take an oath. If he does, then he will get judgment in his favour. But if he too declines he has by that thrown away his right and the court shall confirm the ownership of the first party who is holding possession, but who refused to take an oath as the owner of the property.

If the judge discovers that the property in dispute is not in the possession of any of them but on the hand of a third party or not in the hand of any body at all, while at the same time the evidence they both give are equal in weight or that none of them has any witness in his support. In this respect, the judge shall demand each of them to swear to an oath to confirm his claim, then if they all agree to do so, or refuse to do so, the judge shall by that confirm that the thing belongs to them both and has to divide it equally among them. However if one of them declined to take an oath he will have no judgment in his favour, and has by that lost his right and so his case shall be dismissed and his opponent shall be given judgment as the owner of all the disputed properties. The above explains further how distinguishing the party in a case before a Judge assists him in application of proof before him and administration of oath.

If both refuse to take the oath, the property in dispute shall be shared between them proportionate to their respective claims to it, where each party is claiming the whole property, it will be shared equally between them.[1] In *Sarhuna v. Lagga*[2] however, the same Court of Appeal held that, the crude concept of "no victor no vanquish" approach, has no place in our judicial procedural law and substantive law in our court in Nigeria. There must be a winner and a loser. The import of this decision is that a trial judge must explore the process of accessing the weight of evidence of the claimants for the purposes of according it probative value it deserves.

Also in *Hunare* v. *Nana*, it was held where each of the contending parties is laying claim over property as belongings to him and each called evidence in support of his claim, the judge shall rely on, and prefer the more reliable evidence in taking his decision. In *Binta* v. *Ado Mainasara* it was clearly stated, thus; because possession in Islamic law is regarded as having one witness. In law he should be asked to take complimentary oath to have judgment in his favour. The decision went on..." in other words where the witnesses of the parties are equally balanced or on the same footing or even the same nature then the judge will offer the oath of affirmation of his claim to the person in possession (*Zoo – Yaddi*). If he subscribes to it there and then judgment will be entered in his favour. If he rejects or turns it down, the same oath will be offered to the other party and then

---

[1] *Song* v. *Song* (2001) FWLR (Pt. 44) 447
[2] (2002) 10 NWLR (pt.164) 227

if the latter takes it, the court will give him judgment. In a situation where both parties refused to take the oath (*Nukul*) the property in dispute must be shared equally between them.[3] Similarly, a Kano High Court while sitting on appeal held: (1) in Islamic law when both parties are in possession when both are entitled to call witnesses and if neither has a witness then both are entitled to take oath; and (2) if both or neither takes the oath then they become co-owners of the property.

Only if one takes the oath and the other refuses will the ownership of one be confirmed, per Jones S.P.J.[4]

These principles have been variously illustrated by the courts. For instance, in *Usman* v. *Kusfa*,[5] Wali, JSC stated that:

> "Under Islamic law where each party is a plaintiff in his own case each will be entitled to call witnesses to prove his case. If both produce credible witnesses the court will examine and see whose witnesses are more pious and trustworthy and give weight to their evidence, this is what is called "Tarjih" in the Islamic law of procedure. But where the witnesses of the parties are equally balanced, the judge will ignore the evidence and offer the oath of affirmation of his claim to the person in possession. If he takes it judgment will be entered in his favour, if he turns it down, the oath will be offered to the other party."

PART II
Conflicting claims how proved

The procedure laid down under Islamic law for trial in civil cases in a conflicting claim is as follows:

a. suits can be commenced by causing the plaintiff first to produce his proof through witnesses;
b. the defendant then states his side of the case, and produces his witnesses, and if he cannot do so the judge shall enter judgment against him;
c. it is not all cases under Islamic law that a defendant is asked to swear straight away;
d. if the plaintiff fails to establish his case by calling the appropriate number of witnesses, e.g. two men or one man and two females, then the defendant shall lead evidence for his defence;
e. where the defendant fails to do so, and the plaintiff has only one witness, the plaintiff will be called to offer complementary oath.[6]

---

[3] Ibid.
[4] *Balarabe D/Zungura* v. *Dano D/Z* (1973) NSNLR 1
[5] (1997) 1 SCNJ 133
[6] *Olomu* v. *Humani, Shiwa* v. *Hasbala, Isa* v. *Alabi*

A conflicting claim between two persons over a divisible subject, i.e. money, or estate and which is not in possession of either of them and neither of them has witnesses to prove their respective claims or on the other hand, if each of them produces equally credible witnesses, or decline their right to take oath, or each of them claim possession of the subject matter of claim. It is required that the subject matter of claim shall be shared between them equally.

Where a subject is disputed by two or more persons, whether the subject is an estate, edible or animal, etc., and each of the claimant's claim to himself and none of them is in possession of but in possession of third parties and none has two credible witnesses to prove his claim over the subject, it is required that the subject of dispute be shared between or among them, after oath is administered to each of them. However, if any of them refuses to swear he loses his claim.

On the other hand, where none of the claimants is in possession, or has no credible witnesses or all the claimants have possession over the subject and all have two witnesses each or each of them refused to swear to an oath in such situation each will lose his claim/possession and witnesses and the subject shall remain as there was never a dispute or claim at all.[7]

Where each of the contending parties is laying claim over a property as belonging to him and each called evidence in support of his claim, the judge shall rely on and prefer the more reliable evidence in taking his decision.[8]

But where any one of the claimants is in physical possession (with uninterrupted usage) and none of the other claimants has proof for his claim, the possession remains as if it were with him.

But if a plaintiff who is not in possession has witnesses to prove ownership he succeeds in his claim because possession cannot supersede ownership.

PART III
Assessment of the weight of evidence in conflicting claims

In any conflicting claims a trial judge is mandated to access the evidence adduced from either of the parties and accord each, the weight they each deserve and base his judgment thereon.

1. In a claim of ownership where each party testifies in his favour and the witness of one of the parties went further to say for instance I know that the person I am testifying in his favour purchased it. The party whose witness stated how he came by his ownership should have preference over the one whose witnesses testify to ownership only or where the testimonies of the

---

Akande v. *Atanda* (1961-1989) SLRN and *Mala Baba* v. *Baba Mohammed* (2007) 3 SLR 184
[7] Ihkam Al-Ahkam p. 47
[8] *Haruna* v. *Nana* (1996) 1 SCNJ 135

either party appear to be of equal weight but the other party testified that they know that the party at whose instance they testify came by his ownership on a certain clear date their evidence will over weigh the other in view of clarification as to date.

2.   Where the evidence of either side is weighty but one of the other party mentioned a date or year superior to the other "*Qidamul Tarih*" the evidence which says that he knew that *Musa* got his ownership one year ago should be more preferred against the one that says I know that *Ali* got it six months ago.

3.   Assessment of witnesses on the bases of credibility "*Adala*" by means of "Tarijih" where witnesses of both parties appear to be of equal weight the judge is mandated to ascertain which of the witnesses is more pious, more credible and prefer it over the one whose evidence is of law credibility.

4.   Preferring and giving weight to evidence of two male witnesses over that of one male and two females. Where a party produces two male witnesses and the other produces one and two female witnesses, the judge is to accord the testimony of two male witnesses superiority of weight over the other.

5.   Preference is also given to the party with two male witnesses over one with one male witness with complementary oath.

6.   Evidence which discloses originality of the articles in dispute weighs above that which simply talks of ownership but is short of stating that the article originally belongs to the one of the parties.

7.   Evidence of possession "*Yadd*" is superior over one which does not prove ownership.

Chapter 8

Admission or Confession – *IQRAR*

PART I
Introduction

*Al-Iqrar*الإقرار or *Al-Itiraf* الاعتراف means admission or confession which jurisprudentially, is that voluntary declaration or acknowledgement made by a competent Muslim for the avowal of the right of another, which binds him upon fulfilment of some necessary conditions.[1] It is either oral, written or by conduct which could suggest an admission. In *Fathuul Aliyyul Maliki* Vol.1 P.39-40, admission is defined as "a binding declaration by its maker in favour of another. It must be clear and devoid of ambiguity." Applying this principle in *Hada* v. *Malumfashi*, Wali, JSC held, *inter alia*, "For the principle of "*Iqrar*" or admission to apply, such an admission must be clear, devoid of any ambiguity or equivocation. It must be amenable to one and same interpretation at all time...Where an admission (its wording and context) is clear, it is binding on the court to act upon it."[2]

It is trite Islamic law, that a confession of crime by a sane, adult, which is made freely without any element of compulsion, binds the maker. "Where an adult in a state of health, makes an admission in favour of another, such an admission suffices."[3] An admission, once voluntarily made by a mature and sane against his interest in favour of another is binding and enforceable against its maker. It is trite in Islamic law as well as in the common law that what is admitted requires no further proof, and an aspect admitted need no further proof by the principle of *Iqrar*. Confession or admission is the strongest means of proof in Islamic Law whether civil or "*Hudud*" criminal offences. Jurists are reported to have said:

"Admission is a better form of evidence than calling of witnesses."[4]

الاقرار اولى من الشهود

---

[1] *Kausani* v. *Kausani* (2003) SLR 49 Okunola JCA
[2] *Hada* v. *Malumfashi* (1993) 7 NWLR (Pt. 303) 14
[3] See pages 263-275 of the Mujelle
[4] *Alhaji Ari Wakili* v. *Haruna Dundu Gumel* (2006) SLR 106; *Baba* v. *Baba* (1991) 9 NWLR 248; *Jushi* v. *Jushi* (06)

Under the Islamic Law of Procedure, every civil claim or criminal offence punishable by "*Hadd*", "*Qisas*" or "*Tazir*" other than the crime of "*zina*" is proved by the evidence of the two witnesses and in case of "*zina*" four witnesses or by the *confession* of the defendant or accused.

As provided by the Hadith of the Prophet (SAW), confession takes precedence over evidence. The Quran epitomized the significance of confession in various verses, some of which are as follows:

"Let him who incurs the liability dictate, and must fear Allah, his Lord, and diminish not anything of what he owes."[5]

In another verse, Quran provides:

"O you who believe be staunch in justice, witness for God even though it is against yourself..."[6]

The Prophet on the other hand is reported to have said:

"*Speak the truth even though is against yourself.*"

قل الحق ولو على نفسك

Sirajul Saliki Vol. 11 p.162 on the other hand, provides that; an admission of liability made under duress or circumstances where the man who admits the liability is not in control of his senses or affairs, or he is under age (minor) or he is not allowed by Islamic law to exercise full control over his property, will not be used as basis to enter judgment in favour of the claimant/plaintiff.

PART II
Confession of Civil Liability

A confession made by matured, sane, responsible and free person claiming or admitting his indebtedness to another person not related to him when he is not under any obligation to confess or extraneous influence is bound by his confession.

If his confession is to a person related to him by blood and he is not sick at the time of such confession there are two views: (1) the first view is that, his confession shall not be effectual for he might have done so to deprive some heirs of their likely rights over his estate; (2) The second view is that his confession is

---

[5] Qur'an Cap.2 v.282
[6] Ibib., v.28

effectual since he is healthy, i.e. not sick, others add that the subject of confession must be paid at his death but if nothing is left in his estate because of debt the person in whose favour it is made shall accept his fate along with other creditors who are unable to be paid.[7]

If the maker of the confession is seriously sick and claims that a person to whom he is neither related nor a friend to lent him money his confession is admissible and he shall be inherited as one who died living no heirs that will inherit him.

If the maker of the confession confesses in favour of his friend or a relation who is not qualified to inherit him such as his uncle or aunt because he has no son or daughter his confession is illegal but if he has a son or daughter his confession is legal. Another view is that a confession during illness in favour of one's son or stranger is acceptable or admissible if there is ground or convincing reasons for that.

A confession of a sick person in favour of his beloved wife or his dearest is inadmissible without any convincing reason advanced to support the genuineness of the confession. But if the confession is in favour of his wife who is not so fond of, it is admissible because he will not be expected to favour her for any reason.

If however it is uncertain whether he loves such wife or not and he confesses that he owed her any sum such confession shall be inadmissible. These principles apply to wife much as they apply to the husband.

Testimony on confession

A person who hears the confession of another on a fact known to him alone is a competent witness against such other person. It does not matter whether he was asked to witness the confession or not. The condition of the witness is that he must have heard the confession from beginning to an end of the confession. IBN Asimi says of this principle thus:

"A witness can give a testimony over an avowal against a litigant, without having to call a witness to see that according to a chosen view of jurists. However he must be able to report the whole of avowal from the beginning to the end."[8]

ويشهدالشــاهــــدبـــالإقــــــــــــــــر   من غيراشهاد على المختار
بشرط ان يستوعب الكلام   مـــــــــــن الـــــمقر البدء والتمام

---

[7] Ihkam Ahkam p.
[8] Tuhfa R.121 & 122 at p.31

If however a person is the type that cannot make a confession in the presence of another, except when he is alone then someone could hide for the purposes of hearing such confession and be qualified to testify to what he heard.

PART III
Confession of Guilt in Criminal Cases

In Islamic Law, confession of a crime punishable by "*Hadd*", "*Qisas*" or "*Tazir*", unlike all other confessions must be in a court of law and before a judge. However, the Criminal Procedure Code of the Northern States Sharia Judicial system, provides for two types of confessions that are admissible in criminal trials; the first is under section 125 which permits a police officer to take the confession of any person in the course of an investigation or after the close of investigation before commencement of any trial who confesses to the commission of an offence, record such confession in the case diary in his own hand writing in the presence of the person making the confession and after reading over to that person such record shall require him to sign or seal it and the police officer shall also sign it.

Secondly, section 155, provides that "if the accused admits that he has committed an offence of which he is accused his admission shall be recorded as nearly as possible in the words used by him and if he shows no sufficient cause why he should not be convicted the court may convict him accordingly."

Provided where the accused appears before the court by himself and makes the admission of the commission of the offence, the court shall before convicting him satisfy itself that the accused has clearly understood the meaning of the offence in all its details and essentials; the effect of his admission, and in addition, the court shall inform the accused of his option to retract his admission." It is significant that a judge before whom such confession is made should apply outmost caution in admitting and applying confession on "*Hadd*" cases.

In *Safiya Hussain Tungar Tudu* v. *Sokoto State*,[9] the Sharia Court of Appeal, while setting aside the decision of Gwadabawa Sharia Court which sentenced Safiya, (the appellant) to death by stoning held: (1) it was wrong for the police to spy on the appellant and then charge her to court; (2) it was wrong not to have briefed her of the reason for her arrest; (3) no evidence that the lower court ascertained her state of mind when she allegedly confessed to have committed the offence before sentencing her to stoning; (4) the lower court did not inform her of her rights under the sharia to withdraw her confession; (5) no evidence that the appellant properly understood the meaning of "*Zina*" and the gravity of its punishment before admitting guilt; (6) the lower court did not find out the date,

---

[9] SOK/SCA/CR/ AP/2000

time and place/location of where the offence was allegedly committed; (7) the lower court did not explain to the appellant what "*zina*" is how it is committed and its punishment.

The Islamic Jurists are of the view that confession is a proof only against the maker and not against anyone else. In Hadith, *Sah'l bin Ma'aden* said, we are told that a man came to Prophet (SAW) and confessed that he committed "*zina*" with such and such a woman. The Prophet sent for the woman and asked her if what was said by the man was true, she denied the charge. The man was punished and she was set free.

Essential Conditions for Admission of Confession

In Sharia Court proceedings, a confession will be admitted if the following conditions have been satisfied:

1) it is the essential condition of admission of confession for the establishment of criminal offence that it must be crystal clear. If the confession is so brief that it is capable of more than one interpretation, the offence so confessed of is not established. The offender should be called upon to explain in detail what he is actually guilty of after he confesses of crime.[10] For example, if someone confesses to have killed a person, his confession may not be admissible to establish criminal liability or guilt unless he tells how and with what weapon he committed the homicide, what he told his victim to do and the place and at what point he killed him. If he is confessing for committing theft for instance, the confession must contain the detail about the place, time, colour and proper description of the thing stolen. This is based on the Hadith of *Ma'iz* wherein it was narrated by *Ibn Abbas*, that the Prophet is quoted as asking *Ma'iz* if he copulated, to which he replied in the affirmative. The Prophet questioned him again if he had penetrated into her like the rope into a well. His reply was in the affirmative. The Prophet asked him again, "Do you know what is called "zina" adultery?" *Ma'iz* replied "yes, it is what a man does with his wife; I have done illegally with that woman." The Prophet (saw) then asked him," what do you mean now?" He said, "Please purify me", thereupon the Prophet ordered him to be stoned;

2) it is essential that the maker of confession must be sensible; if the person confessing is out of senses, his confession will not be accepted as genuine, nor will he be called to account. For example, if the maker of a confession is under the influence of some drug or intoxicants or is drowsy or is in a feat of insanity, the said confession will not be accepted. But if after his recovery he

---

[10] The *Criminal Law of Islam*, Vol. 3 p. 286

repeats his confession his fresh confession is admissible against him. However, intoxicant may not necessarily be wine. It could be anything by which a person loses his senses;

3) the confession must not have been made under duress; duress means an act that deprives a person of the freedom of choice and he is conscious of the fact that what is being done to him is detrimental to him.

Duress is of two types: *"duress proper"* and *"duress semi-proper."* The first deprives the victim of the freedom of choice. This is where the victim is threatened with death. The second is where the consent of the victim is not affected but his freedom to choose is taken away, i.e. threatened with imprisonment and detention, but not with death.

Condition necessary for plea of duress
A plea of duress emanating from confessional statement can only succeed upon the fulfilment of the following conditions:

a) any threat or intimidation should pose a danger and neutralize the willingness or consent of the person compelled, e.g. the threat of beating detention imprisonment and starvation is enough proof.

b) A threat is no duress if it does not require something to happen immediately. If it is tied to something that will happen in future, such duress will not have effect on the confession. In effect the threat has to be of immediate nature.

c) The person exerting intimidation or threat must have the capability or power to carry out his threat. Where the power is none existent it will not amount to duress.

d) The person under duress must have no means of escape from the duress and that unless he acts death may be the probable consequence of his refusal to act.

Consequences of confession under duress
The legal consequence of confession under duress is that the confession so made would be void and the maker will not be held accountable to his deeds. This is in accord with the Quran (16:106) where Allah says:

"Except that a person is compelled but contented with faith, his heart is..."

Besides, the Prophet (SAW) also said:

"Things done by my Ummah inadvertently, forgetfully, and under duress are forgiven."

Shuraih is quoted to have reported:

"Tying up is compulsion, imprisonment is compulsion, threatening is compulsion and beating up is also compulsion."

Ibn Shihab is cited to have said that he observed about a man who was confessed after being scourged…that such a man is not liable to "*Hadd*".

Imam Malik, also viewed that, in theft case, if an offender confesses due to beating, detention he shall be guilty of theft but his punishment shall be a return of the thing stolen and a "*tazir*", "*Hadd*" punishment cannot be inflicted.

Confession under duress is therefore void even if it can be proved to be right or wrong.[11]

If a well known responsible and respected person is accused of theft for example, and it has never been shown that he has ever been known to be of such character, the accusation shall be disregarded and there will be no need for investigation, if the accuser is unable to call two credible witnesses. He may take proceeding for defamation against his accusers.

If the accused is known to be of bad character and identified with theft Imam Maliki is of the view that he shall be beaten and detained. This is applicable to an accused whose conduct is not known at all. If he confesses as to the commission of theft as a result of beating or detention his confession is admissible. So also is the confession of habitual criminal.

But if a matured person freely confesses committing crime, e.g. theft of a valuable property (*Nisab*) from legal custody having all conditions precedent to stealing satisfied he shall be punished with amputation.

PART IV
Essentials of Admission

There are five (5) essential ingredients of admission "*Iqrar*":

1. the formula;
2. place of admission;
3. the person making admission;
4. the person in whose favour the admission is made;
5. the subject matter of the admission.

---

[11] Tabsiratu Al- hukkam Vol;11 p.30 & Criminal Law of Islam

a. The Formula

The required formula for an admission is that *"Iqrar"* should be direct and not based on a future happening it should be in clear and precise words without ambiguity, it may be oral or in writing.

Writing, where an oral admission is made it could be reduced into writing. Writing is more secure and more reliable. Without formalities, it can be deposited in court to prove facts admitted without difficulty. See the chapter in documentary evidence.

i) Gesture

A gesture by a dumb person is enough admission on condition that it will be understood by majority of the audience. Maliki School admits a gesture by the dumb in proof of "*Hadd*" related offences.

ii) Silence

Silence does generally constitute admission if the maker can speak. It is seldom accepted but to a virgin girl in the acceptance of a husband and the dowry, this is because the Prophet (P.B.U.H.) is reported to have said: "It is enough for a virgin girl to maintain silence on being consulted to marry such person for such *sadak,* but if she does not approve of either she should speak."

b. Place of Admission

An admission of crime punishable by *Hadd* should be in court and not outside, where made outside court for it to be acceptable must further be repeated in court.

c. The Acknowledger

The person making admission must have the following qualifications:

(i)   he must be adult;

(ii)   he should be sane;

(iii)   he should make the admission voluntarily without undue influence or duress;

(iv)   he should not be under restraint, i.e. he should not have been under a decree made by a court;

(v)   the subject matter of admission must be a thing of value;

(vi)   the person making admission must be conscious of what he is doing and sober;

(vii)   the person making admission should not be drunk;

(viii)   the admission should be probable and reasonable.

d. The person in whose favour the admission is made must be

(i)   known and identified. He may be an individual or legal person, corporate or incorporate;

(ii) he should be human being and not an animal or mineral however his condition or mentality or maturity might be. Admission in favour of embryo is valid provided reasonable explanation is given for that purpose.

e. The subject matter of admission

(i)   must be lawful and customarily of use and value; and

(ii) It should be known and identified.

Withdrawal of Admission

Once an admission is made in favour of an individual, or a legal body it cannot be withdrawn. But if the withdrawal is in respect of admission for crimes punishable by "*Hadd*", the Maliki jurists are of the view that a withdrawal is permissible. It is however required that he must furnish reasons for his action.

If one of the opposing parties admits before a judge, i.e. in open court and the court takes a decision on the basis of the admission, then he turns round to deny his admission, that judgment is final. His denial does not help him; this is the view of the majority. However, Ibn Jallab expressed minority opinion, that if the judge remembers that he adjudicated and the party denies it, (court's decision or its accuracy) the judge's claim shall not be accepted without an evidence to support it.

Chapter 9

Evidence

PART I
Testimony or Evidence

Testimony is "*Shahada*" while Evidence is "*Bayyinah*" but the two words are interchangeably employed in the administration of justice. Jurisprudentially, however, evidence is the true information in court of law about something perceived in order to establish a right or a claim in favour of or against another. It must always come from a neutral source, i.e. a witness.

It is accepted both in Islamic Law as well as in English Law that evidence remains the surest means by which facts are proved before a court of law either in civil or criminal proceedings. The success or failure of a party in establishing his claim may depend on whether the rules of evidence have been properly adhered to. If it is contravened, it may result in the rejection of a piece of evidence.[1]

Evidence be it testimonial or confessional is of supreme importance in the administration of justice, this is in view of the saying of the Prophet (SAW) that

> "If people's claims were to be accepted on their face value some persons would claim other people's blood and property; but proof is upon he who asserts and oath is upon he who denies."

Evidence of a witness does not become proof until it is rendered by a witness "*Al-Shahid*" and received by a judge in court.

The witness must state that he bears testimony. If he says 'I know' or 'I believe', such a testimony will not be accepted as evidence.

It could be by means of hearsay evidence. It is recognized by the Quran in verse 282, chapter 2 where it says:

> "...and get two witnesses out of your own men and if there are not two men then a man and two women such as you chose for witnesses."

---

[1] Comparative Analysis of Burden of Proof under Islamic law and Common law by I.T. Muhammad at judges' conference 2002 Kongo Campus ABU Zaria.

Further, verse 2 chapter 65, Quran says of the requirement of witnesses in commercial transactions thus:

"But take witnesses whenever you make a commercial contract..."

The Prophet (P.B.U.H.) is also reported to have said; "your proof evidence or your oath "Bayyinatuka aw yaminuka".

(بينتك اويمينك)

PART II
Judicial Proof under Sharia

Much as the nature of claim determines the party upon whom the burden of proof rests, so also is the nature of claim determines the type of evidence the plaintiff would use to support or prove his claim even if it shall flow from the party himself by means of admission. Under Islamic Law, claims as well as crimes are established by means of either (1) confession, (2) testimony/evidence, (3) taking oath, and (4) circumstantial evidence.

a) Confession or Admission
It is trite Islamic Law, that a confession or admission by a sane, adult, which is made freely without any element of compulsion binding the maker. (See Cap. 13).

b) Testimony or Evidence
i) Four Witnesses
The proof of allegation of "*zina*", adultery or fornication demands the evidence of four male witnesses who should be unanimous about the details of the act. F.H. Ruxton observed that "the tendency of this rule is to make it impossible ever to convict.[2] The position of the Sharia is that since, the punishment for the offence range from flogging 100 lashes to stoning to death and the offence is such that could be easily and falsely imputed on one, it has to be proved beyond reasonable doubt. As such, the standard of proof of four male, reliable, adult sane and Muslim witnesses who must have been eye witnesses of the actual penetration in which case the sexual intercourse is complete such as piston in a cylinder, pestle in a mortar or a rope in a well.

ii) Two Male Witnesses
The Sharia requires the testimony of two unimpeachable male witnesses in all the claims involving:

---

[2] *Maliki Law* by Ruxton F.H. p. 299

i. personal status;
ii. the claim of consanguinity (*nasab*);
iii. marital status;
iv. claim involving "*Hadd*"; i.e. the fixed punishment for the sake of rights of Allah "God"; and
v. claims involving "*Qisas*"– just retribution in the case of rights of fellow beings.

In criminal complaint, it was narrated by Amr bin Sho'eb that one Ibn Mohisa al-Asghar was killed at the doors of Khyber. The Prophet (SAW) asked the complainant, "Bring two witnesses to testify against the killer and I will hand over the killer to you."[3] Islamic Jurists made distinction between crimes punishable by "*Hudud*", "*Qisas*" and "*Tazir*", i.e. those whose punishment range from amputation, lashes, *qisas* imprisonment and *tazir* and those whose punishments are pecuniary, like *diyah* and compensation. Thus, all offences punishable by "*Hudud*" and "*Qisas*" can only be proved by the evidence of two just and fair male witnesses because *Hudud* and *Qisas* are punishment which involves loss of life and vital part of the body, therefore a measure of caution is required in the testimony of the witnesses. And it is conditional that it must be of two just, fair and honest male witnesses. Therefore evidence of one male and two female or one witness and an oath of the victim is not sufficient.

In Maliki School however, Homicide is of two types intentional homicide "*Amd*" and unintentional homicide "*Khata*", the testimony required on the first is of two just, fair and honest witnesses and on the second, evidence of one witness and the oath of the victim suffices. For example, in *Ibari v. Kano Native Authority*,[4] it was held that Maliki Law requires that the offence of wilful homicide ("*amd*") should be proved in one of these ways: (1) a confession that the homicide was intentional; or, (2) two eye-witnesses be brought; or, (3) one witness be brought supported by the oath of a blood relative that he is a reliable witness and 50 *qasama* oaths. Also, in *Hako v. Adamawa Native Authority*[5] it was held: in unintentional homicide "*Khata*" that the oath of *Qasama* ought to have been sought for to establish that the homicide was intentional.

In respect of offences punishable by payment of compensation, it can be established by the evidence of two male witnesses or two female witnesses with one male witness as well as the oath taking by the plaintiff.

iii) Two Male or One Male and Two Female Witnesses
All matters relating to property and wealth are established by evidence of either,

---

[3] Nailul Autar vol. 6 p. 310
[4] (1958) NRNLR 61
[5] (1957) NRNLR 113

i. one man and two women; or
ii. one man and claimant's oath; or
iii. two women and claimant's oath.

In this category of claims are loans, debt, time and terms of repayment of loans, admission of financial liability, rights to inheritance and disputes arising from the fixtures of price of goods etc. To this type of proof, F. H. Ruxton, says: 'In all questions relating to property, judicial proof is complete by the evidence of (a) one man and two women or (b) one man and the claimant's oath or (c) two women and the claimant's oath."[6] Also, in *Ramatu Aduke Issa* v. *Issa Alabi,* A.B. Wali, JCA *(*as he then was) put it thus: the judicial proof is effected by the evidence of (a) two male unimpeachable witnesses; or (b) one male witness and an oath or (c) one male witness and at least two female witnesses or (d) at least two female witnesses and an oath, or (e) admission by the defendant.[7] Where *"Tazir"* punishments other than those prescribed in either Quran or Hadith is to be inflicted for the offence of theft evidence of one male witness together with the oath of the plaintiff is conclusive, but not where *Hadd* is to be inflicted. In case of theft for instance, the requirement is that the two witnesses must concur in their testimony as to the colour of the property stolen, time, date and place of the theft. Unless this is satisfied amputation is not inflicted.[8]

iv) *Two Female Witnesses*
The evidence of two all female witnesses is required to prove all cases of dispute on issues which are personal and peculiar to women folk such as child birth, pregnancy, gynaecological matters, the evidence of two female witnesses is conclusive evidence and such proof is sufficient in all cases of heredity or filiation without the claimant's oath.[9]

c) **Expert opinion**
Known in Islamic Law as *"Mukhbir"*, i.e. professional opinion. It is sought by Sharia Court to assist it to arrive at meaningful justice when both facts at its disposal and the knowledge of the law can not alone or jointly be relied upon to attain the desired justice in a matter before the court. Hence it assumes a prominent position and status in the adjudication of such matters calling for expert or knowledge. *Sheikh Ali Al-Tasuli,* in *Bahjah,* commentary on Tuhfa emphasized the importance of expert's opinion stating:

---

[6] *Maliki Law* by Ruxton F.H. p. 300
[7] *Ramatu* v. *Issa Alabi* (1961 – 1989) SLRN p.
[8] Ihkam Al-Ahkam p. 316
[9] *Maliki Law* by Ruxton p. 300

"Ordinarily, expert opinion is a class of "Shahadah." Evidence Making it part of evidence is only because it installs the right on whoever it favours without resorting to or needing oath taking to support or rebut it."[10]

The testimony of an expert or expert evidence/opinion (Al-Shahadatu Bil Qafa) is given in relation to some scientific, technical, or professional matter by expert, i.e., persons qualified to speak with some amount of authority by reason of their special training, skill, mastery or familiarity with the subject matter in question. Opinion of such a person is valid and admissible without regard to the sex of the expert. It constitutes one of the reliable means of proof, one expert is ordinarily sufficient in cases of expression of opinion, but two are preferable for the purposes of having second opinion. Interpretation is also part of evidence of an expert, for the purposes of accurate interpretation two interpreters are required. In *Garba Maina* v. *Hajia Falta & Al. Abana*,[11] the lower Sharia court dissolved a marriage on the strength of the allegation that the husband of the appellant got married to a lady identified to have been infected with HIV/AIDS, although his test showed he is negative. The Sharia Court of Appeal allowing the appeal held that no matter the gravity of these allegation, the lower court acted on mere speculation as what it ought to rely on was the test report which showed that one year after discovery that the appellants second wife was HIV/AIDS positive, he the appellant (husband) was still negative of the symptom of the disease and that could not have affected his marriage.

d) Children's Evidence
Evidence of small children is valid to prove allegation of crime such as homicide, manslaughter against other children such evidence is used in the absence of the evidence of adults provided:

 i. they are male children;
 ii. the pieces of their evidence are unanimous;
 iii. they have not dispersed from the scene of the incidence by the time the evidence was collected from them;
 iv. an adult has not had an opportunity to influence them.[12]

e) Oath
Oath of denial, rebuttal is a means of prove available to the defendant as a defence where the plaintiff is unable to prove his claim against him.[13]

---

[10] Bahjah Vol. 1 p. 113
[11] BOS/SCA/CV/73 2003
[12] *Aishatu Obalowu* v. *Jimoh Adisa* (1987) KWS/SCA/CV/116/87
[13] Chapter 13

Chapter 10

The Characteristics of Judicial Proof

PART I
Direct and Complete Evidence

Proofs which satisfies all the conditions of admissibility in terms of its quality and quantity and the person in whose favour it is given need not take oath and is entitled to judgment in his favour, except where the claim is against the dead or a person whose whereabouts is unknown then oath of *Qad'a* is administered on him, are of six types:

i.   Evidence of four witnesses required in trial of (*Zina*) fornication, where the 4 witnesses concur that they saw Ali's penis in the Fati's vagina without contradiction by any one of them on the modus of the fornication. Here the offence is proved. The claimant is not required to subscribe to any oath.

ii.   Evidence of two unimpeachable just and truthful witnesses on any claim other than "*zina*" or fornication such as money or property, tangible or intangible, the claimant is not required to subscribe to oath.

iii.   Evidence of one male unimpeachable and just witness and two female unimpeachable and just witnesses on money or money worth, to it no oath is required from a claimant.

iv.   Evidence of two females unimpeachable and just witnesses in a claim the proof of which is peculiar to women, i.e. men cannot be asked to give evidence on the subject such as menstruation, child delivery, no oath is required from any claimant.

v.   A report submitted by an expert or a delegate appointed by a judge to represent him where oath is being administered, or to confirm the existence of prescription (*Hauzi*) on a house, farm or economic tree or a report submitted by a doctor whether he is a Muslim or not and a translator or a person appointed to sniff smell from a drunkard's mouth. In all these, oath is not required to confirm the report. It is however preferred if the report is prepared and submitted by two persons who are of proven integrity. "*Mubarriz*"

vi.   Evidence given by children about what happened among them in terms of a sustained injury or death which occurred in their midst, their evidence does not require oath of confirmation, if it satisfies these conditions:

    a)   Where the children are smart and wise.
    b)   Where the children are males as against females.
    c)   Where their testimony is about what   happened.
    d)   The children have not dispersed.
    e)   Where any matured fellow has not entangled with them or mixed with them.
    f)   Where all the children possess freedom, i.e. not slaves.
    g)   Where they are confirmed Muslims.
    h)   Where two or more of them testify or give evidence as against evidence of only one.
    i)   Where the children giving evidence are neither close relation nor enemy to the person on whom their evidence is against.
    j)   Where their evidence is in favour or against children of same age but not in favour or against mature fellows who are not of the same age.

PART II
Direct and incomplete evidence with oath

Evidence which though satisfies all the conditions of admissibility yet, the person in whose favour is given does not get judgment in his claim except with complimentary oath, is in the following four types.

One witness with complementary oath as proof

1)   Where a claimant is under obligation to produce two credible witnesses in a claim of money or chattel or like claim and was able to produce only one witness who meets the requirement. He is required to take oath to complement his proof otherwise he loses.

2)   Where a claimant is under obligation to produce two credible male witnesses but was able to produce two female credible witnesses. Here again he is required to swear to an oath of confirmation.

Custom with complementary oath as proof

A claim which is based on custom or practice of the people such as:

(i)   Where a married couple made a valid retirement in a room in a manner which raises a presumption of consummation of their marriage and for whatever reason divorce occurs. If the bride claims that the husband had conjugal relation with her and he denies that he did so, she will be required to subscribe to an oath to complement her evidence. The fact of locking themselves up in a room stands as one evidence and oath she will subscribe to will compliment it. This will entitle her to her full dowry. It doesn't matter whether their seclusion in a locked room is during Hajj, Umrah or during fasting. Other views are that if the locking up is during periods when love making between two couples is prohibited her claim should be discountenanced.

(ii) Where *Musa* pledged his book to *Ali* for the sum of ₦200 and after the expiration of the period of the pledge, *Musa* says the amount given to him was not ₦200 but ₦100 and *Ali* insisted that it was ₦200.00 the fact that *Ali* is in possession of the book is (a) customary proof of pledge he will be required to subscribe to an oath to confirm his ₦200 claims. The fact of possession of book is one proof and oath is the second proof for him to be entitled to the ₦200.

(iii) Where *Isa* is in possession of a house for a long period and has been identified with the house as the owner having been managing the property for such a long time as the rightful owner. Suddenly, "*Kamal*" appears to lay claim over the house such that the dispute goes to court. The practice is that "*Kamal*" shall be required to furnish proof of his alleged ownership of the house if he fails "*Isa*" shall be required to subscribe to an oath of confirmation. Possession is a first proof and oath completes the two witnesses required. If that is met the house shall remain his; or

(iv) Where "*Kamal*" was also to furnish two credible witnesses whose testimonies as to his ownership of the house were accepted by the court. And in the other hand "*Isa*" who has been in long possession also called two credible witnesses to prove his ownership as well and the court accepted their testimonies. Here the testimonies of the witnesses called by *Isa* shall be abandoned and judgment shall be entered in favour of *Isa* in view of his customary possession of the house; or

(v) Where "*Isa*" had been in long possession of the house (years) and "*Kamal*" appears and lays claim on the house, when required to produce two credible witnesses he failed to do so, even when he is allowed time enough or reasonable time to do so by the trial court and having failed the court shall require "*Isa*" to subscribe to an oath for the house to remain in his possession on the principle of "proof is on he who claimth and the oath is on who denith."

Surrounding Circumstances with Oath as Proof

The forth type, where surrounding circumstances could be treated as proof or evidence where there is none, e.g. where a person as a judgment debtor is not able to pay the judgment debt and there were no credible witness to establish his wealth or poverty, reliance may be placed on the surrounding circumstances, i.e. his resilience to hunger or cold or to any other thing he could not ordinarily have resisted. This will be considered as a proof of penury and he will be required to subscribe to complementary oath for him to secure temporary discharge.

In alternative, where the claimant insists that his debtor is solvent and therefore capable of paying his indebtedness, he shall be required to call two witnesses to establish the solvency. If the two credible witnesses prove before the court that Judgment debtor has the means, after providing their reasons for coming to such conclusion. The circumstances leading to the conclusion could be accepted as one proof. The claimant shall then be required to complement the proof with oath so as to secure the enforcement of judgment against the judgment debtor.

Further, a wife who complains of cruelty against her husband, and has constantly reported such cruelty and her desire to seek divorce to the neighbours in view of such cruelty, shall be obliged to call two witnesses, one witness who offers evidence on such and circumstances of the constant report by the wife. These circumstances are enough proof and the wife shall be required to subscribe to complementary oath for her to secure judgment.[1]

PART III
Insufficient Evidence and its Consequences

Evidence, which has satisfied conditions of admissibility but can not by itself secure judgment because of its insufficiency, can give rise to preservative order, injunction or interim order to secure a subject of dispute. Example: Where a *prima facie* case is made by the testimony of a single witness who has passed the test of purgation and is credible, a judge can on his own or on application of the plaintiff issue an order to secure or preserve a subject matter of the case from being disposed. This process is of two types:

(1) Where doubt is created in a testimony or a witness is secured but is less credible, a claimant can apply that the judge should issue an order to secure or preserve the subject matter of dispute from being disposed or misused i.e. change the structure of the subject matter or its colour or where it is a building adding another building to the existing one or pulling down any part of the

---

[1] Ihkam Al-Ahkam p. 34- 48, Bahjah p. 110-138

building etc. but he will not at that stage dispose off the subject matter. This is because complaint *per se* does not create this right; a *prima facie* case must have been made before such injunction can be granted.

(2) Where the plaintiff establishes his claim in conflicting claim with two credible unimpeachable witnesses but the defendant insists that he will furnish further grounds that could outweigh the evidence of the plaintiff. There, the defendant will be entitled to an adjournment to enable him accomplish that but the subject matter of dispute shall be stayed (taken away from him) pending his establishment of his grounds. If the subject matter is a house it shall be locked, if it is farm land he should not farm it, if it is a rental shop, court shall collect the rent. As for his evacuation from the shop he is entitled to three days grace within which to vacate the house, he may be given additional days if he claims to have things that might be difficult to remove within three days.

(3) If a person claims a house, farmland or a tree from another, the jurists have different view on the required practice:

(i) If it is a house and the plaintiff seeks that the defendant be restrained from further use of the house or evacuation of his belongings from the house, the judge has discretion to set a time limit within which he will evacuate his belonging and the house locked up pending determination of the rightful owner of the house;

(ii) If it is a farmland, the person in whose possession it is, is to be restrained from farming it until determination of the rightful owner;

(iii) If it is in any moveable item such as grinding stone or things similar to it, it could be seized;

(iv) If it is an economic tree such as mango or its likes, then the fruit could be sold and the money realized paid into the court;

(v) If it is a rental shop the rent could be collected and deposited with the court pending determination of the respective rights of the parties;

(vi) If it is part of building that is being disputed, the part so disputed can be deposited or stayed until the ownership is determined;

(vii) If it concerns edibles, or animals it shall be placed in the custody of any trustworthy person. Until such a time, the court will finally determine rights of the parties;

(4) A plaintiff who claims ownership of property, a house or farm land which:

(a)   is in the possession of another and called a credible witness who gave evidence in his favour but when called upon to subscribe to a complementary oath he declined claiming that he should rather be given time to call the second witness. In this regard the subject matter could be suspended…he shall be directed not to part with possession until he calls the second witness. If it is not perishable he will be restrained but where perishable it could be sold and money deposited, but the subject matter cannot be taken out of his possession.

(b) A plaintiff who claims ownership of property, be it a house or farm and calls two witnesses whose credibility is unknown to the judge, and on the same premise seeks for an injunction on the subject of dispute, such   an order of injunction may be granted but ownership cannot be taken away from the defendant who is in possession until the judge established the credibility of the witnesses. Same applies to moveable properties such as edible, animals, or clothes, it can be placed in the custody of any trustworthy person during the period of the injunction or an order of stay and the judge will set a time limit within which he will ascertain the credibility of the witnesses. He must however in exercise of such power consider the followings:

   i)   the distance of a witness to be called,
   ii)   his closeness,
   iii) time limit,
   iv)   sufficiency of time,
   v)   the value of the subject matter in dispute,
   vi)   volume of the subject matter of dispute.

(c) If a subject of dispute is a perishable item such as mango, banana, assorted meat and the claimant called two witnesses whose credibility is not known during the time the judge is required to ascertain their credibility or administer purgation on the witness, the judge shall order for the sale of the perishables and deposit the sum with any trustworthy person for safe keeping. When he ascertains the credibility of the witnesses or purged them the money so realized from the sale shall be paid to the party that is successful in the case.

(d) Whoever sees a slave, horse or donkey and claims ownership of either of them and produces two witnesses who testified to the effect that they know that the claimant has announced the loss of any of them or produces two witnesses who testified that they heard the news of the loss of the claimant's slave, horse or donkey and the claimant also claims that he has witnesses he could call who are resident within the jurisdiction of the court and in addition   seeks the preservative order over the subject of dispute pending when he will call those witnesses, the judge could grant him such preservative order and adjournment for five (5) to seven (7) days.

(e) If however the witnesses are distant witnesses then preservative order or injunction cannot be granted but the person in possession will be required to subscribe to an oath that the claimant does not have claim over the subject matter and they shall be left in his possession with the order not to sell them or part with them in whatever manner until judgment.

(f) Also where one witness testifies that he knew that the claimant had announced the loss of his slave, horse or donkey but the second witness could not be produced due to the distance of his residence if he is allowed time to produce the second witness he cannot be granted suspension on the subject of dispute in such a case the defendant who is in possession could be sworn on oath that the defendant's right over the subject is not known to him, then the subject will be left in his custody with an order not to sell or part with possession until judgment.

(g) A defendant does not lose custody of a subject matter in dispute which is in his possession except on the following grounds:-

(i) Where two credible unimpeachable witnesses have established that subject matter is the property of the plaintiff before final submission "*Izar*" the subject matter shall be preserved by an order of court pending judgment.

(ii) Where the credibility of the witnesses is uncertain and they are subject of purgation, the subject matter can be stayed by court order pending the occurrence of the two proceedings of purgation and before judgment.

(iii) Where the witnesses are not credible while the plaintiff is entitled to further right to call additional witnesses. The subject matter can be stayed pending exercise of such right before judgment.

(iv) Where the claimant has secured one credible and unimpeachable witness but seeks for an adjournment to call the second witness during such period of adjournment the subject matter in dispute can be stayed by an order of injunction pending judgment.

PART IV
Incomplete Evidence
Evidence which though of quality but not enough to establish a claim except with an oath are permissible in the following situations:

(i) Where a woman sues her husband claiming that her husband has divorced her, she will be required to call two credible unimpeachable witnesses but if she calls only one male or two females who testified that they heard the divorce and are unable to complete the requirement, the divorce will neither be confirmed nor will she be called upon to swear to an oath or be compelled to live with him and neither will the claim be set aside. In the circumstances the husband and the wife shall be separated. But if the husband declines to swear he shall be imprisoned for upward of one year. If after the expiration of one year and he refused to divorce the wife while she remained unable to produce the remaining second witness, the husband shall be left alone with his God. The wife is never debarred from bringing forward proof of her alleged divorce whenever it becomes available. Under this circumstances the wife will be compelled to go back to her husband's house with an order that she must abstains from having intercourse with him and must not make enticing appearances to him and that she should release herself through the process of "*Khuli*" by payment to him of certain amount of money she can afford.

(ii) If a slave claims that his master has emancipated him which claim the master disputes and the slave was able to produce one witness who supports his claim one male and two females who testify that they heard that the slave is emancipated this testimony can neither confirm the freedom nor can the slave be required to swear to an oath or the complaint be struck out. In the circumstances the slave master shall be required to swear to an oath that he did not emancipate his slave so as to knock off the evidence already before the court of one male or two females. If he swears then the slave is not free but if he declines to swear he shall be imprisoned for upward of one year. After the one year however and the slave is still unable to complete or produce the second witness (one male or two females) the slave should be left to himself and his God with an order that the slave should go back to his master.

(iii) If "*Musa*" alleges that "*Ali*" defamed him "*Qazaf*" and he produced one credible unimpeachable witness or two credible unimpeachable female witnesses who testified to the hearing of the defamatory words from *Ali* but *Ali* still denied the allegation, here *Ali* shall be required to swear to an oath to knock off the testimonies. If he swears he succeeds but if he declines he shall be imprisoned for upward of one year at the end of the term he shall still be required to swear if he refuses and *Musa* was still unable to complete his witnesses, the case will be dismissed and defendant left to God.

Injunction

Under the general law, in any matter or cause before an Area or Sharia Court, pending final determination of it, it shall be shown to the satisfaction of the court that any property which is in dispute in the course or matter is in danger of being wasted, or damaged, alienated or otherwise injuriously dealt with by any party the court may issue an injunction to such party commanding him to refrain from doing the particular act complained of, or alternatively, may take and keep such property in custody pending the determination of such cause or matter.[2]

PART V
Incomplete and Imprecise Evidence

Where *"A"* sues *"B"* for money had and received which is disputed, *"A"* calls two witnesses who testified that they saw when the money was paid to *"B"* by *"A"* but did not know how much was the money or that they saw the money in notes but did not know in which denomination was the money. Maliki is of the view that such claim is subject to two decisions:

i) The claim should be struck out as if the claim was never presented/filed but the defendant should be required to swear to free himself.

ii) The defendant shall be compelled to say how much the money was or in what denomination it was. The compulsion is however by means of imprisonment/detention, is either that he states the amount before his detention or after his detention. If he says something and the claimant accepts it he will be required to pay but if the claimant disputes what he said then he should be made to swear that what he said was the correct positions of things. If he swears he shall be ordered by the court to pay what he swore that he knows not the full amount.

If however, the defendant refuses to say what he knows even after being detained or he says what he knew but the plaintiff objected to what he said the defendant shall be required to swear that what he said was correct, or declines to swear then the judge shall compel the plaintiff to state the amount he is claiming from the defendant. If he states the amount, the judge is obliged to consider his means to ascertain whether he could own such amount so much as to lend someone and in addition he should be ordered to swear that he lent *B* the total amount before judgment could be entered in the sum.

If the plaintiff states the total amount lent to the defendant and the judge asked him to swear and he declined to swear or when he could not state the total amount lent because he did not remember the figure and adds that the document containing the total amount was missing, the judge shall dismiss his claim.

Another unpopular view is that his case shall not be dismissed since he already had proof that the defendant was indebted to him rather the defendant shall be detained until he states the total amount of the debt.

---

[2] S.38 Area Court Law Jigawa State/ O. 17 Area CPR

If the plaintiff states that he owns part of the property in which the defendant stays on and when asked to identify the extent of interest or boundary of his part and he fails, the defendant should not be detained, rather he shall be required to state the boundary owned by the plaintiff, otherwise he shall be ejected from the property until he states the boundary of the part belonging to the plaintiff in addition to the oath he shall take.

Another view is that the plaintiff shall not be detained nor shall he be compelled to swear to an oath, therefore the evidence already given for the plaintiff, shall amount to nothing, the defendant will remain as if he was never challenged.

Outright denial of claim can not entitle the defendant to proof any claim relating or resulting from the initial claim, e.g. A plaintiff sued a defendant claiming ₦100.00 which he lent him, when asked by the judge the defendant out-rightly denied owing the plaintiff any money. If plaintiff calls two credible witnesses who testify that they saw, when the plaintiff gave ₦100.00 to the defendant and in reaction thereto the defendant calls two credible witnesses to prove that he had paid the plaintiff his ₦100.00.The judge is required not to accord the latter testimony any significance because the defendant lied earlier by his outright denial of the claim.[3]

Superiority of date is in its self a form of proof of ownership, e.g. a plaintiff sues a defendant claiming something from him and calls two credible witnesses who testified that they know that the plaintiff owns the thing for upward of two years whereas the defendant on his part calls two credible witnesses who also testified that he is the owner of the thing and that they know his ownership for one year. A judge is required to accord the claim of two years superiority over the claim of one year. It does not matter whether the thing claimed is in possession of either of them or not.[4]

Disagreement of Witnesses in their Testimony

If the witnesses disagree in their evidence as to time, place, instrument in such details in cases punishable with "*Hadd*", such as adultery and theft including murder, in view of such contradiction the evidence will be inadmissible but admissible in cases of "*Qazaf*" and drunkenness says Maliki.[5]

If the witnesses differ in ordinary business transactions, where one witness gives evidence as to ₦3,000 and the other as to ₦2,000 and the claim is of ₦3, 000. The two witnesses could be taken as if both agreed on a lesser amount of ₦2, 000.

---

[3] Ibid page 131
[4] Ibid page 139
[5] Tabsiratul Hukkam Vol.I p.240

PART VI
Unreliable Evidence

This is the evidence which is inadmissible in all cases civil or criminal, as it is unreliable. It does not establish rights nor does it de-establish one such as:

i) False evidence;
ii) Evidence of a son against or in favour of his father and vice versa;
iii) Evidence of wife against husband or in favour and vice versa;
iv) Evidence of an enemy against or in favour of his adversary.

PART VII
Retraction of Evidence

Retraction of evidence could be made under three instances:

1. Retraction of evidence before judgment;
2. Retraction of evidence after judgment but before its execution;
3. Retraction of evidence after judgment and its execution. For example:

a) If a witness gives evidence on a matter or for the proof of a case before a judge but later comes back to retract the evidence either that he was initially lying or that he misconceived the facts of the case, whether he furnished any reason for his conduct or not he shall be permitted to retract his evidence but where his evidence is to the effect that a person committed fornication or adultery (*Zina*) he shall be punished for defamation by inflicting on him 80 lashes.

b) If a witness gives evidence on either civil claim or "*Hadd*" offence upon which a judge relied and gave judgment but before the execution of such judgment the witness retracts his testimony, some jurists such as Ibn Kasim are of the view that the judge should proceed with execution of his judgment and the witness who claimed to have lied should be charged to bear responsibility and pay compensation of any loss suffered as a result of heir lies by means of restitution in monetary value or on loss of blood, except where untruthfulness of his testimony manifested clearly such as where "*Musa*" falsely testified that Ali was killed by "*Abu*" and after judgment and before its execution "*Ali*" surfaces, the retraction shall be accepted by the judge or where *Musa* falsely testified that "*Ali*" had carnal knowledge of *Fati* and after judgment before its execution it was confirmed that *Ali* is impotent in such situation retraction can be permitted and relied on.

c) If a witness retracts his testimony after judgment and execution his retraction cannot be accepted and the testimony shall be treated as if it was never retracted. Any loss suffered as a result therefore shall be bone by the lying witnesses.

PART VIII
Circumstantial Evidence

Circumstantial evidence is defined by Nnamani, JSC, thus:…evidence of surrounding circumstances which by undersigned coincidence, is capable of proving a preposition with the accuracy of mathematics.[6]

Under the Islamic law, it is known as Al-Qarain though it is used in some cases; however, it is a guide for further investigations. According to Oudah A.Q., in most of the cases circumstantial evidence does not provide positive proof if it is not supported by textual injunctions. It is therefore rather ambiguous and doubtful but used with cautions.

Circumstantial evidence both in the Sharia and Common Law is evidence based upon inference conditional and conjunctional to the situation, contingent upon deductions of the pieces of elements necessary to establish the case. Islamic Law allows the application of circumstantial evidence "*qarain*" to arrive at a justice. This is based on Quran. Chapter 55:41 where it states; "The guilt will be seized by their forelocks and their feet." Caution is however required in the application of circumstantial evidence i.e. it shall not be used in administration of justice unless it is conclusive "*qariatun*". For example, pregnancy is a conclusive proof of *zina* against the unmarried.

In the Maliki School, appearance of pregnancy is a justification for *Hdd* purnishment. *Ashalul Madarik* vol. III, p.179, provides; "Lashing for the offence of zina is only applicable upon confession or appearance of pregnancy."[7]

ولا يجلد الزانى الا با عترا ف اوبحمل يظهر

In homicide cases, it is a strong presumption "Lauth" and indeed Circumstantial evidence to find a dead body in a pool of blood with an accused in the same room, or find his hand stained with blood or find him with a stained knife or an interval between a blow and death or dying declaration is made by the victim. In such situations oath of *qasama* is required in addition to the evidence of two witnesses to establish the circumstances of death. The post-mortem examination, dying declaration, recovery of blood-stained cloth, razor, knife, spear lathe, chopper, etc., injury on the body of the suspect or accused, recovery of a gun or other weapon can be considered in murder or homicide cases as circumstantial evidence which can be linked and corroborated with other circumstances. Circumstantial evidence of theft is finding of the item stolen in possession of an accused if the circumstances does not suggest otherwise.

---

[6] *Circumstantial Evidence in Nigeria* Okekerefere A.L.2000
[7] Tabsiratul Hukkam

Chapter 11

Witnesses

PART I
Competence of Witnesses

Under Islamic law, the significance the law attaches to evidence is the same as one it attaches to a witness who is called to render such evidence. A witness is known as "*Al-Shahid*" he must have certain qualifications approved or stipulated by the law; he will be subject to "*Tazkiyah*" purgation and or "*Tajrih*" this is despite that all Muslims are presumed "*Adil*".

In Islamic law, the quality and integrity of a witness is high. It is stated that the qualification of a witness is as high as the qualification of a judge.[1] The authority of a judge is not valid, unless he possesses the qualifications necessary of a witness; that is unless he be free, sane, adult, a Muslim and has never been convicted of slander. It follows that whosoever possesses competency to be a witness is also competent to be a judge.[2]

For a person to qualify for appointment as a judge he must possess the attributes of "*Adil*", likewise a witness, to qualify as a competent witness he must as well be "*Adil.*" Perron, made efforts to accord correct English translation to the word "*Adil*" when he said:

> "The word 'eligible to give evidence' do not quite render the Arabic expression '*Adil*'. This word in its primitive sense signifies justice, equity, he who has the sentiment and love of justice hence; in the language of their law, it means wishing to do right in justice and equity, only wishing to testify in favour of truth; he who is a just man, the unexceptional man because of his sincerity cannot be doubted."[3]

Accordingly, an "*Adil*" is an honourable and pious individual, male or female, whose personality commands respect and qualifies him/her to be a competent witness. He abstains from all grave sins and avoids as far as possible,

---

[1] Muwatta Malik, Vol II p. 438
[2] The Hedaya p. 334
[3] *Maliki Law* by Ruxton F.H. p.293

the light and minor offences. He/she eschews even what is allowed when it is contrary to propriety. The witness must be self respected and should have no stake or interest in the dispute. A person who has been convicted for an offence is not competent to testify in a crime similar to that which he had been convicted of. Evidence of a parent in favour of his child and vice versa are not admissible so is also the evidence of spouses.

The principles in Islamic law are that a witness must be Muslim, sane, credible and intelligent not stupid and must be steadfast in his testimony. It is also required that a witness must be of proven integrity "*Adil*" and must be free from slavery as the positions of a witness, judge and Imam who leads in prayers must only be occupied by a free person. A slave has no independence or freedom to enjoy except that as is given to him by his master. A just or credible person is one who avoid, committing offences such as fornication (*Zina*) taking of interest (*riba*) stealing and banditry, he is also one who avoids,   similarly smaller crimes and conducts that are unbecoming of a responsible person, such as passing urine in public place, eating in the market, walking without having shoes on. These conducts also determines the competence of a witness under Sharia.

Qualities of a Witness

The Basic qualities required of a witness are (a) *Tahammul* and (b) *Ada'a*. The first refers to his ability to perceive an event he sees or hears and his capability to retain it in his memory, the second refers to his ability to narrate or relate accurately before a judge of the events which he saw exactly as he saw them.

However, inability of a witness to render accurate testimony does not make his evidence inadmissible:

1. Evidence of witness as to sale which he witnessed but could not remember the amount or price of the sale does not render his evidence in admissible.

This is based on the principle of Islamic law which says:

الشهادة بالشراء دون تسمية الثمن صحيحة تامة

A trial judge is required under the circumstances to invite two experts who are to value the subject matter of sale independently. If they agree on a price, that shall form the basis of the judgment.

2. A testimony which increased or decreased a disputed amount is admissible where the error is correctable it could be corrected before the conclusion of such testimony but where the evidence or testimony is duly completed in error it shall be rejected.

(إن الزيادة اوالنقص فى الشهادة لابيطل الشهادة ان وقع عند الاداء او اثناء الأداء, أما إذا وقعت الزيادة
او النقص بعد الأداء فذالك مبطل)

PART II
Evidence of non-Muslim

Islamic jurist, have divergent views on the competence and admissibility of the evidence of a witness who professes a faith different from Islamic faith before a court administering Islamic law. The differences are due to their interpretation of three verses of the Quran that represent most important sources of authority on evidence, the chapters are 5:106, 2:65 and 2:282 respectively:

1. Chapter 5:106 reads:
"Oh ye who believe the right evidence among you when death comes to one of you, at the time of making a will is of two just men from you or two others not from among you in case you be on journey in the land and the calamity of death befalls you."

2. Chapter 2:65 also reads:
"Then when they are about to reach the limit of their prescribed term, retain them with kindness or part with them in a suitable manner, and call to witness two just persons from among you".

3. Then Chapter 2: 282 reads:
"Oye who believe; when you borrow from one another for a fixed period, then write it down... And call two witnesses   from among your men, and if two men are not available then a man two women of such as you approve as witnesses..."

Those relying on these verses of the Quran are of the view that it is categorical that the witness should come from among male or female adherents of Islam. And that the clear intendments of the verses imply that witnesses who hold a faith other than Islamic faith are not competent witnesses in the courts applying Islamic law. This remains the general view in Maliki School. Maliki School however accepts the testimony of non-Muslim expert such as Medical Doctor as of necessity, where his testimony is expression of his expertise. In such a situation the testimony of a single doctor is acceptable as against two witnesses generally required for proofs. Maliki also does not accept the testimony of non Muslim against Non Muslim. But Hanafi accept the testimony of Jews against Christian and Christians against Jews. The Shia sect does not accept Jews against Christian or Christian against Jews. The wisdom in all these is to ensure prevalence of justice as the evidence of one religion against the other religion could be unsafe and liable to suspicion or bias and partiality.

The holders of the contrary views among whom are Nigerian jurists and judges opine that the wordings of verse 5:106 *or from among you of two others not"* refer to the witnesses professing faith other than Islamic faith, and that the meaning could be applicable to the circumstances of necessity. Ambali, GK. argued: The simple analogy (referring to the verse) is that the multi religious nature of our society where Muslims and people of other faiths freely intermingle in all spheres of life could be logically reasoned as a factors making the evidence of non Muslims acceptable as it was laid down by Quran 5:106 in the circumstances of being on a journey, threat of death or other factors of necessity.[4]

Further, that in so far as Qur'an had allowed the evidence of the witnesses from the other faith it is fait accompli. In *Tela R/Dorawa* v. *Hassan Daudu*,[5] the then High Court of North Western State sitting in its appellate jurisdiction over a decision based on such principle of Sharia by an Area Court. In its decision on appeal Per Mohammed AG.J:

> "It is proper in Islamic law for an area court to admit the evidence of a non Muslim witness as of necessity; because Nigeria by its Constitution is not an Islamic Country. It would be impossible to do justice in litigation if a distinction were drawn on the religion a witness adheres to before he could give evidence in a case, and that would be contrary to section 28 (1) of the 1963 Constitution of the Federation."

Referring to *Al-tashria al-jina'i fi al-islam* vol. II page 406 of Hambali Orthodox School of Islamic law he concluded:

> "Ibn Taimiyyah and his disciple Ibn A-Quayyim are of the opinion that the evidence of a non-Muslim against a Muslim is acceptable in all cases of necessity (on matters happening at home or in the course of a journey)) and in all situations...as given in a analogy in acceptance of their (non Muslim) evidence has been accepted in bequest (of wills) on necessity. Therefore their evidence is also acceptable in another case of necessity."

11.10 The Court of Appeal in *Alhaji Umaru Haruna Mai-aiki* v. *Danladi Maidaji*[6] held, Per. Okunola, JCA. "Evidence of a non-Muslim is acceptable and reliable against a Muslim"...but referring to Dasuki's commentary on Mukhtasar vol. 4 page 171 and Khurishi commentary on Mukhtasar vol. 7 page 184 concluded that "Religious animosity will not be regarded as a ground of impeachment" consequently holding that evidence of "Izala" sect against "Darika" which the lower trial court rejected when challenged on the ground of animosity between the two sects is contrary to the principle (*supra*).

---

[4] *The Practice of Muslim Law in Nigeria* p.
[5] (1975) NSNLR 81
[6] (2004) FWLR (Pt. 188)

PART III
The Blind and the Dumb

A blind is a competent witness on clarification of words in special instances such as:

1. Where the evidence is required to distinguish the voices of the defendant where his voice is subject of determination in court.

2. Where hearsay evidence is admissible, such as cases of marriage, paternity of a child, divorce and death.

3. As an interpreter in court, this is because interpretation is a form of expert opinion.

4. Where the blind is to testify on incident perceived by him before he became blind if he could give an accurate account of it from the beginning to an end.[7]

The Dumb
A dumb is a competent witness if his gestures could be understood in court.

PART IV
Tainted Witness

Generally, in Sharia evidence of a person interested in the outcome of a case is not admissible and he is not competent to do so in view of existence of element of suspicion. More so, that he is susceptible to "*Naqad*", i.e. impeachment. This is based on the principle which states "*wala Wala tajuzu Shahadatu Jarin Linafsih Nafan, wala Dafi'in Anha tabaran*" ("the testimony of an interested party is not admissible).[8]

ولا تجوز الشهادة جر للنفس نفعاً ولادفعاً عنها تيرعاً

Generally, under Islamic law, the evidence of a near relative of a party is admissible in favour of that party if:

a) the witness will not derive some benefits from such evidence; or
b) by giving such evidence, the witness may not escape some harm or loss; or
c) there is no suspicion or bias in that he will not remove some defects or loss from himself or derive some benefit, for example where he is solely dependent on the party; or

---

[7] Tabsiratu Al- Hukkam Vol.ii p.80
[8] Per Coomassie, ref. to Thamaradani p. 610 in *Aidami* v. *Bukar Kusumi* (2007) 3 SLR 208

d) The witness excels his peers including the party calling him in integrity, except where suspicion becomes manifest.

Near Relations and Close Associates

Where, bias, benefit or suspicion is manifest in a witness he becomes incompetent and his evidence may be subject of impeachment. The relations whose testimonies are susceptible to suspicion are:

a. Evidence of near relation raises suspicion.
(i) Descendents to ascendants and vice visa not acceptable.
(ii) Son's wife or daughter's husband not acceptable
(iii) Husband to wife and vice-visa so also son of the wife to her father not acceptable.[9]
(iv) Brother to brother generally acceptable unless suspicion of benefit or deprivation is manifest.

b. Evidence of a friend, generally acceptable unless the friendship is close or intimate and raises suspicion.

c. Evidence of partners, co-owners which is beneficial to the partnership is suspect and unacceptable.[10]

d. Enmity; which is in respect of worldly affairs is suspect and evidence from either of the enemies is inadmissible except where it is based on dispute arising out of the same religions differences such as I*zala, Qadiria, Tijjania, shiat,* etc.

e. Evidence of employee against his employer is suspect.

f. Evidence of an apprentice or disciple against the master is suspect.

g. Evidence of a debtor to a creditor is suspect.

The jurists of the School of Imam Malik, stipulate the condition that the testimony of a brother in favour of his brother should not be in respect of the family matters of the brother in favour of whom the evidence is given. It can be only in matters or causes having to do with money or damages relating to it or testifying to his good conduct. It shall not be in favour of his claim of consanguinity."[11]

---

[9] Al–Khirshi, Vol. 5 p.170
[10] Hashiyyat Al-Dasuiki, Vol. 4 p.169
[11] *Gunbi* v. *Doro* (1992) 3 NWLR pt.228 190

PART V
"Mubarrizi" A Person of Proven Integrity

A person whose commendable conduct is well known and excels his peer in integrity is called *Mubarrizi*. His features are that, once his name is mentioned, the drawable conclusion is that of recognition or acceptance. His evidence is admissible in favour or against his brother except where suspicion is manifest or in claims of "*Nasab*" consanguinity.[12] Whenever he gives evidence in Court his testimony is unimpeachable except impeachment which borders on enmity or hate in anything mundane or enmity between him and the person whose testimony is against or between his relation and the respondent.

"*Barazah*" is not presumed but must be proved.

A person who could be described as just but is short of being *Mubarrizi* can be impeached on a simple allegation of hatred, or allegation of simple offences or conduct which is judicially condemnable such as theft, fornication (*zina*) or an allegation that he permits his wife to roam about or go out to the markets without any compelling reasons or an allegation of selling ingredients with which wine is made from.

A witness (Mabarrazi) who testifies that Musa is indebted to Ali to the tune of ₦100,000.00 for example and later says that the amount is ₦80,000.00 or ₦120,000.00 his second testimony is required to be accepted against the earlier testimony, and the judge should enter judgment in the sum mentioned later which is either above the earlier amount or lower. But if the witness is not a known witness of truth the judge is required to accept a lower amount against any higher amount mentioned by him.

PART VI
"Tazkiyya" - Purgation of Witness

Purgation is a process in Islamic Law of Evidence by which a witness whose credibility is unknown "*Majhulul Ha'l*" is identified through secret enquiry from respectable members of the public so as to accord credibility to his evidence. This process is now being replaced by a process of administering oath of witness "Yaminu Al-Shahid". However, the following witnesses are subject to purgation or purification they are:

1. a person whose appearance present him as responsible and pious but not known as such to the generality of the people, his testimony must be subjected to purgation by testimony of two male witness or more who could give evidence to the effect that the witness is just and reliable;

---

[12] Ibid.

2. a witness whose appearance gives impression of irresponsible conduct, if he testifies his testimony shall be purged;

3. a witness who exudes traits of misconduct can neither be allowed to testify nor subjected to purgation;

4. a witness who has uncertain conduct (*Majhulul-Hal*), i.e. is neither known to be credible nor known to be incredible, his testimony should be subjected to purgation by two witnesses. If they establish that the witness is credible then the court should admit his evidence if on the other hand they establish that he is not credible his testimony is to be rejected. Where however, there was no purgatory evidence and the court is left to consider the testimony of the uncertain conduct the court is urged to discard his testimony." See Cap. 13, Pr. 13.09 (7).

Uncertainty of the credibility of a witness

A witness in respect of whom there is uncertainty as to his credibility has four judicial tests applicable to his testimony in court, e.g.:

a) If he has a clear and well reputable conduct
b) If he has a clear and un-reputable conduct
c) If his conduct whether reputable or un-reputable is clear
d) If his conduct is clearly condemnable.

i. In respect of the first category, his testimony is admissible in the place where he resides upon purgation by two witnesses who will testify to his conduct that he is credible and just. If the testimony is that he is not credible his testimony is only admissible on condition of his being a traveller.

ii. In respect of the second category his testimony is inadmissible either as resident or a traveller.

iii. In respect of the third category his testimony is neither admissible as a resident nor as a traveller except his testimony is purged.

iv. In respect of the forth category he is not qualified to give or be called a witness at all.

In any claim involving a house or farm in respect of which two witnesses produced by the claimant are subject of purgation. Until they are purged or "*Tazkiyya*" is administered on them the subject matter of dispute is to be withheld by the court until the purgation is concluded.

A witness who is well known to the judge and likewise to the generality of the people can be purged in court or in his absence.

A witness who is neither known to the judge nor to the generality of the people can only be purged in his presence and in the court if however he is absent then:

(a) If he is within the jurisdiction of the court his purgation must take place in the court room.
(b) If he had travelled out of jurisdiction on a long journey he may be purged in his absence.[13]

Credibility of a Witness: How Established

Credibility of a witness is established by two credible witnesses chosen by a judge, with an order to enquire secretly about the conduct of each of the witness mentioned by any of the litigants or a judge personally investigating to know the conduct of a witness from his neighbours in the neighbourhood, or in the market, and such private investigation shall be conducted among responsible members of the society, and must be randomly made in the midst of more than one person to avoid creating enmity or hatred between a witness and one to be purged.

A witness impeached must be told of the reason advanced for his impeachment so also a person against whom the testimony is given.

A witness offering "*Tazkiyya*" purgation is only expected to say one of the followings, i.e. "He is credible or he is reliable"; or, say both, i.e. "He is credible and reliable."

If witnesses offering purgation differ, some testify that a witness is credible and others testify that the witness is not credible, a judge is required to discard the ones that say he is credible and accept the other that say he is not credible.

If a witness who testified at a proceeding and was subjected to purgation was further invited to testify in another proceeding different from the earlier proceeding and despite his earlier purgation the defendant insists that he should still be purged the judge is required to once more repeat the purgation on him. He shall do so once more even if the period of the earlier purgation is less than one year. But if the witnesses to offer purgation are not found the judge is required to proceed on the earlier purgation.

A credible and reliable witness can testify for or against his brother except where it is feared that he might favour or injure his said brother or his testimony may be tainted with favour or injury. Islamic law forbids the testimony of the following for the fear that their testimony may be tainted with favour or injury; they are:

a) Father for or against his son or daughter;
b) Son or daughter for or against their father;

---

[13] Ibid.

c) a person to his maid or her maid;

d) a person to or against his mother's husband;

e) a person to the father of his wife or her mother;

f) a Person to the wife of his father (step mother);

g) mother to her son or daughter;

h) maid to the husband of his mother;

i) woman to the son of her husband or daughter of her husband;

j) husband to his wife and vice versa;

k) woman to the father of her husband;

l) enemy against his enemy;

m) opponent in a litigation against his opponent;

n) testimony of endowed against the beneficiary of the will and vice versa;

o) testimony of a bankrupt debtor against his creditors.

Father and son can jointly give evidence in a cause before a court in cases such as marriage and divorce if both satisfy the requirements of witnesses, a judge is required to admit their testimonies.

Some jurists are however of the view that the testimony of a father and son is a single testimony.

PART VII
Compellability of Witnesses

Testimony in court is not mandatory, it is *fardul kifaya* if witnesses are in abundance but where none exist but one, it is obligatory (*fardul ain*) in which case it acquires status of five daily prayers against prayers on the dead which is (*fard-alkifaya*). Quran verse 282 chapter 2 provides:

"The witnesses should not refuse when they are called."

Further, in verse 283 chapter 2, it provides:

"Conceal not evidence for whoever conceals, his heart is tainted with sin."

The jurists are in consensus that a witness is duty bound to give evidence when called upon to do so in cases relating to right or individual rights. But in cases relating to rights of God, i.e. offences punishable with *"Hadd"* a witness is at liberty to respond to the call or not. This is in accordance with the saying of the prophet narrated by Muslim, which goes; "Verily it would have been better for you, if you had concealed it."

Furthermore; he is also reported to have said:

"Whoever conceals the vices of his brother Muslim shall have God conceal his crimes in the next world by the Almighty God."

In all other cases such as divorce, emancipation, custody of a child, etc., it is obligatory that when called upon to give evidence a witness must respond. Generally, a witness not called upon to give evidence should not give; in other words witnesses should not give evidence unless called upon to give evidence, but he may express his willingness to testify to a litigant if called upon. This is because the prophet said: "The worst of witnesses is that who gives evidence before he is called upon to do so."

شر الشهود من شهد قبل ان يشهد (الحديث)

The Prophet further said: "The best generation is the one in which I live, then the generation after that and then the next one, but after that there will be people who will give testimony although they are not invited to give it."

Under the Nigerian Legal system however and particularly by provisions of section 35 and 36 of the Area Court Edict 1967 and Order 13 Rule 1 of the Area Court (Civil Procedure) Rules 1971 vis-à-vis section 19 of the Sharia Court Law 2000 and Order 13 Rule 1 of the Sharia Court (Civil Procedure) Rules 2000 Area Court and Sharia Court. Judges have the powers to summon on their own motion any witness to give evidence. These provisions have been given judicial approval, per Muhammad JCA (as he then was) in *Abodurin* v. *Arabe*, thus:

"Having regard to sections 35 and 36 of the Area Court Edict 1967 and in particular the provisions of order 13 Rule (1) of the Area Courts (Civil Procedure) Rules 1971, the Area Courts are not bound to obtain the consent of the parties in a case before the courts exercise their power to summon witnesses as such, the trial is neither irregular nor void. This was what was decided by the Supreme Court in the case of *Awoyele* v. *Ogunbiyi*.[14] Its proceedings were not vitiated thereby as its conduct in this respect was within its powers under the law."[15]

---

[14] (1986) 2 NWLR (Pt. 24) 626 at 636
[15] (1996) 5 NWLR (Pt. 393) 77 at 93

Chapter 12

Documentary Evidence

PART I
Introduction

A "document" means any matter upon any substance by means of letters, figures or marks, or by more than one of these means, intended to be used or which may be used for the purpose of recording the matter. It includes written, painted or inscribed material which gives information.[1]

Documentary evidence is that evidence derived by the court from the inspection of some documents produced before it. It connotes that piece of evidence of facts reduced into writing and contained in form of a statement and that document of facts tendered before the court at a trial as proof of the facts contained therein.[2]

Islamic law, Pen and writing are shown to be immeasurably of great significance as Allah (S.W.T.) swore by them as in Chapter 68 verse 1 of the Holy Quran when. He says:

ن والقلم ومايسطرون

"*Nun wal-Qalam wama Yastroon*" (by the Pen by the Record which men write)"

At the advent of Islam, the art of writing was very scarce and only few could read and write. As such the Prophet (P.B.U.H) encouraged the early Muslims to learn the art, so much that he made it clear to many captives in the battle of Badr that anyone of them who could teach ten of the young Muslims writing he will be set free. This shows the significance Islam attaches to writing and document.

Further Quran chapter 2 vs. 282 states:

"O ye who believe when you deal with each other in transactions Involving future obligations in a fixed period of time reduce them to writing."

---

[1] Al-Taruq Al-Hukumiyyah, by Ibn Qayyim; p 204-213
[2] S. 2 (1) 91, 93, 94, 95 96 and 97 of the Evidence Act

What could be distilled from the meaning of this verse is that in order to prevent doubts and disputes and for the record purposes, writing is enjoined and that whatever is in writing is suitable as evidence and could be adduced to prove:

a)   the existence of transactions;
b)   identify the parties involved in the transaction;
c)   signature of any signatory to a document;
d)   the handwriting of a maker of document who is either dead or cannot be found and to create obligations.

Generally, early jurists put little weight on the documentary evidence and in its stead placed more emphasis on admission, oath and oral evidence as the means of proof, maintaining that evidence of hand writing/documentary evidence is a weak form of evidence which could only be relied upon when there are no other means. Later some of Maliki jurists, accorded documentary evidence significance even though according to them it is unreliable, as writing may be resemble, one and another, they however accepted it saying: "*Al-khutub Tajuzu shahadat alaiha wa in Kana yash-bahu ba'aduha ba'ad*" (evidence of handwriting is admissible even if they resemble one another).[3]

الكتب تجوز شهادة عليها وان كان يشبه بعضها بعضاً

They maintain that oral evidence is primary evidence, the original means of proof which the court must rely on in the absence of admission and that documentary evidence is secondary evidence that can only be resorted to in the absence of the oral evidence.[4] They observed that its application should be limited to the property and monetary claims, cases of marriage, divorce, emancipation and *wakf,* as such admissible on transactions, but inadmissible in cases relating to "*Hadd*" punishment.[5] An example is where a husband writes his wife a letter of divorce, the letter is admissible in evidence unless denied by him but if two witnesses give oral evidence identifying the writing to the husband, he is bound by the content of the letter.

The position of documentary evidence in Islamic law under Nigeria Legal System is that it is generally admissible. It is admissible in connection with property cases as well as cases relating to marriages, divorces, emancipation and *wakf.*[6] The rule is that whoever writes something by his own hand is bound by the contents therein. This rule is founded on the principles of documentary evidence

---

[3] Tabsiratul Hukkam vol.1 p.356. 3. p.243
[4] Al Khitab vol. 6 p.188.
[5] *Kabara* v. *Kabara* (2006) 3 SLR 115
[6] MCA/CV/120/190 (unreported)

which says: "Whoever wrote something by his hand then died or denied it shall be held bound by what he wrote." - *"Wakatibi bi haddihi ma sha'a wa mata ba'ad au aba imda'ahu"*

وكاتب بخطه ماشاء ومات بعد أوأبى إمضاء

While upholding this principle of law, the old Muslim Court of Appeal of the Northern Region held in *Opara* v. *Joseph Onwara*[7] in the case, the appellant claimed that he only loaned £4.15 from the Respondent but because he could not write he asked the respondent to write for him and append his signature but it turned out that the content of the document he appended his signature to was that he sold his house to the respondent which he never did. Furthermore the document had two witnesses. The court entered judgment in favour of the respondent saying that since the appellant in his right senses signed the document he is bound by it emphasizing that "whosoever wrote something by his hand then died or denied he shall be held bound by what he wrote."[8]

Decision of a court (court record or record of proceeding) – duly certified in accordance with section 111 of the Evidence Act can be admissible evidence so also is statements of witnesses. A written document by a deceased person or by a person who cannot physically be present himself before the court can be admissible if two male witnesses testified to the hand writing. If a person wrote something and later denied writing it but two witnesses testify that it is his writing, the content of the writing can be admissible in evidence.

It is not in all respect that documentary evidence is entertained in proceeding before the court. The three notable instances are as follows:

1. A document written and signed by the defendant, which contains his admission of certain facts but later denies the hand writing or the signature, consequently denying the admission, while the plaintiff has no witness to offer oral evidence. In the circumstances evidence of two witnesses may be admitted to prove that the defendant is the maker of the document.

2. A document written and signed by a person who is dead and there is no oral evidence, two witnesses may be called upon to prove the deceased handwriting.

3. A document written and signed by a person whose whereabouts is not known or known but his presence cannot be secured easily before the court because of the difficulty in transportation or the risk involved in travelling to secure him,

---

[7] MCA/CV/120/190 (unreported)
[8] Tuhfa R. 132

oral evidence of two witnesses may be admitted to prove that the writing and signature are his.[9]

PART II

The processes of admission of evidence of writing are as follows:

a. If a well known personality makes a statement under his hands or recorded evidence in writing but while testifying in court, he forgets the content of the recorded document he may be shown the writing or signature or any impression, or mark on the recorded document, if after words he identifies the document as the one made by him or identifies his signature or mark, he can give evidence on the writing, provided the writing is not defaced or torn, such as will create doubt in the mind of ordinary person.[10]

A record of a court is as authentic as evidence or testimony if a judge makes a record under his hand writing and could not remember that he made it and could not procure evidence on the content of such record then the jurists are of the view that such record or judgment has become an evidence on the matter except if there is doubt created on the face of the record. Others are neither of the view that such recorded judgment can neither be considered a judgment any more nor to be taken as evidence because there is difference between judgment and evidence;[11]

b. If any credible witness whose credibility is known to the judge who is either dead, or had travelled on a long journey or whose whereabouts is unknown writes a letter, a judge is required to make do with evidence of two witnesses to establish his hand writing on monetary or endowment claims.

The form of their testimony should be thus: "we have looked at the writing of Malam Musa, who is dead or travelled on a long journey or whose whereabouts is unknown and we have carefully observed the hand writing and have come to the conclusion that the hand writing is his."

Other jurists are however of the view that such testimony of two credible witnesses on a hand writing is valid in all civil   claims and criminal offences, such as *Hudud* offences, civil cases like marriage and divorce. Female witnesses are however not competent to give evidence on hand writing;

c. If a person on his own free will and right senses makes a note under his handwriting and in such document confirms his indebtedness to another or confirms a trust given him by another fellow etc. if afterwards he dies without

---

[9] Hashiyyat Al- Dasuiki vol. 4 p. 192-1939
[10] Ihkam Al- AHKAM p.32
[11] Ihkam Al- Ahkam p.32

paying his debt or unable to return the trust and his heirs raise objection thereto, or he during his lifetime denies that he ever wrote such letter, a judge is required to accept evidence of two credible witnesses to establish the writing against him, and give judgment against the maker without asking for additional oath or (*Yaminu Qdaia*) because testimonies on handwriting are equivalent to the requirement of proof by two witnesses on claims. The witnesses must however be well acquainted with the writer and his signature. Others are of the view that oath must be administered in addition to the evidence of two witnesses.

PART III
Current position

The current position of documentary evidence is that it has acquired the status of oral evidence since writing/documents have become of common use in all official and business functions and hand writing or signature experts are more available now than before. Further legislations have been made to strengthen genuineness and authenticity of official documents thereby making documents duly certified as valid as oral evidence. In *Hajiya Talle* v. *Bagobiri Bakari*[12] it was held, per Maidama, JCA, that under Islamic law, a document in support of the testimony of a witness stands like a complimentary oath, there was therefore no need to ask the appellant to subscribe to the judicial oath, therefore the letter from the land officer together with the witness evidence accepted by a trial judge completes the required proof of ownership of the house in dispute.

Affidavit Evidence

Affidavit evidence is rooted in the old English law and practice. The use of affidavits is a newer development than the use of oral evidence. The word "*Affidavit*" has its origin from the Latin word "*Affidare*", which then simply meant 'to pledge one's faith or *Fides*'. The said pledge was normally done in writing. It could be concluded therefore, that affidavits came with the age of literacy and writing unlike oral evidence, which have been there in every culture.

On the other hand, an oath is a solemn confirmation of a state of affairs; a solemn undertaking to speak the truth or to act in conformity with an expected virtuous pattern, it is a voluntary invocation of the wrath or judgment of the divine.[13]

While an affidavit is to an extent of its application, an assertion, an oath is not. Under the Islamic law of evidence and procedure it is trite, that affidavit

---

[12] *Hajiya Talle* v. *Bagobiri Bakari* (1989) ILR P.80
[13] Chukwumerije, A. I.; *Law and Practice of Affidavit Evidence*, pg 133-153

evidence is not regarded as being inviolable or taken as conclusive proof of the matter in dispute. Affidavit evidence remains as an assertion which is subject of proof once it is disproved, challenged or contradicted.[14]

It is only in Order III Rule 8 of the Sharia Court of Appeal Rules that a reference is made on the use of an affidavit in support of applications.

---

[14] *Abebi* v. *Ambali Alao* KWS/SCA/CV/M/IL/02 98

Chapter 13

Hearsay Evidence

PART I
Introduction

Evidence is the testimony of a person who is present and saw in person the occurrence of a certain thing. Such person is called or identified as "*Shahid or Hadir*".

الشاهد او الخاضر

The general rule is that one should not give evidence in court unless he has actually in person seen the incident himself and that he was sure of all what happened This is in accordance with Hadith which says:

"*Iza Ra'aita Mithlal Shamsu Fash'had*" ("Unless you saw as clear as sun do not give evidence.")

اذا رايت مثل الشمس فاشهد

Under Islamic law there are two types of evidence:

a) Direct evidence, "*Shahadatul Qatee*": is one which a witness relates what he personally saw, the fomulae; is thus "I was present at a so place and I saw "A" beat up "B" or collected the sum of ₦10.00 from "B". It was in my presence that the whole incidence happened. This is also referred to as "*Shahid bi-ma'ana Hadir*" a witness present when a fact happened. It is the strongest means of proof, next after admission.

b) Hearsay evidence, "*Shahadatul simmai*' : this is one which one or more witnesses relate what they heard from the generality of people generally conveying the occurrence of certain act which is common knowledge.[1]

---
[1] Ihkam Al-Ahkam p.43

PART II
Acceptable Hearsay Evidence

The jurists provided for exception to the general rule   as will take care of certain incidents which are mostly effected in privacy, such as delivery or horrific thing like death. So in such incidents and other incidents of like nature, jurists allowed testimony based on hearsay evidence with some qualifications. There is concurrence of jurists on the acceptability of hearsay evidence to establish the followings.

1. Pregnancy

Hearsay evidence is admissible where a slave woman alleges that her master is responsible for her pregnancy and witnesses testify that i.e. we have been hearing that *"B"* is pregnant for *"A"* and that the news of such pregnancy is wide spread. This type of testimony is admissible to qualify the lady of the privileges accruable to slave woman who is impregnated by her master.

2. Marriage

Hearsay evidence is admissible to establish valid marriage between two couples where *"B"* claims that he is married to *"A"* while she denies the claim. *"B"* can call two credible, unimpeachable witnesses to testify that they have been hearing from responsible members of the society that *"B"* and. *"A"* are married and that the marriage has been a common news in the town. This testimony is valid whether *"A"* is in the house of *"B"* or not. Other jurists argue that it is only admissible where "A" is in actual control of "B" where he treats her as such.

3. Breast Feeding

Hearsay evidence is admissible to prove relationship of two persons by way of breast feeding. If *Musa* shows his intention to marry *Hawa* and she claims that she is related to *"Musa"* by means of breast feeding, i.e. that she shared the same breast with *Musa* whereas two credible witnesses testify to the fact that *Hawa* was breast-fed by *Musa*'s mother that they have been hearing such from the public, such evidence is admissible to impede marriage between two of them. Or where *Hawa* alleges that *Musa's* wife breast-fed her and the witnesses testified that they had been hearing people say such it is admissible evidence to prevent marriage between two of them. Or where hearsay evidence is to the effect that *Musa* was breast-fed by *Hawa* it is admissible to impede marriage of the two. This is before formal intercourse has occurred between them, otherwise the hearsay evidence will be inadmissible.

4. Menstrual period

Hearsay evidence is admissible to prove pendency of menstruation, i.e. if *Musa* divorces his wife "Talaq Rajee" with the option to return her, during her menstrual period the husband (*Musa)* dies and she claims to be in her menstrual period so as to be entitled to inheritance and the other surviving heir argue that the legal waiting period (*Idda*) has expired and the dispute goes to court. If the heirs of the late *Musa* call two credible and unimpeachable witnesses who testify that they heard people say that the wife menstrual period has expired before the death of her husband their testimony will be admissible, judgment could be entered in their favour.

5. Inheritance

Hearsay evidence is admissible to prove right of inheritance, i.e. if Musa dies and Ali comes to allege that he Musa's master/lord or that Musa is his slave, and calls two credible witnesses who said that they heard from the public that Ali's claim is true and that the news is popular among the people. He succeeds in his right to inherit Musa. Also if Ali alleges that Musa is the son of his uncle, that they have the same grandfather and he calls two credible witnesses who testified to the fact that he news of such relationship is popular among the people and that they heard from the people that Ali's claim is true. This proof is admissible to entitle him to inherit the estate of Musa.

6   Birth

(a) Hearsay evidence is admissible to prove delivery of a child, e.g. If *Hawa* a slave woman alleges that she delivered for her *lord/master,* who denies the allegation and she calls two witnesses who say that they heard from people that *Hawa* gave birth for her lord *Musa*, that the news is a popular one among the people. Judgment will be given in her favour and in support of her claim.

(b) If a woman who is in a waiting period (*Idda*) and claims that she has delivered and her husband disputed the claim, if she calls two credible, witnesses who state that they heard from people that the woman delivered such testimony is admissible and she will be entitled to judgment on the ground that her waiting period had stopped.

7. Islam

Hearsay evidence is admissible to prove that a person has embraced Islam. *If Musa* dies and it was alleged that he died a non-Muslim and his relations called witnesses who testified that they heard people say that *Musa* died a Muslim that the news is a common knowledge, this testimony is admissible.

8. Apostasy

hearsay evidence is admissible to prove that a person who was hitherto a Muslim has converted to other religion (*ridda*) a testimony of two credible witnesses that they heard that Musa has converted to other religion is admissible.

9. Impeachment

"*Tajrih*" of a Witness: hearsay evidence is admissible to impeach the testimony of witnesses, e.g. If *Musa* alleges that he loaned ₦10,000 to *Ali* and *Ali* disputes the loan and *Ali* called two witnesses of character who testified that they have been hearing that the two witnesses called by Musa to prove his allegation are not credible and reliable. The evidence of character though hearsay is admissible to impeach the character of the *Musa's* witnesses.

10. Credibility of a Witness

Hearsay evidence is admissible to establish credibility of witnesses. If *Musa* sues *Ali* claiming the sum of ₦10,000 from him and he *(Musa)* call two credible witnesses to establish his claim and they confirmed that they saw when *Musa* delivered ₦10,000 to Ali. Ali has sought to impeach the two witnesses on the grounds that they are not credible. *Musa* now calls two witnesses who informed the court that they heard people say that the two witnesses who gave evidence for *Musa* are credible and that it is common knowledge.

11. Guardianship (*Wali*)

Hearsay evidence is admissible to establish right to be guardian. If *Musa* and *Ali* claim right to be guardian of *Hawa* as to have the right to give her out for marriage and the dispute is brought before the court. If two credible witnesses are called and each gave evidence that they heard from people that *Musa* and *Bello*, *Bello* who is the father of *Hawa* are of the same father and mother, the evidence is admissible.

12. Maturity/Stupidity

Hearsay evidence is admissible to establish that a person is matured or that is stupid. If *Bello* before his death entrusted his son *Musa* and all that he left for him in the hands of his friend *Ali*. After some years the said son claims that he has come of age and that he is capable of taking charge of himself and all that belonged to him and Ali disputes the claim. The said son called two witnesses who testified that they heard people all over saying that the son is matured and can take charge of his affairs. Or that he is still stupid and cannot manage his affairs; the court can accept either hearsay evidence.

13. Will

Hearsay evidence is admissible to establish existence of a will. If *Musa* claims that *Ali* bequeathed to him a will placing in his care all his children or made a will of

₦10,000 from his estate to him, after his death and a dispute arose from the members of the family of *Ali*. And two credible witnesses testified that they heard it all over that the will existed in favour of *Musa*. The evidence is though hearsay is admissible.

14. Prescription
Hearsay evidence is admissible to prove prescription. If *"A"* is in possession of property/house or farmland for upward of 20 years or more and makes uninterrupted use of the property and *"B"* who is either available or not for unforeseeable reasons could not challenge *"A"* for such possession but having overcome unforeseeable reasons now claims that the property is his and that he acquired the property by way of purchase or gift etc. and called two witnesses to establish his claim. On the part of *"A"* who has been in possession for over 20 years also called two witnesses said that they have been hearing from people that *"A"* acquired the property which he occupies by means of purchase or gift from B or his heirs and were able to explain how the property came into A's possession, the testimony though hearsay is admissible.

15. Endowment
Hearsay evidence is admissible to establish endowment or trust if a property is in the possession of a group of Muslims, such as house or compound, for over 20 years and later some people or persons come to claim that the property belong to their ancestors. The group of Muslims may call two credible witnesses who could state that they heard from people over the years that the property is on endowment or a trust property to the group.

16. Removal of a Judge
Hearsay evidence is admissible to prove the fact that a judge has been removed from office. If " A" claims that a judge by his judgment dated 20/7/2007 awarded him a house at Hotoro and "B" who disputes the claim called two hearsay witnesses who established that people say that the said judge was removed from office on the 2/7/2007 such hearsay evidence is admissible.

17. Appointment of a judge
Hearsay evidence is admissible to prove appointment of a judge. If "A" claims that a judge by his judgment dated 20/7/2007 awarded him right over a property and *"B"* claims that as at 20/7/2007 the said judge had not been appointed and he called hearsay witnesses who testified that they heard from people that as at the time the Judge was not appointed such testimony is admissible.

18. Cheating, cruelty between spouses
Hearsay evidence is admissible to prove the fact that husband is cheating or impairs his wife. *Hawa* sued her husband *Dauda* that he hurts her and *Dauda*

denies the allegation, two witnesses who heard from the people that *Dauda* hurts *Hawa* and that is common knowledge is admissible to prove cruelty.

19. Emancipation

Hearsay evidence is admissible if proved that a slave has been emancipated provided the news is wide spread among large number of people.

20. Bankruptcy

Hearsay evidence is accepted to establish that a debtor is bankrupt provided the news about the bankruptcy is widespread.

21. Purgation of a witness

Hearsay evidence is admissible if it establishes that a witness is just and reliable.

PART III
Conditions Precedent to the Admissibility of Hearsay Evidence

Hearsay evidence is only admissible under the following conditions:

1) the news must be wide spread among the people, the number of those who heard the news must not be known;
2) the people from whom the news was heard must not be identified;
3) witnesses must say that they heard clearly credible and not so credible people talk of the incidence;
4) the testimony must be free from mistake, lies and doubts. Thus if two witnesses give evidence (hearsay) and over or about 100 people of the same age with the witnesses say that they have no knowledge of the fact it is inadmissible;
5) large number of credible witnesses is not required but only two credible witnesses;
6) the condition precedent to the admission of hearsay evidence of two witnesses is that it must be strengthened by the oath of the claimant otherwise it cannot be acted upon.[2]

---

[2] Ibid.

Chapter 14

Oath

PART I
Introduction

Oath in Islamic law is a form of evidence; this is in view of the maxim *Al-Bayyinat Alal Muddai Wal Yaminu Ala Man Ankara*:

البينة على المدعى واليمن على من انكر

That is, the Onus of proving an allegation is upon the plaintiff and if the plaintiff fails to prove the allegation by calling credible evidence, then the defendant should take the oath to clear himself; this type of oath is called oath of rebuttal or denial of liability or *"Nukul"*.

Generally, oath occurs to dispel a claim or an allegation in the absence of evidence *"Alyamin Inda Ajzi anil shahada"* اليمين عند العجز عن الشهادة but not otherwise. Unlike the common law system where a witness is free to either affirm or take oath before he starts testifying and such evidence could be relied upon. In Islamic law, if a witness starts by swearing before he gives evidence, his testimony will be taken with a pinch of salt and the judge may not rely on such evidence to decide the matter - per Musdafa.[1] The modern day jurist have accepted what is referred to as *"Yaminu Al-Shahid"* as a form of purgation where a witness has a trait of uncertain credibility.

Oath is therefore administered where a plaintiff is unable to produce two credible witnesses and the defendant is required to rebut the claim or where the plaintiff fails to produce the required number of witnesses to prove his claim, i.e. one witness he will be offered an oath to complete his proof of the claim. It is however mandatory that oath shall only become due when transaction is established. This is on the principle *" Wala Yamin Hatta Yasbutul Khuldatu Awil Dhinal"*. ولايمين حتى تثبت الخلطة.

Oath is testimony or to swear by the name of the Almighty Allah viz: *"Billahil Ladhi la Ilaha Ila Huwa."* It being another form of proof is administered by court in a Juma'a mosque in any claim in the nature of Sharia the value of

---

[1] *Maigari* v. *Bida* (*supra*)

which is not below ¼ of Dinar on party to a dispute whether he freely agrees to swear or not.[2]

Oath taking must be by the name of the Almighty Allah; this is in conformity with the saying of the prophet which goes: "Whoever shall take oath let it be in the name of Allah otherwise he should abstain therefrom." Oath does not become apparent until transaction "*Huldha*" is established or accusation is established.[3] In *Soda* v. *Kwinga*,[4] it was held:

> "Under Islamic Law, the onus of proving allegation is upon the plaintiff. If the plaintiff fails to prove his allegation and the defendant denies the charge, the defendant must take an oath to clear himself. However, the taking of oath cannot be considered until it has been confirmed that some transaction has taken place between the litigants or when there is a strong suspicion that a transaction has taken place between the parties."

Before a party is called upon to take an oath under the Islamic law, the court is bound to explain to him the implication of his refusal to take such oath.[5]

If a party who is under obligation to take oath is a male, the oath shall be administered at any time of the day or such time as may be fixed or determined by the judge. If however, the person is a female who is in purdah and so does not go out in the day time, it shall be administered in the night.

Oath is administered while the party taking the oath is standing facing Al-Qibla. Should any party refuses to be sworn in the Ju'mat Mosque, standing and facing the Qibla he shall be considered to have declined the oath taking and the oath shall be reverted to the other party. But where there is no Mosque in the city any place chosen by the judge which is revered can be considered suitable for the administration of oath. A non-Muslim Jews or Christian may be sworn in a place which he reveres such as Church or Synagogue, where inevitably they are parties before a Sharia court, and the oath is to be administered against each any one of them.

PART II
Types of Oath

In order to do justice at all cost, Islamic law of practice and procedure approves various kinds of oath-taking known as *Al-Yamin* and are as listed.

---

[2] Thamaradani p. 604
[3] Ibid.
[4] (1992) 8 NWLR (Pt.261) p. 632
[5] *Saya Saya* v. *Saya Saya* (1990) 7 NWLR (Pt.164) 652

1. Oath of accusation *"Yaminu Al-Tuhmah"*

This is the oath taken by an accused of criminal offence to exonerate himself from the charges against him. It is administered for self-defence in criminal trials. Some jurists of the Maliki School attached the condition that the allegation should be very strong before the oath of exoneration is imposed. If the suspicion is strong, the oath of exoneration should be imposed. Oath of accusation is administered where prima facie case of theft, robbery or defamation is made against the accused and he still disputes. But where none is established he shall be discharged.

If *prima facie* case is made and the accused persists in his denial he shall be required to take oath. If he takes it he is freed but if he declines the oath there will be no reversal.[6]

But the majority view is that the oath should be imposed once there is a kind of association. In *Amudatu Adunni* v. *Fsasi Atanda*[7] the plaintiff claimed ₦960.00 as damages from the defendant for using acid water to destroy her belongings. She did not have any witness to support her allegation. As a result, the court imposed the oath of exoneration on defendant because:

a) "There was association of marriage between them and it was when she was attempting to divorce him that the incident happened";
b) "The incident happened in the house where the defendant /respondent had overall control when the plaintiff/appellant was away";
c) The room where the clothes were kept was forced open;
d) The destruction was as a result of pouring acid on the clothes; and the defendant respondent was a commercial vehicle driver.

2. Oath of judgment *"Yaminul Qadai"*

It is administered in a claim against a deceased or missing person and imposed when an assertion is made against a dead person, or against anybody who is in position of a minor and a man of unsound mind, in such a situation the ordinary proof of providing two competent witnesses will not suffice. The law requires that *Yaminul Qadai* should be taken by the plaintiff in addition to satisfying the ordinary method of proving an allegation, e.g. for instance where Musa claims some money or property against Ali (the deceased) for money had and received and was able to establish his claim after calling two credible witnesses, he shall in addition be required to take an oath that he has not been paid the debt.[8] As per U. Mohammed JSC) oath of judgment is not to be administered when right to claim is not proved per Wali JSC in *Kofar Jatau* v. *Mailafia*.[9]

---

[6] Ibid.
[7] (1984) KWS/SCA/CV/3/84
[8] *Kada* v. *Yawa* (1998) 7 SCNJ 171
[9] (1998) 1 SCNJ 48

3. Oath of rebuttal or *"yaminul Inkar or Munkar"*

It is due when a plaintiff's claim has to do with money in which case he is expected to substantiate his claim with two male witnesses or at least one male competent witness and two female competent witnesses, but failed to bring the full proof before the court. For instance, if he produced one male witness or two female witnesses only, then he has failed to satisfy the requirement of the law. In event of such failure, the defendant is liable to take the oath of rebuttal or denial of liability. If the defendant declines to take the oath, the plaintiff will be called upon to take it. And if the plaintiff, like the defendant, declined to take oath, the claim will be dismissed. This is because the plaintiff failed to substantiate his claim and declined also to take an oath. It is held until otherwise proved.

4. Complimentary oath (*Yamin Ma'a shahid*)

This is an oath to support or compliment the evidence of one single witness. It is in case where the plaintiff who is obliged to produce two witnesses (competent) in support of his claim but was able to produce only one, he shall be required to take a complimentary oath or oath of perfection. This type of oath is applicable to claims having to do with money.[10] Complimentary oath is further defined as that oath sworn to by a plaintiff in order to complete the minimum number of witnesses required by the law. It can occur in any of the following circumstances:

(i) where the plaintiff has one male unimpeachable witness, then he swears to an oath to complete his witness;

(ii) where the plaintiff has two female witnesses, then he compliments them with an oath;

(i) where the defendant refuses to swear (*Nukul*) and the oath reverts to the plaintiff; if he swears it is a complimentary oath. It complements the refusal of the defendant to swear (which is regarded as an evidence in favour of the plaintiff) the defendant's refusal and the plaintiff's oath amounts to the minimum evidence required which entitles the plaintiff to his claim.

(iv) in a situation where the two parties call evidence and the evidence of each of the parties is equal in terms of cogency to that of the other and the subject matter in dispute is in the hand of one of the parties (usually the defendant) then he shall be required to swear to a complementary oath to entitle him to what is already in his possession.

5. Oath of *"Istihqaq"* - Entitlement

This is administered where a plaintiff discovers his property moveable or immovable in possession of another and claims that to the best of his knowledge,

---

[10] *Kabara* v. *Kabara* (2006) 3 SLR P. 115

he has never transferred the property to the person in possession he shall call witnesses to prove his claim and swear in addition, to oath of entitlement in respect of the movable property. (See Chapter thirteen part ii for more details).

6. Oath of the conjurators (*Qasama* Oaths)

it is administered in trial of homicide in Sharia Court based on Islamic Law, when the evidence reaches the stage of establishing a grave presumption of guilt of the accused person. It is still necessary for the oath to be taken in order to establish full proof and that on the facts the guilt of the accused had been fully established subject to the completion of the full proof by the oath of the conjurators.

Maliki Law requires that the offence of wilful homicide (*amd*) should be proved in one of these ways: (1) a confession that the homicide was intentional; or (2) two eye witnesses; or (3) one witness supported by the oath of a blood relative that is are liable witness, and 50 *Qasama* oaths.[11]

7. Qasama Oath

is only administered when death was unintentional, or the wound which led to the death is in the nature that death would not ordinarily have resulted and it is accepted as a substitute for direct evidence.[12] The Prophet (SAW) was reported in both Bukhari and Muslim to have said when a claim alleging homicide was made before him he said "if you tell us the name of the killer and fifty of you take oath we will hand over the killer to you."

8. Yaminu Al-Shahid (Oath of Witness)

This is Oath which is sworn by a witness before he renders his testimony so as to give credibility to it. This type of oath is common practice these days. It is administered as a modern form of purgating a witness.[13]

Features of Oath

The feature or modality of oath shall depend on what the oath is intended to dispel or confirm. It must clearly relate to the issue before the court. If the subject matter of claim is of a value, less than *j* of Dinar, oath can be administered at any place, it will not be necessary to be in the Mosque, the oath taker may stand or sit facing Al-Qibla or not.[14] For a Christian or Jews in oath taking, it is required that their respective oath shall have or make reference to their respective books, i.e. Bible or Torah for the purposes of instilling fears in them and must be administered in a Church or Synagogues. For instance, for a Muslim the term of

---

[11] *Katsina N.A.* v. *Kago* (1930) 12 NLR 49

[12] *Ibani* v. *Kano* (1958) NLNLR 61

[13] Fiqh Al- Islami Wa Adillatuhu Vol.6 p. 600

[14] Ihkam Al-Ahkam p. 46

his oath is "*Billahil Lathi Lailah illa huwa*" if however it is discovered that he might not be scared by the oath but known to harbour fear of certain areas or Mosque then the oath shall be administered at the area or mosque.[15]

Oath of non-Muslim in a Dispute with a Muslim

The rule is that the Islamic practice of oath taking to discharge the onus of proof applies where the dispute is between Muslims, thus if one of the parties is not a Muslim, oath cannot be administered in order to discharge the onus of proof. There is no provision under the Sharia which allows oath taking to be offered to a non -Muslim, who in any case does not believe in Sharia and therefore is not bound by the rules and procedure of Sharia.[16] In *Sarhuna* v. *Lagga*[17] it was held: that: "The procedure of oath taking in Area Court to discharge the onus of proof applies where the dispute is between Moslems. It will not be applicable where the dispute is between a Muslim and a non-Muslim."

PART II
Reversion of oath

The circumstances when oath can be reverted to either party in a case.

The unique feature of Islamic Law of Procedure is such that a dispute can be resolved on the basis of denial "*Nukul*" of either of the parties (plaintiff or defendant) to subscribe to an oath when confronted with one. Such may occur on either of the following:

1) where the plaintiff is unable to discharge the burden of proof on him, the defendant shall subscribe to the oath of denial;

2) where the defendant denies the oath, the plaintiff may be required when the oath is returned to him to establish the truth of his claim; or

3) where the plaintiff refuses or declines to subscribe to the oath the defendant shall be discharged of any liability arising out of the plaintiffs claim in view of his inability to provide proof or swear to an oath.

Examples

If "A" claims that "Z" is indebted to him which claim "Z" denies while "A" has no witnesses to prove his claim "Z" shall be required to take oath if he declines to take oath, the oath shall revert to "A". If he however declines the claim shall be dismissed, there shall be no further reversion to "Z, "or where "A" claims that "Z" is indebted to him, and "Z" admits the indebtedness but claims that he paid "A"

---

[15] *Ahmadu* v. *Bashir* (1997) 10 NWLR (Pt.523) 81
[16] *Ahmadu* v. *Bashir* (1997) 10 NWLR(Pt.523)81
[17] (2002) 3 NWLR (Pt.759) 322

the money. If "A" could not prove his claim by witnesses "Z" shall be required to take oath if he declines, the oath shall revert to "A", if he "A" declines he loses his claim, the oath cannot revert again to "Z". This is in compliance with the maxim, *Al-Nukul Ba'adal Nukuli Tasdaiqi Li Nakili Awal* النكول بعد النكول تصديق للناكل الأول , which means if the defendant declined to swear to clear himself, the oath could be given to the plaintiff and if the plaintiff takes the oath, he gets judgment in his favour but if he declines as did the defendant, his claim is dismissed as his refusal confirms the position of the defendant.

Refusal to subscribe to oath

Refusal to subscribe to oath could be practical as well implied: It is *practical* when oath becomes apparent on a litigant and when confronted with it, he replies: "I cannot swear or subscribe." On the other hand, it is *implied* when so confronted he maintains silence, neither accepts to swear nor decline it.

On the former, the practice is for the judge to announce to the litigant, thus: "I will offer you oath unless you take it I shall give judgment against you." The judge shall make the pronouncement three times for the litigant to respond by saying, "I cannot swear" to each of the offers. Repeating the pronouncement three times is to ensure that the offer is well receipted and clear to the litigant and is a condition precedent to a valid judgment. Therefore, if the offer is pronounced once or twice and the judge proceeds to give judgment his judgment is liable to be set aside. But when a litigant is offered an oath as prescribed and he seeks for time he shall be given three days within which to take a decision if after words at a first count he declines while on second day agrees to swear and on third day says he does not agree. It shall be recoded against him that he declined the oath.

On the latter, the practice is, when the litigant is offered the oath three times and he maintained silence on each of the three occasions of such offer, it shall be recorded against him as he has declined the oath. That shall be after the judge has ascertained the mental or physical condition of the litigant, i.e. whether he has any hearing infirmity or ailment which could prevent him from hearing.[18]

Claims of Gift or *Sadaka*

Baba claims that *Dauda* gave him a shoe out of his free will while *Baba* is not in possession of the shoe at the time of his claim and *Dauda* denies the claim. *Dauda* cannot be required to swear to an oath. But if at the time of the claim *Baba* is in possession of the shoe while *Dauda* claimed that he did not give him, *Dauda* shall be required to swear to an oath in view of the fact that Baba has the shoes in his possession.

---

[18] Mueen El-Hukam by Aalal Deen Abil Hassan Ali bin Khalil p 188- 189

Claim of a Definite Nature

Baba claims money against *Dauda* which *Dauda* denies, *Baba* could only call one witness, *Baba* shall be required to make a definite statement in his complimentary oath to the effect that he is definite that he lent *Dauda* such clear amount of money. Or *Baba* claims and *Dauda* denies the claim and *Baba* had no single witness while *Dauda* is asked to swear an oath but he declines and oath was reverted to *Baba*, his oath must therefore be with definite pronouncement that he gave *Dauda* such clear sums of money.

PART III
Claimants on whom Oath could be administered

There are five types of claimant on whom oath could be administered:

1) Matured/responsible

The general rule which applies to any claimant applies to his oath. It can be administered to him at the moment the need arises.

2) Young and immature/an infant

If he claims against the dead/deceased or missing person and he calls two witnesses who established his claim while it is required for him to swear to an oath, his oath taking shall be delayed until he attains maturity or puberty. The subject of dispute shall be stayed/suspended pending his oath. If he swears judgment shall be entered for him, if he declines the subject of dispute is released to the other party. If on the other hand he attains maturity but remained irresponsible, the first view says that he shall be sworn, the other view says his swearing shall be suspended until he turns out responsible.

3) Matured and Stupid or/Irresponsible

Be him free or slave if he claims against any one and produces one witness only, the general rule of supplementary oath taking is applicable to him notwithstanding that he is stupid or irresponsible, if he declines then the oath reverts to the respondent. Oath taking cannot be delayed for him until he attains responsibility.

4) A boy /young

An immature boy who claimed a thing against a matured person, and produced a credible witness who testified for him whereas the matured maintained his denial of the claim, the matured shall be required to swear that he has no obligation on him from the young boy, if he swears the subject of dispute shall be stayed and placed in the care of any trustworthy person or the treasury. The judge shall preserve the recording of the testimony and the administered oath, the proceeding in writing, he shall appoint two witnesses on the record as he might be transferred or may die or the witness who had testified may die or either of the parties may die. In all these circumstances the judge succeeding him shall continue with the proceeding or successor to either of the parties may take over the place of his father etc in the proceeding.

If however the person disputing the claim declines to swear, the subject of dispute shall not be stayed as there will be no need for such and the subject shall be returned to the young boy because the person against whom the claim is made had declined oath in addition to one witness already secured for the young boy. But if the subject is delayed until the young boy matures but afterwards he declined to swear the subject matter shall be returned to the person claimed against.

5. Young Lady (Girl)

A matured young girl who claims for a subject against a person who disputes the claim and produces one witness who testified in her favour, she shall be required to swear to an oath to compliment her witness; if she declines to swear the oath shall be reverted to the person, if he swears he succeeds.

If a matured girl got secluded with her husband such that the door was shut against two of them in the house as is the tradition/custom, if she claims that she is pregnant for her husband and he denies the pregnancy, she shall be required to swear to an oath to add to the proof established by the custom. If she declines the oath on the ground that he had divorced her, she shall be entitled to half of her dowry.

If she is not matured what applies to immature boy applies to her, which is that the oath shall be stayed until he or she attains maturity, this is the popular view. The other view however is that:

(i) the father shall swear on his behalf as he is the custodian of all his belongings, he takes care of him in the time of sickness and otherwise and his properties whether in event of its increase or decrease; or

(ii) The immature girl shall be required to swear despite her young age because staying oath allows for persistence in the dispute which is unhealthy and no one fore tells the future. This view is in favour of absolute control of the property of the young girl in terms of its management.

Chapter 15

Hauzi (Prescription) and *Istihqaq* (Claim of Entitlement

PART I
"Hauzi" - Prescription

Definition

Prescription "is when a man claimth anything for that he, his ancestors or predecessors or they whose estate he hath, have had or used it all the time whereof no mind is to the contrary."[1]

"*Hauzi*", in Islamic Law, is when a stranger establishes control over a property (moveable or immoveable) either by means of purchase, inheritance, gift and remains in physical possession for a period legally recognized acquires title over the property.

In law *Hauzi* is two-fold. The first is one to which the person in possession is ignorant of the original owner. Under this type, ten or more months could confer title whether or not the property is moveable or immoveable. The second is one in which the person in possession knows the original owner or owners under this type ten or more years confers title on the person in possession of immovables such as house of farmland and two years in respect of movables such as animals, slaves and cloths. In all of these instances, possession must be for uninterrupted and undisturbed years while making use of same in a manner which shows ownership, while no one though present watches and say nothing whether in dispute or otherwise or kept away from the property, when he is not hindered by fear, infancy, insanity, threat or use of force, such person acquires title over the property and no one shall have right of claim over the property except where he is able to establish that the person in possession acquired his right through rent, loan, pledge, or right or permission to occupy the property for the rest of his life. In these situations the ten (10) years prescription will be inconsequential.[2] Nigerian courts have always identified *Hauzi* as prescription.

---

[1] Strout's *Judicial Dictionary* Vol. 4
[2] Bahjah Fi Sharhi Tuhfa, Vol.11 p. 252

The procedure is that the judge shall put a question first to the person in possession and ask him if he has reason for so being in possession, perhaps he may admit that the plaintiff owns the property, or that he is a tenant or has been on the property on loan. But if he insists on his possession saying 'I am in occupation, am in control and in possession for 10 years now" in case of immovable property or two years in case of moveable insisting thereof, of undisturbed possession while the claimant is around and silent, he shall not be compelled to offer further explanation because such possession is in itself a form of proof.

The claimant shall be bound to prove his claim[3] by calling witnesses whose testimony shall be as follows:

1. I have always known the property to belong to the claimant;
2. the property is part of the claimant's properties;
3. he is always identified with the property;
4. has owned the property and nobody has questioned his ownership;
5. to the best of their knowledge he has not transferred his ownership until now that someone else claims possession.

All these questions must be answered if one is missing proof is unacceptable by court.

If the claimant who has been silent until the period of long possession was over, claims that his silence or inaction was due to the fact that the property was loaned to the person, or that the person is permitted to be staying on it, or it was given to him for life, or rented out to him, his right in that respect will not lapse. He shall however be requested to bring witnesses to prove his allegation. If he does that, the court shall give judgment in his favour. But if he fails, the defendant, i.e. the person in possession shall be made to swear and if he does, he holds on to his possession. If however in the process, the one in possession alleges that he either bought it, or given as a gift, he will not be believed.

Period of "*Hauzi*" in case of non-blood relation

The period of prescription under Islamic law is 10 years the exception to the rule are those situations where the parties are related by blood or marriage.[4] Ten years peaceful enjoyment of possession of a landed property without let or hindrance bars all actions against an un-blood related possessor, except:

1. where the claimant establishes his residence or is away outside the area of the property the distance of which is a journey of seven (7) to eight (8) clear days;

2. where the property is situated within an enemy territory;

---

[3] Ibid
[4] Ihkam Al-Ahkam p. 260

3. where the claimant is female who is away to a place whose distance is a journey of two days. But if the claimant is male his claim will not be considered because a journey of two days to a male is not any difference to one residing in the jurisdiction of the property.[5]

Where a claimant alleges that he has repeatedly sought for his property/claimed his property during the period of ten years whether such claim was made before a court or not, the acceptable view is that he can only be heard if the claim was before a court otherwise not.

Period of *Hauzi* in case of blood relation
The period of prescription in case of close relation differs, depending on the nature of ownership exercised by the person in possession of the landed property in dispute when it concerns   occupation of a house or cultivation of a farmland, the period applicable is forty years or more.[6]

The longest period of prescription among them (relations) which bars the claim of the claimant is forty years and above. Any of the relations who take up possession for the period or more, then the claimant shall have no case against him.[7]

Exception available to blood relation
1. Where the claimant is a blood relation the possessor's period of prescription is *forty* years if throughout the period there was no instance of enmity or misunderstanding between the two otherwise the period of *ten* years shall apply.

2. Where the claimant is a blood relation and the possessor of a slave makes use of the slave for up to 10 years and the claimant made no claim even when the slave is being sold his 10 years period is applicable.

3. Where the claimant is a blood relation, who watches the possessor pull down his house and rebuild the same, or creates a road on the claimant's property or rents out the property without complaining, two views are applicable to the situation:

(a) One is that 10 years period is enough in view of the changes (destruction and rebuilding);

(b) The second view is that 40 years period is applicable view of the existence of relationship.

---

[5] *Haruna* v. *Nana* (1996) 1 SCNJ 144
[6] Tuhfa p. 261
[7] Ihkam Al-Ahkam p. 9, 133- 134

The Islamic principle of *hauzi* (prescription) is applicable in equity. Under the English law of equity, the period of prescription is extended to 20 years.[8]

General Exceptions

Generally, the principles of *Hauzi* do not apply where an issue of pledge, mortgage, trust etc, crept in the principles of "*Hauzi*", حوز out of necessity. Where they do, the position would have to change. Any of the above issues will then constitute an exception to the general rule that is where a defendant possesses a land, farm or a house, and using same as his own and which fact is within the knowledge of the true owner for ten or more years such defendant acquired title to that land by prescription. The plaintiff then will not be heard to complain, his claim on those facts will be dismissed.

a) Pledge

Where the plaintiff in such a situation is able to prove the existence of pledge to the defendant or trust and so on, then that element will defeat the claim of *Hauzi* by the defendant.[9]

b) Inheritance

Whoever claims ownership in fee simple of a property in the possession of another and alleges that it is part of estate he has inherited, the possessor shall not be asked to explain anything until the claimant has established the death of his deceased predecessor from whom he claims to inherit the estate and proves also how he becomes an heir of the said deceased predecessor in respect of the said estate, per U. Mohammed, JCA.[10]

c) Gift

Where an alleged claimant establishes by evidence that a property belongs to him and the person in possession or occupation alleges that some one else gave him a gift of the property, in that case he shall be required to prove the claim of gift by evidence if he fails to do so the claimant shall be required to take oath in his claim and that he did not make a gift of the property.

For a claim of gift to succeed in *Hauzi,* "it must be complete delivery to or for donee and acceptance of gift by donee." A donee of title to a house therefore shall acquire title only if the donor relinquishes to him absolute title. If he resides therein he shall vacate it or pay rents to the donee otherwise the donee will establish no title or *Hauzi* whether he be a father or son, mother, brother, etc.

---

[8] *Saidu* v. *Akinwumi* (1959) 1 FSC 107
[9] *Hada* v. *Malumfashi/Balarabe* v. *Audu* (1997) 10 NWLR (Pt.524)/ Mayyara Vol. 2 and Bahjah Vol. 2
[10] *Ahmed* v. *Jibrin & Ors.* FCA/K/35S/81

d) Purchase

If an alleged claimant claims established by evidence that the property is his but the occupier argues that he bought it from the owner he shall be required to take oath on his claim in addition to proving the payment. If the alleged claimant alleges that he bought the property from the person in possession/occupation and the occupant also claims that he repurchased the property from the claimant, he shall be required to take oath to the effect that he repurchased the property.

Exceptions to the Rule of "*Hauzi*"

Where a person has been in an undisturbed possession of real property for 10 or 40 years without opposition from the true owner whether claim is from a stranger or blood relation he acquires ownership. However, this principle of *Hauzi* or prescription under Islamic law permits of exception such as where:

i) under immense fear of the person in occupation where the person is his leader, a leader too powerful to be confronted;

ii) a strong relationship;

iii) in-law;

vi) under the care of the occupant -

    a. cogent reasons are adduced for not complaining in time, for example blood relationship or fear of harm from authority;

    b. the claimant is a minor;

    c. the person in possession is put in possession by the claimant either as free or fee paying tenant;

    d. the person in possession is put in possession as a trustee;

    e. the claimant is a relative, or a partner or co-proprietor to the person in possession;

    f. in the case of a house the possessor is in permissive occupancy only.

Trust or loan defeats *hauzi*. This is because evidence of ownership takes priority over that of undisputed possession because the former is stronger than the later. This is based on the principle which provides:

"Evidence of ownership takes priority over that of undisturbed possession, because the former is stronger than the latter."

In Ihkam Al-ahkam, page 47 it is provided:

"Wa iza kana ligairil haizi bayyinat bil mulki fal kaulu Kauluhu, li annal mulki la yan quli bil hauzi."

وإذا كان لغير حائز بينة بالملك فالقول قوله لأن الملك لاينقل بالحوز.

("If the person not in possession has proof of ownership his claim takes priority because long possession does not take away ownership.")

Hauzi is ineffectual in a property owned by a woman or a property in which she has vested interest if she is married to a husband who is harsh, stern and placed her under strict control and does not at all permit of her going out of matrimonial home.[11]

Prescription on Movables

Where a person has been in undisturbed possession of moveable properties such as clothes, animals, slaves or slave woman, etc., he needs only to establish physical possession for the following periods:

(i) two years in respect of clothes;
(ii) two years or more in respect of animals;
(iii) three years or more in respect human (slave or house maid) or domestic servant where used for domestic services;
(iv) the fact of intercourse is enough proof of possession on slave woman it does not matter whether the possessor has used her for a long period or not.

Under Islamic law, a house that belongs to another cannot be acquired by mere possession however long except where the party in possession of the land deals with it in all manners just like the owner, e.g. demolishing and rebuilding it or planting or harvesting it, showing complete ownership like his personal property. A plaintiff who can show that his house which is in possession of the defendant is merely on loan or for lodging or tenancy for life will not be precluded from claiming it by mere expiration of the period of prescription.[12]

Under Islamic law, if a person sells property belonging to another person and that other person was around and was fully aware of the transaction or came to know about it but stood by and did not take any action to recover his property or have the sale set aside and kept silent for up to one year, then he forfeits his right to recover both his property and the purchase price.[13]

PART II
Istihqaq (Claim of Entitlement)

Istihqaq is when a person claims entitlement over a property in possession of an adverse party who claims ownership of the some property. The plaintiff is required to prove his claim by calling the required number of unimpeachable

---

[11] *Dauda* v. *Asabe* (1998) 1NWLR (Pt.532) 102/ *Gulma* v. *Bahago* (1993) 1 NWLR Pt.272) 766/ *Salati* v. *Dogola* (*supra*)
[12] Bahjah Fi l Sharhi Tuhfa p.255
[13] *Sani Magatakarda* v. *Bature Gando Isa* CA/K/12/87

witnesses, and the person in whose possession the property is found shall not be under a duty to explain how he came into possession.[14]

Proof Required From the Complainant and the Defendant

The burden is on the plaintiff to establish by two unimpeachable witnesses that the chattel belongs to him the witnesses must explain how it came to be the plaintiff's, i.e. that he, (the plaintiff) never parted with his ownership, that for the past ten months the witnesses have always known the plaintiff with the chattel or that the chattel is part of the plaintiff's belongings. That he never parted with it either by way of sale or gift or loss but suddenly found it in possession of the defendant. It is mandatory that the witnesses must state exactly as above. Until the plaintiff's claim is established, the defendant will not be obliged to say anything because he is in possession or if not at all it is about maintaining his right of claim to possession. This principle is laid by Tuhfa of Ibn Asimi when it said:

> "Whoever claims ownership of a property in possession of another shall be bound to furnish proof. The proof shall be adduced without the person in possession being compelled to offer explanation as to how he came by his possession. Oath is not required where the claimant establishes his claim on immovable property "Al Usul" الأصولBut he shall swear after establishing his claims on moveable properties."

المدعى استحقاق شىء يلـــزم   بينـة مثبـــــتة مـــــا يـــــزعم

من غـــــيرتكليف لـــمن تـملكه   من قبل ذا بأى وجه ملكه

ولايـــــمين فى الأصول مااستحق   وفـــى سواها قبل اعذار يحق

    It will be sufficient for the defendant if he insists on his prescription or possession and the burden shall remain upon the plaintiff to prove his ownership. If the plaintiff's claim is that he is the owner of the subject of dispute, then the proof of such could be either admission or denial of such claim by the defendant, but if the defendant maintains his right of claim to possession he will not be compelled to offer any proof other than claim of his possession.

    If the plaintiff's claim is that the subject of claim belongs to his grandfather in that circumstances proof on the part of the defendant may not be complete by his admission or denial until the plaintiff proves the death of his grandfather and his right to inherit the property. If he establishes the death of his grandfather and his right to inherit him, then the defendant may admit or deny the claim. But if the defendant insists on his possession, he cannot be compelled to admit or deny.

---

[14] Tuhfa p.264 / *Agbebu* v. *Bawa* (1992) 6 NWLR (pt. 245) 80

In the circumstances, the plaintiff will be directed to prove his grandfather's title over the subject of dispute or else the defendant will not be compelled to go beyond his claim of possession.

If at the mention of claim and before proof, the defendant respond that he purchased the property but subsequently claims his ownership and possession, such reversal is permitted.

If the plaintiff establishes his ownership or ownership of the property by his grandfather and also established his right to inherit the property and the defendant maintains his hold on possession for the period of ten years, that the plaintiff was aware and did nothing to disturb his ownership yet could not impeach any of the plaintiff witnesses, then he shall be required to state his source of ownership. If he establishes his claim by calling at least two witnesses regarding his claim of 10 years undisturbed possession, the court shall exhaust (*izar*) the plaintiff, if the plaintiff is unable to impeach the defendant witnesses, judgment shall be given against him.

But in a situation where the defendant did put up defence of *ten* years undisturbed long possession or he did but could not call witnesses to establish it but established lesser years, in such circumstances he must state his source of ownership.

If the defendant claims ownership of the property through purchase or gift even before the plaintiff is born or before the property became due for inheritance in the circumstance he shall be called upon to prove such by evidence. If he proves that and the plaintiff could not discredit the evidence he wins.[15] The defendant's and the plaintiff's claim shall be dismissed but if he (the defendant) is unable to prove his claim, the judgment shall be entered for the plaintiff after he has taken the oath of *Istihqaq.*

When Oath (*Yaminul Istihqaq*) is Necessary

If the plaintiff proves his ownership through witnesses he shall as condition precedent to requiring explanation from the person in possession take oath, *Yaminul Istihqaq* which will be thus: "*Wallahi Tallahi billahi Lazi La Ilaha Illa Huwa; Huwa,* والله تالله بالله الذى لاإله إلا هو (This property is mine, I have never parted with possession until now.') Then the person in possession (defendant) shall be required to state the circumstances of his ownership and its source. He (the defendant) may discharge the burden on him either by subscribing to an oath or by other forms of proof such as calling witnesses as well, thus:

---

15 Bahjah Vol. 1 p. 264- 265

a) If the claim of ownership is in connection with moveable property such as grains, animals, farm produce, etc., oath is required as most preferred proof; but

b) if this claim of ownership is in connection with immovable properties, such as house or farmland, oath is not necessary. Therefore proof by means of calling two credible witnesses should be most preferred because there can be no secrecy in the disposal of real property (house, farmland, shops, etc.).

If oath is apparent in the circumstances it is better administered on the person in possession before *"Izar"* (اعذار) final allocutus and before judgment or after *Izar* (اعذار) allocutus before judgment.[16]

Where the property is immovable such as house, farmland, shop or anything attached to land, oath shall not be required to prove his ownership but where the property is moveable such as grains, animals or similar properties before *"Izar"* allocutus or any further explanation by the person in possession, the claimant shall swear to an oath of *Istihqaq* after evidence by two credible witnesses who shall state that the property is his own, he did not sell it nor give it out as a gift and he has never under whatever circumstances parted with ownership legally and that he is still the owner.

The procedure where property is in possession of a third party

Where a property is found with a person and another person claims the property and calls two credible witnesses to prove his ownership of the property and still the person in whose possession it is found did not resist the claim or show that he has no reason for being in possession of the property which will over weigh the evidence adduced by the claimant, he in whose possession the property is shall be required to collect back his money from whosoever sold it to him. But if he raises any objection or argues otherwise or shows he has reasons or grounds that will outweigh the earlier evidence, the judge is required to allow him time/adjournment to enable him prove his right over the property. If he does provide proof that is accepted he shall be allowed to keep his property.

If the period of adjournment lapses/expires and he is unable to furnish ground or proof of right of ownership or he provides proof but which did not favour him, the property shall be confiscated from him and returned to the claimant and he shall lose his right to collect back his money from whosoever sold it to him because he showed a resistance and challenged the witnesses called by the claimant to show that the property is not his.

---

[16] Ihkam Al-Ahkam p. 265

If *Musa* claims that the immovable (house) occupied by '*Dauda*' is his and urges the judge to attach the house until he finds two reliable/credible witnesses to prove his claim or title , he shall not be granted the attachment until he furnished good and convincing reason such as: providing for two credible witnesses who testified for him before *"Izar"* final submissions and judgment or he secured only one male credible witness and was yet to furnish the second witness or finds two male witnesses who are subject to purgation but have not been screened.

If however, the subject of dispute is moveable such as animal or cloth the judge shall attach it and place it in the hand of any trust worthy person if the claimant states that he intends to call witnesses that are not too distant away.

Any such subject of dispute which is moveable such as animals grains, clothes as against house, farmland in respect of which evidence is to be given must be produced in court, this is to enable witnesses identify them.

Further any such subject of dispute which is immovable such as house or farmland in respect of which evidence is given, the judge shall proceed with the proceeding if he is satisfied with the evidence before him he may not necessarily visit/inspect the locus in-quo personally.

It shall be enough if he directs any trust worthy person to do so, on his behalf, and take the boundaries of the property or deliver the property to any successful party. These shall be in the presence of witnesses.

It is preferred if the judge appoints two persons to do so on his behalf where the boundary of the property is disputed by litigants, where no dispute exists as to the boundaries there shall be no need to send a representative of his to deliver the property to any successful litigant.

Gifts, arms and endowments cannot legally be valid unless "*hauzi*" (physical possession) is established over it. Where however, before physical possession is established the death of the giver or endower occurs, the property given reverts back to the estate of the deceased.[17]

"A" claims a land which has been in possession of "B" or that the land belonged to his late father and calls two credible witnesses who gave evidence to the effect that they know that the land is "A's" land or that it belonged to 'A's" late father but that they do not know the boundaries. "A" can also call another set of two witnesses who will give evidence as to the boundaries. The two sets of witnesses could be used in a proceeding and are both admissible if they satisfy the required conditions.

Further the two sets of witnesses could be used if the disputed place is a very popular and well known place identifiable to "A" or his late father or grandfather

---

[17] Thamaradni Fi Taribil Ma'ani Shorhi Resalat Ibn Abi Zaidi Al-Qirwani

the court may proceed on its investigation and there upon appoint two of "A"s representatives in addition to the testimony of the two witnesses to entitlement and two witnesses to boundaries and prescription and decide on the case without calling on the claimant to swear to an oath since the claim is about the entitlement (استحقاق) *istihqaq*.[18]

The procedure where the claim is of measurable items

A buyer who pays for say, grain or wheat or anything which is measured and somebody else comes to claim *one-third* of the items, claiming that its his own, and establishes his claim by two credible witnesses and the judge confirms in his judgment that such belonged to the claimant, the buyer has two options, either to accept the remnant after *one-third* is deducted as what he has paid for or returns the remnant to the owner and collect his money. But if the item is less than *one-third* he may retain the remnant and claim the money due for the balance.[19]

The procedure where the claim is of valuables

If the subject of purchase is one that can be valued such as cows, horses or clothes and a buyer buys five cows or clothes for ₦5,000 and the seller agreed to the sale, suddenly a third person comes and claims entitlement, i.e. that the biggest of the cows or the most beautiful cloth is his own and he establishes the claim by two credible witnesses upon which court rules in the favour of the third party, the sale shall be revoked and set aside even if both the seller and the buyer agree to continue the sale without one of the cows or cloth because it will be difficult to ascertain the value of the one claimed from the rest. But if the claim by (استحقاق) "*Istihqaq*" is not as good as the others a value shall be made of that and the difference paid to the buyer.

The Procedure Where the Claim is on a Divisible Property

A buyer of a property which is divisible who pays for (e.g., a piece of land) and after payment to the seller another person who claims entitlement (استحقاق) claimed *one-third* or *j* of the land and established his claim with credible witnesses and the judge enters judgment in his favour, the buyer is entitled to the portion of the house cut off from the main land and the money due in respect of the portion cut off, whether the land is for rent or personal use.[20]

---

[18] Ibid.
[19] Ibid.
[20] Ibid.

Where the Claim is a small Sized Property

If however the house or land is small in size and may not be conveniently divided or shared and someone lays claims of *Istihqaq*(استحقاق) entitlement the buyer shall have the option of either to return the house and collect the money due, for the claimed part on its face value or claim his money, etc.[21]

Recovery of Damages arising out of *Istihqaq*

There are *five* instances where damages are not recoverable in claim of *Istihqaq*:

1. any *Istihqaq* claim where a person is in possession of a house and lived with an animal which he used or a machine which he used for farm projects suddenly someone came to claim that such thing is his and establish his entitlement with *two* credible witnesses and judgment is entered against him for the return or vacation of the house or animal. He shall not be required to pay rent or pay any money for the use of the animal or machine;

2. where a purchase is made of a car, house and the sale was declared illegal or void for reasons of illegality in the transaction and thus nullified by the court, the buyer shall not after returning the subject pay any damages for the use of the car or, etc.;

3. where a person buys something such as animal or car after claiming the subject and made use of it and discovers a serious defect or fault which could vitiate the sale, upon return of the subject matter he shall not be required to pay for the period he used the subject;

4. where a person buys a cloth or a bicycle to be paid later, while using the subject matter and before payment and the subject matter is attached along with his other properties through a court order and the seller lodges a claim on his properties and court granted him discharge of attachment over the properties, the buyer shall not be required to pay for the use of the property;

5. also where a person buys a portion of a property from another while he is using it, a third person claims right of pre-emption over the property and succeeds the buyer shall not be made to pay anything for using the said portion.

Proof of Ownership of Deceased's Property

In a case of distribution of estate of deceased under Islamic law, the practice requires that certain facts must be proved:

---

[21] Ibid.

i)   proof that a person whose estate is about to be distributed died in fact and in law;

ii) that the estates he left behind were his during his life time;

iii) that the beneficiaries are his *bona fide* heirs.

A judge shall ensure in any case seeking the distribution of the estate of a deceased person that witnesses are called to establish ownership of the estate to the deceased and that he owned the estate until the time of his death and shall also ensure that witnesses are called to establish relationship between the deceased and his alleged heirs so as to ascertain those with specific shares and those to inherit the residue.

Proof of ownership and prescription (physical occupation) can both be made by two separate sets of witnesses, a set giving evidence about ownership and another set about possession (occupation) and boundaries of the property. At this stage the trial judge is required to make a ruling rather than enter a judgment, as it is only at this stage the actual distribution from which most disputes arise, commences.

Chapter 16

Partition of Hereditament

Partition (*Al-Qismat* or *Tamlikah*), applies to joint property in partnership and to the distribution of inheritance. It primarily distinguishes the rights of one person from that of another. In other words, it is an exchange, i.e. the share or portion which falls to one of the heirs as a result of partition is partly his original rights while part of it is the right of other heir.

Distribution of inheritance is not restricted to the courts. It could be extra-judicial. Whenever its extra-judicial a person to be appointed to distribute the hereditament must be a man of high integrity and justice and must be an expert in the field and must possess particular knowledge on the business of distribution.

Where however, a court is approached by the heirs of any deceased by such a request, it is fundamental that certain legal stipulations be complied with before partition should be made. The courts must establish the following:

a) the death of the person to be inherited must be in fact and in law;
b) whether the heirs are truly his biological children (siblings);
c) whether the items/properties which are subject of distribution are indeed legally the belongings of the deceased;
d) whether the items are indeed present in law and in fact or are not present at all and no one hears of it at all or is present but no one knows its whereabouts.

Partition is permitted on all items that are similar, i.e. of the same species such as animals only; and dissimilar items such as household goods and animals and on moveable and immovables. If the estate comprises of buildings/house and pieces of land, each should be shared subject to its value; and mixing houses and lands is not permitted because they are of different species, said *Ibn Rushd*. Where the items are similar, partition can be made in the absence of one or more of the heirs because each of the heirs can lawfully take his share and enjoy the use of his own portion solely without anyone being able to interfere with his property.

Where on the contrary, a joint property consists of items like articles of different species, it is required that all the heirs give their express consent before partition can fully be made by the court as it cannot be made equitably otherwise, partition cannot be permitted.

It is lawful for several heirs to agree among themselves for partition of their joint property. But if there is an infant among them, it is required that the court act as his guardian or it appoints a guardian to look after and over see his interests.

If the estate which is subject of litigation, is scanty such that if distributed it will separately be of no use, the judge must not order partition unless both heirs acquiescent. For partition is legal only if it benefits the beneficiaries but if by partition that cannot be realized, it should be avoided except the parties give their consents.

It is required for a person undertaking partition, to draw up on a paper a plan of the things which he divides so that it remains a record for him and for the court/judge.

A partition of a house and a piece of land is required to be made separately, i.e. house separate and piece of land separate for it is only by ascertaining the value that justice and equality can be observed.

If two or more heirs are inevitably joined and allotted a share of a property which cannot conveniently be divided among them such as a house or a horse, whence its division will render it not useful while one of the beneficiaries insisted on the subject matter being sold for them to share the proceeds, the law is that he should not be listened to therefore, he should be paid off his share so that the rest of the heirs remain with the property, except doing so will occasion miscarriage of justice.

Where all the heirs are joined in a property which is indivisible and all of them concur on the need to sell the property and proceeds shared to them, a judge shall order for the auction of the same (where various offers will be received until a final offer is made, or at the point of the fall of the hammer if no additional offer that is above the final offer is received, the judge shall direct any of the heirs who has the ability and means to add some amount above the final offer so that he acquires the property). Unless no one is able to pay for the property, it shall not be sold to an outsider.

If the heirs/beneficiaries object to an auction, the judge shall direct a valuer to value the property and thereafter order any of the heirs who might be interested in the acquisition of the property to pay.

If again the heirs further object to any valuation by a valuer, the judge shall make a mandatory order of sale insofar as the property is not divisible and sums realized shared to them.

Where an estate of the deceased is distributed among his three or more heirs and subsequently a third party appears with a claim of one-third ($\frac{1}{3}$) or more against the shares of either of the heirs and proffered credible evidence in support of his claim such that the judge found in his favour and returned to the claimant his property. The judge may on demand by the heir recall all the shares of the other heirs for redistribution or may order other heirs to return to the heir the value of the shares taken from him.

If however, the share claimed is one-quarter $(\frac{1}{4})$ or anything lesser, the distribution shall not be disturbed but his co-heirs shall pay him the value of what is claimed against the estate.

If however what was claimed by the third party amounted to half of the total estate, the whole distribution must be set aside to allow for the redistribution of what is left.

Where an estate is to be shared between or among two, three or more heirs and the estate is such that cannot be divided or if divided it would lose its value and any of the heirs calls for its sale for the proceeds shared to them, the judge should not permit that, he may order the sale of what could be the heir's share to any of his co-heirs.

(a) where the estate is a house or farmland which is used by some of the heirs excluding others the judge may order for the sale of the property and the proceeds shared to all the heirs; or

(b) where the estate which is indivisible is on lease and bears income the judge should preserve it and whatever is generated in terms of rent be shared to the heirs.

Sharia judges in Kano have for the purposes of attaining and doing justice to the heirs devised a means by which indivisible estate can be distributed per stripe, i.e. shared according to the number of deceased wives and sibling of each wife. This indeed has reduced to the barest minimum disputes that arise from such situation.

A duly distributed estate may be set aside or recalled if any of five things happens after such distribution:

1. if defect is detected in the property allocated to one or more of the heirs;

2. a third party claim of entitlement is made subsequent to the distribution and allocation of the property to the heirs;

3. a claim by a creditor against the estate of the deceased after it has been distributed and shared among the heirs;

4. sudden appearance of another heir who claims that he was entitled to inherit from the estate but was omitted or left out; or

5. existence of a will at the time of distribution but was not brought to the attention of the heirs or court until distribution was concluded.

Under these circumstances, distribution must be set aside unless other heirs are ready to make some promises in favour of settling the heir that might have been affected.

If there is a dispute concerning road by heirs where a party desires that the road should be maintained as it were for the common usage while others demand that it should be part of the estate and be shared among the properties provided it is practical so to do, the judge must divide the road otherwise he should not.

Whoever is allocated a share of an estate, whether such allotment is as a result of ballot or agreement of all the beneficiaries and takes his share and appropriates the same for a period spanning one year and afterwards seeks from the judge to set aside the distribution on ground of being short-changed in the distribution of the estate, he shall not be listened to for that amounts to transgression.

Whoever alleges that an estate in which he was entitled had been conclusively distributed among the heirs and a section of the family claims each of the heirs took what he needed and distribution has not. The one alleging conclusiveness should be called upon to prove his claim. If he proves that, the judge shall direct him to keep the portion in his possession but if he fails to prove his claim, the distribution shall be rescinded and redistributed among them again.

Where the estate to be distributed involves ornaments such as gold, diamond or bronze, which are not distributable in sharia, either of the following procedure are pertinent:

(i) either the weight of either the gold, diamond or bronze is taken and shared among the heirs in accordance with the weight; or
(ii) the value of either the gold, diamond or bronze is made wherein one heir takes the ornament and the other takes the value.

In all cases where a professional has to be employed for the valuation of property of inheritance his professional fees shall be borne by the estate.

PART II
The process of distribution of estates immovable and movable

The process of distribution of estate immoveable (houses or farmlands) and movables (clothes, animals, and food items) and indeed any property which is ordinary divisible can be of the following forms:

a) distribution by ballot;
b) distribution by consensus and agreement as 60 equality, value and delivery;
c) distribution by consensus and acceptance with no emphasis on equality, value and delivery.

The first is explained by Ibn Asimi thus:

ثلاث القسمة فـــــــي الاصـــــول   وغير ها تجـــوز مع تفـــصيـــل

قسمــــــة الــــــقرعــــة بـالتقـويم   تسوغ فـي تـــماثل الـمعسوم

ومـــن ابــــن القسم بــــها فيجبر   وجمع حظين بهــا مستـــكر

وكذالك في اختلاف الاجناس   وفي مكيل وموزن المنع إقتفى

ولايـــــزيـــــد بعضهم شـــــناولا   يزادفـــــي حــــظ لكي يعدلا.

Distribution by ballot

Distribution by ballot is applicable on immoveable properties and movables alike, whose values and similarities are the same, or the values though not the same but are close in value. Where the values and similarity are the same there will be no need for valuation. Need for further valuation will arise only if the values are merely close, in such circumstance a professional valuer should be appointed to carry out valuation before balloting could commence.

Any distributable property whose value appear completely different from major properties should be kept aside or kept out of other properties, the heirs should be advised to agree among themselves on how they would want the property shared. If however they fail to agree the court shall order for the sale and sum realized shared to them.

It is required that immoveable such as houses could be shared by means of ballot so also are farmlands and movables animals such as cows, etc., each of the properties should be balloted on separately because they are not of the same species.

Should any of the heirs suggest distribution of estate by ballot which property is in the ballotable category and other heirs oppose such suggestion. The judge is enjoined to compel all to accept balloting.

The shares of two heirs in distribution by ballot are not to be considered as one unit unless the distribution is between a heir with specific share and residuary male heirs. For example a deceased person living only one biological daughter and three (3) residuary male heirs (who are not his biological heirs) in this case balloting could be applied for a daughter whose specific share is $\frac{1}{2}$ (half) and three residuary male heirs who are edited is $\frac{1}{2}$ (half) wherein the daughter could pick her separate share and remaining half which is the residue could go to the males.

Balloting is not applicable on items which are not of the species such as animals, and clothing, placing the two on the same category for the purpose of balloting as well as placing cows and horses on the same category, i.e. to say the value of this horse is this and the value of these clothes is this and balloting is applied in their distribution is not allowed.

Balloting is no allowed on any item that could be measured either by measure and scale or countable such as eggs except they are of the same species and values.

It is not permitted for the organizers of the ballot whether within or outside the court to add any thing to another. For example balloting on two houses one has a value of ₦500.000 and the other has a value of ₦400.000 that whoever wins one of high value would pay the difference to the other with less value.

It is also not permitted in balloting between heirs on two properties which are not of the same value. Where one is valued at ₦1,000,000 and the other ₦900.00 and ₦100.00 cash is added to the one below in value then they are asked to go for balloting.

Balloting is permitted by law and a judge is enjoined to enforce it because its application settles dispute permanently. If thus a section of heirs demand for balloting and a section oppose it, a trial judge is enjoined to make an order in favour of those who demand for its application.

Distribution by consensus

Distribution by consensus and agreement as to quality, value and delivery, is elaborated thus:

لكل مع التعديـل والتقويـم   وقسمةالوفاق والتسليـــــم

وتشمل المسوم كلا مطلقا   وجمع لحظين بـها لايتقى

Distribution based on the consensus and delivery and equality of the distributable item is permissible offer valuation and equal allotment to the heirs while each of the beneficiaries is willing to accept delivery of his share without objection.

It is permitted in his type of distribution to join together two beneficiaries in one share so also are two different types of distinctly different species can be merged in share, e.g. one heir accepts a camel for ₦1000 and another heir takes a cow for ₦1000 or takes five bags of maize at ₦500 while the other accept millet for ₦500.

All properties can be shared on the bases of consensus provided they are properties which are equal in value but if one is higher then the other in value it is not allowed - for example, half a bag of rice to a full bag of corn or maize or corn to be delivered in days to come.

Distribution by consensus is applicable on all cases of heirs, male, female, young, old, orphan or idiot who is under strict care of some else provided such distribution shall be for his benefit.

Whenever, a distribution by consensus is between young ones and their elder brothers under whose custody the young ones are, it is required that distribution by consensus must be carried out by a judge not otherwise. Where, however it was carried out by other person other than a judge, the judge before whom is reported shall annul the distribution forthwith.

Under distribution by consensus it is permitted for one heir to add some money to the other heir if his share of estate is not equal to his in value, e.g. one heir gets a house worth ₦50,000 while his co-heir gets a house worth ₦49,000. It is allowed for the heir with ₦50,000 worth to pay to the one with ₦49,000, 1,000 instantly the difference or seek to pay the difference in a later day. But if any one objects to the payment on a later day his objection will be sustained.

Under distribution by consensus, if a heir complains that he has been short-changed and he did so timorously, his complaint should be considered and the property be revalued and shared to them equality.

Distribution by consent and approval
Distribution by consent and approval with no emphasis on equality, value and delivery:

وقسمة الرضا والإتفاق   من غير تعديل على الإطلاق

كقسمة التعديل والتراضي   فيماعدا الغبن من الإعتراضي

Distribution by consents and approval negates the distribution by consensus only by the absence of the emphasis for equality. The requirement of both consent and consensus are there, but no emphasis on equality or proportional distribution. Complaint by either of the consenting parties cannot be entertained.

Ibn Qasim said, he is informed by the people of knowledge…and I also see it as the saying of Malik, that:

"If a man dies and leaves houses and his heirs live in one out of his houses, and are so identified by people and all the family look up to that house as a family house, that house must be shared among the residuary heirs such that each heir would take his share from it. But if the house left by the dead is not one that is lived in by the heirs, all the houses should be taken inventory of and shared among the heirs so that each heir takes his."[1]

---

[1] Mawahibul Jalil fi Sharhul Mkhtasar Khalil; MJ 5, pg 338

Chapter 17

Izar (Pre-Judgement Plea)

PART I
Introduction

"*Izar*" is a pre judgment plea which enables the parties to a case a final opportunity to go over their respective claims or ventilate their grounds before judgment. It is synonymous to allocutus under criminal justice system of Common Law.

The procedure is that the judge shall ask each of the parties or litigants thus:

"Do you have any more grounds or evidence to give?"

هل بقيت لك حجة تدفع بها ماثبت عليك

The plea shall be sought for and supported by two credible witnesses before the judge proceeds to judgment. The procedure is therefore condition precedent to judgment. Where a proceeding of a court is lacking of this fundamental procedure, the judgment is a nullity and liable to be set aside. In *Nasiru Alhaji Muhammadu* v. *Haruna Muhammadu & 1 other*, the Court of Appeal had this to say:

"The principle of *Al-Izar* in Islamic law is like allocutus in English criminal justice which must be conducted before an accused person is sentenced before and or conviction. "*Al-Izar*" in Islamic law goes beyond that. It is so fundamental that failure of the court to apply it at an appropriate time would make the decision of that court a nullity. It must be applied clearly before the decision or judgment. It enables each party to go over or ventilate its own case so that no party should say in future that he was not allowed to present his case by the court."[1]

The requirement of "*Izar*" does not let in defence witnesses in a case but only enjoins the court to make sure that the plaintiff has proved his case on all

---

[1] (2001) 6 NWLR (Pt. 708) 104

relevant issues.[2] It is the necessary requirement in Islamic law that before giving final judgment a judge is required by law to give a final chance to the defendant to state whether he has any defence that will prevent the judge from passing judgment against him; this is known as "*Al-Izar*" which is contained in Ihkam Ahkam, page 21.

> "Before giving judgment a judge must establish the exhausting of any possible defence (*Al-Izar*) by two unimpeachable witnesses that is the chosen course."

وقبل حكم يثبت الإعذار   بشاهدى عدل وذا المختار

Whenever the plea is taken and anyone of the litigants responds that he has something more to say or proof to adduce, the court shall permit him to call additional witnesses, and shall ask the parties the same question after hearing the additional proofs or grounds before his judgment. In *Wangara* v. *Tsamiyar Kara*,[3] it was held that:

> "Under Islamic law procedure, the trial court must apply the principles of *Al-Izar* throughout where the witness testifies in favour of either the plaintiff or defendant as the case may be, the court must allow a form of cross examination of the witness to take place or else the whole proceedings will be a nullity."

Sometimes to be on the safer side the court would put some questions to such witness to make sure that the principle of *Al-Izar* had been complied with, thus after the witness had given his testimony, the judge will call on the opposing party saying:

> "Have you heard the testimony of the witness? Do you have any question for him by way of impeachment whatsoever? This is not all, as part of the in built mechanism to actualize the principle of fair hearing and to ensure that opportunity for fair hearing had been given actually to all the parties, the court will at the conclusion of trial and before adjournment for judgment ask whether the parties (i.e. the plaintiff and defendant) have finished calling witnesses or either party has any witness to call, or say anything before judgment is delivered. At this period either party has the right to say what he wants to say or call any witnesses to say on his behalf.

---

[2] *Chamberlain* v. *Abdullahi Danfulani* K/57A/75
[3] SLR P. 168

This satisfied the principle of *Audi Ateram Partem* and the Constitutional provision."

Muntaka Coomassie, JCA put it succinctly thus:

"I must say without mincing words that it is wrong for any court to condemn a party unheard. Both common law and sharia law respects the principles of hearing the other party. It was clearly stated in so many words that *Al-Izar* must be announced before the decision. The judge must ask the party whether he has anything more to say before judgment is entered against him or that whether he had more witnesses to call. If *Al-Izar* was not done or done after the decision the whole proceeding becomes a nullity."[4]

It is to be noted also that this requirement of *Al-Izar* is akin to allocutus in criminal justice. The main purpose however is to make sure a party has not been condemned unheard.

Also, in *Suleiman* v. *Isyaku & 6 Ors*, it was held, per Wali, JSC, thus:

"It is a mandatory principle of Islamic law that no one shall be condemned without being afforded the opportunity of being heard. At the end of the parties' cases, the court shall ask them whether they have anything more to say before the court pronounces its judgment. This is what is called *Al-Izar*, something having similarity with allocutus."

Also, in *Hakimin Boyi Umar* v. *Aisha Bakoshi*,[5] it was emphasized thus:

"*Izar*" is akin to allocutus in criminal trial. In Islamic law, *Izar* is quite necessary. It has to be done at the end of trial and before judgment is delivered. Failure by any court to do so would violate the proceedings and judgment delivered without *Izar* would be null and void."

If the opposing party produces additional ground or witnesses, in response to judges *Izar* and afterwards denies that he was ever asked to proffer additional grounds and the claimant in his part argues that the defendant was given such right by the judge and went further to call two witnesses who established that the

---

[4] (2006) 3 SLR, Pt. I P.
[5] (2006) 3 SLR, Pt. I P.

defendant did respond that he has no more to say or proof to offer, the defendant shall not be allowed to impeach the witnesses.[6]

No witness shall be called upon to witness the witnessing of *Izar* that there were no more pleas to be made since doing so will set in motion claims of reaction thereby lead to endless proceeding, similarly witnesses of Izar shall not be called upon to witness the performance of a person ordered by the Judge to administer an oath on his behalf.[7]

Also witnesses shall not be called to witness that hearsay evidence has been given in the presence of a particular person. Further no witnesses shall be called upon to witness the group of people swearing the *Qasama* Oaths (*Qasama* oaths are the fifty oaths taken to buttress an accusation of murder).[8]

The judge shall not call upon anyone to witness the evidence given by a group of people amongst whom there are men of integrity and men of doubtful characters.

---

[6] (1961-1989) SLRN 150-154
[7] (2006) 3 SLR.
[8] Ihkam Al- Ahkam

Chapter 18

Judgment

PART I
Meaning of Judgment

Judgment is a court's final determination of the rights and obligations of the parties in a case, it includes an equitable decree and any order from which an appeal lies. As under Islamic Law it necessarily affirms or denies, that such a duty or such liability rests upon the person against whom the aid of the law is invoked.[1]

The ingredients which are indispensable for a valid judgment under Sharia and which the absence of any one of them renders the judgment invalid are six in number, namely:

> "The judge, the plaintiff, the defendant, the subject matters in dispute and the applicable law leading to the judgment (Quran or Sunnah, texts or the consensus) and lastly the procedure by which such judgment is attained."[2]

يعنى أن أجزاء حقيقة التى لأ يتم الحكم الأ بجميعها و يختل بفقدواحد منها وهى كما قال بعضهم ستة القاضى و المدعى والمدعليه والمدعى فيه والمقضى به من كتابا اوسنة اواجماع بالنسبة للمجتهد...وسادسها كيفية القضاء

Under the Islamic law of procedure, judgment is fundamentally rested on clarity and the understanding of the intricacy in the dispute and secondly on the facts, evidence or oath proffered before the judge. Tuhfa Hukami, of IBN Asimi provides.

> "It is not lawful for the judge to pass a judgment if the nature of the case is not very clear to him'....It is unanimously agreed by jurists that a judge should base his judgment upon what he learnt from the evidence of witnesses..." Imam Malik strictly forbids giving judgments not based upon the evidence of witnesses."

و ليس با لجـــا عز لللـقا ضـــي اذا   لم يبد و جه ا لحكم ان ينف

---

[1] Henry Campbell Black, in a treatise on the law of judgment 2nd Edition, 1902
[2] Ihkam Al-Ahkam, p. 8

وفــى   وفى الشهود يحكم القا ضى بمـــا   يعـلم مـــنهم بــا تفـا ق الـعلـــما

ســـوا هم ما لك قد شـــددا   فـى مـــنـــع حكـمه بغير الشهدا

The rule thus is that the judge shall not give verdict on any matter before him without listening to the entire claim and proof *"wala Yahkumu Hatta Yasma'a Tammul Da'awa Wal Bayyinah."*[3]

ولايحكم حتى يسمع تمام الدعوى والبينة

In determining the nature of a claim in an action in an Area or Customary Court, to avoid undue technicality it is always necessary to look at the totality of the evidence adduced in the proceedings in the Area or Sharia court in order to discover the precise nature and subject mater of the controversy between the parties.[4]

Importance of Evidence to Judgment

"A judge shall on no account rely on facts within his personal knowledge and base his judgment thereon. It is mandatory that judgment must be based on proof proffered before him by witnesses and inferences drawn therefrom."[5] It is trite law that the trial court must decide a case on legal evidence adduced and where it fails to follow this course, an Appeal Court will interfere. *Tuhfat Al-Hukkam*, simply put it that "The jurists are in concurrence that a judge should base his judgment upon what he learnt from the witnesses." On more elaborate note, the commentary on this principle, as on page 14 of Ihkam Al-Ahkam states inter alia; "Imam Maliki, strongly prohibited him (the judge) from basing his judgment upon facts which are not supported by evidence even if such facts took place in his court."[6]

> "In all judicial matters, the judge must endeavour to obtain evidence and consequently to be guided of witnesses, rather than on what he has learnt in court as to the matter under consideration."[7]

The judge is however allowed to decide on moral worth of the witnesses, either from what he knows of them personally or through certifying witnesses personally known to him. Maliki School insists that the judgment must be guided by evidence or confessions or admission only, or in exceptional cases, by the oath of one of the parties. He must even admit the evidence of an *Honourable* witness

---

[3] Irshadul Salik Vol. 111 p. 119-120

[4] *Ajagunjeun* v. *Osho* (1977)5 SC 89 at 103

[5] Ihkam Al-AHKAM p. 13

[6] Ihkam Ahkam p. 13

[7] *Alashe* v. *Ilu* (1964) 1 All NLR 290

when he knows it not to be true and must not accept the evidence of a witness who is not honourable even when he knows it to be true.[8]

Should a credible or two credible witnesses testify for the proof of something which is subject of proof and the testimony turned out to be contrary to the proof a trial judge personally possesses about the case he shall disqualify himself and terminate the case and direct the plaintiff to another court or judge with co-ordinate jurisdiction within the same territory or outside, to afford himself the opportunity to testify to the truth of the facts as he possesses it.[9] In any case it is not for the judge to assure the triumph of truth or justice.

If a witness whose testimony though inadmissible judicially because it does not satisfy the requirements of the law, testifies to the truth of an act which, to the personal knowledge of a judge, is correct, he (judge) shall not admit the testimony in view of the fact that the testimony is also within his personal knowledge. He should therefore reject it.[10] In case of what actually occurred in court in the presence of the judge, he can decide without hearing evidence. This is the opinion of *Sahun*.

Judgment to be After Hearing Parties

In Aqrabul Masalik, Vol. iv page 18-19, the author postulated the procedure, thus:

"The plaintiff makes the statement of claim in respect of definite matter...then the court turns to the defendant. If he admits, the judge calls witnesses to his admission. But if he denies the claim, the court turns to the plaintiff for proof. If he produces evidence the court then turns to the defendant if he has any reason why the judgment shall not be against him."

Further Abubakar B. Hassan El-Kastinawy concluded that

"the judge shall not give verdict on any matter before him without listening to the entire claim and proof. He then asks the defendant to put up his defence. That is to say a Judge shall not give judgment against any party until he hears the full claim from the plaintiff, when he finishes, the judge turns to the defendant for whatever he wants to say about the allegations levelled against him. If he admits it as made by the plaintiff, there is no problem. But if he denies the onus of proof is placed on the plaintiff."[11]

[8] *Maliki Law*, by Ruxton p. 289
[9] *Kausani* v. *Kausani* CA/K/199/3/94
[10] Ibid
[11] Irshadul Saliki, Vol. 111, p. 199- 120

The consequence of this all important requirement of judgment is that the practice of raising preliminary objection with or without notice does not find ready accommodation in Islamic law. Everything a defendant or respondent has to say shall wait until the complainant puts up his claim and proof succinctly before the court, the defendant or respondent then has the whole right to react at the end of the statement of claim and proof by the plaintiff. Further, raising of preliminary objection is by virtue of section 61 of the Area Courts Edict 1976 unknown to the Area Courts, it provides:

"No proceedings in an Area Court, and no summons, warrant, process, order or decree issued or made thereby shall be varied or declared void upon appeal or revision solely by reason of any defect in procedure or want of form but every court or authority established in and for the State and exercising powers of appeal or revision under this law shall decide all matters according to substantial justice without undue regards to technicalities."

PART II
Estopel Per Rem Judicatam

Estopel, is bar which prevents a person from denying or asserting anything that contradicts what he has, in contemplation of law, established to be true. Its elements are: (a) reliance on the acts or representations of another, (b) a deception of that person, and (c) a change of position to the detriment of the person who so relied on the acts or representations.

The doctrine of *res judicata* is that a judgment which decides between the same parties or their privies on the same subject matter by a legally constituted court having jurisdiction is conclusive between the parties and cannot be raised again or litigated upon before another court until such judgment is reversed.

Res Judicata, which is a rule of evidence in English Law, is also known as "Estoppel by record". A defendant could employ the rule by showing by means of a record of judgment that the subject matter in dispute was the same with the earlier question in controversy and that it has been adjudicated upon between the same parties of course by a competent court, as such cannot be litigated upon again.

Some Sharia Court judges, notably Ambali G.K., had decided in *Aremu* v. *Akani*[12] that the principle of *Res Judicata* is unknown and inapplicable in a matter the fact of which is based on the principle of Islamic law. He referred to Ahmed

---

[12] (2002) LRNN 640

Duraid's Commentary on *Aqrabul Masalik,* Vol. iv Page 27 which says, "The verdict of a judge in a matter does not transcend to its kind. Rather, if a suit is repeated/renewed, the judge (if he is *Mujtahid* or an exponent in law) has to look at the same matter or its kind afresh. If the judge belongs to the class of followers of a school "*Muqalhid*" let him repeat the judgment he had given earlier based on the reliable opinion of his school. So it is, even if the matter earlier adjudicated upon is same, for instance, if he annuls a marriage of a woman who contracts herself out in marriage and she repeats same, the matter is open for consideration from the same judge or another judge. The learned Kadi also referred to *Jawahirul Iklil* Vol. ii, page 230 which says if a judge takes a decision in a matter before him and similar matter comes up before him, the former does not transcend the latter. Rather if a similar case to an earlier one decided comes up between the same parties or others, what is stipulated for the same judge or another judge that such repeated matter comes before him is to look into the matter, i.e. (exercise *Ijtihad* on the matter).

Contrary to the decisions in *Aremu* v. *Akani* (*supra*) and in *Shuni* v. *Yarrabi,* on non-applicability of the doctrine in Islamic, the Court of Appeal, per Okunola, JCA, held, *inter alia,* plea of *estoppel per rem judicatam* raised at the trial lower court up to the Sharia Court of Appeal is not strange to Islamic legal system. Referring to the earlier judgment of the court in *Balan Ayye & 1 other* v. *Musa Yar'Adua,*[13] he concluded that

> the rationale for the doctrine is that it is in the public interest that there should be an end to litigation...This multipurpose legal principle common to both the common law and the Islamic law has received the approval of the Supreme Court in a long line of cases, which were considered in our recent judgment...It is necessary at this juncture to point out that the doctrine of *res judicata* applies to both legal cultures, the procedure or method employed by Islamic law differs from that employed by the common law even though the end result seems to be the same, that a case that has been judicially decided cannot be re-litigated again...Thus, the issue of finality of judgment which forms the bases of the doctrine of *res judicata* is common to both the common law and the Islamic law."[14]

It will appear that the principle as produced in the two texts referred to by the learned Grand Kadi is basically hinged on whether the trial judge is in the class of "*Mujtahid*"s or "*Muqallid*". Thus a *Mujtahid* may possess the qualification to reach another decision different to his earlier decision but certainly not

---

[13] (1991) 8 NWLR (Pt. 210) 464
[14] *Shuni* v. *Yar Rabi* (2006) 3 SLR 136

Muqalhid to which most of Nigerian judges belong, as it will appear repetitive and monotonous for a trial Judge who is *Muqalid* to go over and over again the same judgment or try and retry a matter having the same subject matter and parties when appeal system is available. This could also be the situation regarding the invocation of the principles of *functuo officio.*

The rule has its application in Islamic Law under the principle of *Al-Ta'ajiz,* thus a copy of a previous judgment is allowed to be used as estoppel to any future litigation between the same parties on the same issue, except under the following cases:

1. **Endowment** *"Hubs"* - for example, when a property is endowed for a particular use and somebody claims it to be his own but lost his claim for want of evidence. If after the judgment of the court he is able to find evidence in his favour he will be allowed to reopen his case;

2. **Divorce** *"Talaq"* - the example is, when a woman goes to court and claims that her husband divorced her, but could not bring witnesses to prove her claim, which lead to the dismissal of her case as a result she was directed to return to her husband. If afterwards she gets witnesses, her claim can be reopened and heard;

3. **Legitimacy** *"Nasab"* - if a person claims to be the child of somebody but was unable to prove the claim and the court dismissed it on lack of proof. He can reopen his case if he later secures witnesses;

4. **Emancipation** *"Al Itq"* - a slave who claims that his master has freed him, but could not prove the fact after being given time to do so and as a result lost his case and was so adjudged to remain his master's slave, can re-litigate his case whenever he gets a witnesses; and

5. **Pardon for Murder** - a man who committed murder and was found guilty and sentenced to death but before his execution he claims that the family of the victim have pardoned him and was ready to call witnesses in proof of his claim, he can be listened to and heard.

Whether a Judge Can Reverse His Judgment

Generally, the judgment of a court can only be reversed by:

a. a superior court; or
b. the same court; or
c. another court of coordinate jurisdiction with the one that originally pronounced the judgment.

Under Islamic law, a judge can reverse his own judgment *suo motu* under some exceptional circumstances, so also is a judge of the same jurisdiction with the original court in the following circumstances:

1) he discovers that another decision would have been more equitable for example where he has misapplied the law which led to miscarriage of justice;

2) he discovers that he has deviated from his genuine perception of the facts of the case;

3) he discovers that he has applied the principle of another school of thought to the principle applicable in his court.

Review of Judgment by another Court

As to another court reviewing the judgment at the instance of a party who has had judgment delivered against him, the law is that the judgment is conclusive in so far as it is reached with due reference to the text of law on which its relies. No court therefore can re-hear the case for the litigation no longer exists.[15] This is based on the doctrine of a "Well-Judged Judgment". Thus it means that no fresh judgment by another court can be pronounced on any case that has once been judicially decided, unless:

a. it is clear that the judgment was wrongly based;[16]
b. the judge acted without or beyond his jurisdiction;[17]
c. miscarriage of justice is clearly manifest in the judgment.[18]

Section 7 Order 11 of the Sharia Court of Appeal Rules 1960 states:

7 (2)..."The court may re-hear or re-try the case in whole or in part and may;
(g) Do or order to be done anything which the court below has power to do or order."

Section 59 of the Area Courts Edict 1967 also confers power of review, reversal or confirmation of decision of lower courts by appellate court and states:

59(1) Any court exercising appellate jurisdiction in civil matters under the provisions of this law, may in the exercise of that jurisdiction.

---

[15] *Maliki Law*, by Ruxton pp. 286-288
[16] *Kausani* v. *Kausani* (*supra*)
[17] Ibid.
[18] *Balarabe* v. *Balarabe* (2006) 3 SLR 248 per IT. Muhammad

(a)   After rehearing the whole case or not, reverse vary or confirm the decision of the court from which the appeal is brought and may make any such order or exercise any such power as the court of first instance could have made or exercised in such case or as the appeal court shall consider that the justice of the case requires.

The Sharia Court Law 2000, did not provide for a similar provision but only stated in Section 7 thus: "the practice and procedure to be applied in Criminal and Civil matters by the courts shall be in accordance; (a)...(b) the principles of Islamic law and procedure (c) Any codified practice and procedure of courts made by the Grand Kadi pursuant to Section 279 of the Constitution."

The practice and procedure in Islamic law as related in Tabsirat Al-Hukkam; provides: "that a judge can amend, or reverse his earlier judgment where mistakes are apparent" It further states[19] thus:

"Ibn Habib said: Muttarraf informed me and Ibn Majuishun (reporting) from Malik may Allah bless him , and from other learned jurists of Al-Madina, about a judge who delivered judgment but later discovered a decision better than the one earlier delivered and he wants to revert to that better decision, he is free to do so, so long as it is within his jurisdiction. These principles of law was considered and applied by the Court of Appeal."[20]

PART III
Execution or Enforcement of Judgment

An Area or Sharia Court has ancillary powers to enforce any judgment or order made by it by seizure and sale of the property of the judgment debtor or by such other methods of enforcing judgments and orders as may be prescribed by rules of the court.   An Area or Sharia Court shall carry into execution any orders or Decrees of:

a) the Supreme Court;
b) the Court of Appeal;
c) any High Court;
d) any Magistrate Court;
e) the Sharia Court of Appeal;
f) any Area Court or Sharia Court established under or in pursuance of the Law; or

---

[19] Vol. 1, p. 63
[20] *Balarabe Mazadu* v. *Sule A. Garba* (2006)3 SLR 21

g) any other court or tribunal of any other part of the Federal Republic of Nigeria, which may be lawfully directed to them and shall execute all warrants and serve all process issued by any such court and directed to it for execution or service.

Order 18 Rule 2 of the Area Courts (Civil Procedure) Rules 1971 made provision for execution against person and Order 19 against property. The said Order 18 of the Area Courts (Civil Procedure) Rules 1971 provides:

> "On the application of a judgment creditor for the enforcement of any order for the payment of money by the imprisonment of the judgment debtor, the court shall issue a summons calling upon the judgment debtor to appear before the court on a day and at an hour specified in the summons to show cause why he should not be committed to prison."

Order 17 Rule 1 of the Sharia Courts (Civil Procedure) Rules 2000 provide for execution against person while Order 18 made provision against property: Order 17 however made distinction between person with means and person without means: Rule 1 provides thus: "Where execution is against a person with means he shall be ordered to pay the judgment debt there and then or attach his properties, e.g. moveable property" and Rule 2 also provides "where execution is against a person without means, the court shall after due investigation allow him time within which he will pay at the discretion of the court."

Sharia Court of Appeal is also not without such powers of execution or enforcement of judgment, because Section 10 (2) of the Sharia Court of Appeal Law states:

> "For all purposes of and incidental to the hearing and determination of any appeal and the amendment, execution and enforcement of any judgment, order or decision made therein, the court shall have all the powers, authorities and jurisdiction of every Area court of which the judgment, order or decision is the subject of an appeal to the court, and without prejudice to the generality of the foregoing, shall have the powers conferred upon Area Courts exercising appellate jurisdiction under any Area Courts Law."

These are in consonance with the position under the Islamic law as expounded in *Fathul Aliyi Al Maliki*,[21] which provides:

---

[21] Vol. 1, p. 116

"Execution is distinguishable from both finding and judgment. Finding is the first phase. The second phase is judgment and the final which is the third phase is the execution."

Execution; known as '*Tanfeez El-hukum*' means; 'carrying out by means of enforcement one right against the other or taking away something from one and putting it into the hand of another.'

Execution may be carried out by the judge who gave the judgment, and it could be by another judge, stranger to the judgment who might not be within the same jurisdiction with the trial judge but is approached with a request to execute the judgment. There is certainly no difficulty if the trial judge himself is the executing judge but where however, the judgment is to be executed by another judge or at a place outside the jurisdiction of the trial judge, it is required that the trial judge sends a letter to the other judge which must carry an inscription, 'I have given judgment in the case between this and that person.' The said letter must be read in an open court to the hearing of the bearer and the person seeking execution in his favour. This is because a letter from a judge to another is in the nature of evidence. Or as it now obtains, a certified true copy of the record of the proceeding or certificate of judgment duly issued under the hands of the trial judge is sent to the executing judge.

In all respects, injunction as provided for by Order 17, 18 and 19 and enforcement are within the realm of the powers of Area and Sharia courts.

Execution of Criminal Sentence

Section 406 of the Kano State Criminal Procedure (Amendment) Law 2000, which is with utmost similarity with Zamfara and Jigawa States Criminal Procedure Laws provide, in case falling under section 124-134 of the Sharia Penal Code where death sentence or amputation of hand is passed the court shall as soon as possible after passing such sentence send to the Governor through the Attorney General report upon the case together with all the documents(record of proceedings) in respect of the case and the sentence shall not be carried out unless it is confirmed by the Governor, within the period of 90 days. Further, item 48 and 57 of the Constitution of the Federal Republic of Nigeria retained prison, service and execution in a State of the civil and criminal processes and judgments in Exclusive Legislative List to the Constitution. Item 57 particularly provides that:

"Service and execution in a state of the civil and criminal processes, judgment, decrees, orders and other decisions of any court of law outside Nigeria or any court of law in Nigeria other than a court of law established by the House of Assembly of that State."

PART IV
Stay of Execution

Stay of execution is a temporary arrest of a judgment of a court pending the outcome of an appeal. It is known under Islamic law as "*Al-tauqif*". Unlike in English law, the process in Islamic law is employed not only to arrest a judgment pending appeal but also employed to arrest a subject matter of dispute pending judgment.[22]

At any time after an appeal has been lodged until the determination of the appeal the Sharia Court before which appeal may lie, on application of the appellant or on its own motion, order that the execution of the order or judgment appealed against be stayed or suspended. Upper Sharia Court shall have power to stay the proceeding before final judgment in any cause or matter before a Sharia Court upon a motion or oral application by any party in the case where there is apparent miscarriage of justice. When such order of stay is granted the notice of it shall be served on the court below or to the person or authority enjoined to put into execution the lower courts order or judgment. The judgment may be stayed either with or without the appellant furnishing security should the appeal fail.[23]

The Powers of the Court

The power of courts to grant or refuse a stay of execution is discretionary. But the discretion must be exercised judicially and judiciously and not arbitrarily. An application for a stay of execution bears the burden of showing that the grant of stay of execution will not result in the determination of the issue, subject matter of the appeal.[24]

Conditions for Grant of Stay

In a judgment involving money, the terms upon which the court would grant a stay of execution are easier to determine than in other judgments where the *res* is perishable or prone to destruction. The terms are:

(a) Whether compelling the applicant to satisfy the judgment would affect his financial position in such a way that he could not prosecute the appeal;

(b) Whether it would be difficult to secure the refund of the judgment debt and costs from the respondent, if the appeal succeeds, for which purpose the financial ability of the respondent is taken into account.[25] These terms are relevant in English Law much as they are in Islamic Law.

---

[22] See Chapter 3, part III

[23] Order iii, Rule 8, Sharia Court of Appeal Rules

[24] *Fatoyinbo* v. *Osadebe* (2002) FWLR, Pt. 110 1770

[25] *Gov. of Oyo State* v. *Akinyemi* (2003)1 NWLR, (Pt.800)1

Principle for grant or Refusal of Stay of Execution

The principles governing such application under Islamic law of procedures are fundamentally the same with the principle in English Common Law as enumerated here below. Further emphasis is placed on the balancing of the conflicting interests of the two parties with fairness and equity as the applicant must not suffer any injustice while the successful party should not be unduly deprived of the fruits of the judgment in question. Also to be considered, whether to grant or refuse stay under Islamic law, is the nature of the subject matter of dispute, whether perishable or non-perishable objects with the view of doing justice to all. And the outcome of the appeal is not rendered nugatory. In all the circumstances, there must be proof that appeal has been filed and attached to the application before the court considering it.[26] While referring to the ruling of Tabai JCA in *Leaders & Co. Ltd* v. *Adetona*[27] stated:

"The principles for the grant or refusal of a stay of execution are:
1) Unless a judgment is patently illegal or wrong, there is a presumption of its being correct until the contrary is proved and consequently, the courts will not normally deprive the successful litigant of the fruits of his success.
2) A substantial and arguable ground of appeal is a strong circumstance in favour of granting a stay of execution.
3) Poverty or difficulty in paying the judgment debt does not per se constitute special circumstances to warrant granting a stay where however paying the judgment debt would render the appellant/applicant incapable of prosecuting the appeal, a stay should be considered.
4) Where, in the case of monetary judgments, there is strong indication of the judgment creditor's inability to repay the judgment debt in the event of a successful appeal, a stay ought to be granted.
5) Stay of execution is a discretionary relief and its grant or refusal depends by and large on the peculiar circumstances of each case.
6) The court in considering whether or not to grant a stay of execution must exercise that discretion judicially and judiciously depending on the circumstances, of each case. And because no two cases can be identical in facts and circumstances the exercise of discretion in one case cannot be binding precedent for another case."

---

[26] Tabsiratul Hukkam Vol. I p. 172-182
[27] (2003) 2 WRN 33

The Conditions for Grant of Stay under Islamic Law

Order 5 Rule 8 of the Upper Area Court of Appeal rules as well as that of the Upper Sharia Court of Appeal Rules provide that upon receiving a Notice of Appeal the Upper Area or Sharia Court may on application made by the appellant, make any such order as it thinks fit upon "as to a respite of sentence or stay of execution…"

Similar application may be made by the appellant pursuant to order iii rule 8 of the Sharia Court of Appeal Rules. No court grants what it is not prayed for. There must be an application seeking a stay of judgment in his favour before a court can do so. The reasons must however be justiciable and justifiable.

At any time after an appeal has been entered until the determination thereof by the court, the court:

a) may, on the application of the appellant or of its own motion, order that the execution of the order or decision appealed from be suspended with or without security for the eventual performance thereof should the appeal fail; and

b) shall send notices of all such orders to the court below, or to the person or authority empowered to put into execution that court order or decision.

It is instructive that the rule did not state the mode the application will take. It did not state that such an application must be by way of motion on notice as could be supported by an affidavit. It states however, that the record of the judgment to be stayed must at least be attached.

PART V
Recovery of Debt (Bankruptcy proceedings)

Islamic Law laid the procedure for enforcing recovery of judgment debt and categorized debtors into four types:

1) a debtor whose appearance shows affluence/means, i.e. he wears new and beautiful clothes, pays for the services of aids or house maids or recognized to be affluent but has neither houses of his own nor farmlands, or any landed property shall not be allowed any reprieve from paying his debt for his neglect to pay his indebtedness is wickedness, he may be imprisoned. If however he applies for reprieve he shall be entitled to only two to three days within which to pay and then he must furnish a surety. If he request to be allowed to show cause or that he has no means to pay he shall furnish a guarantor "*Dhaminun Wajhi*"

2) a debtor who has landed properties such as houses, farmland, etc., but is not in a position to pay his debt for lack of cash shall be accorded reprieve sufficient enough to sell his property to settle his indebtedness. For if he is not given enough time he might face difficulty;

3) a poor debtor who established his poverty by calling two credible witnesses shall be giving enough reprieve (mandatory) this is in view of the verse of Quran which says: ("*Wa Inkana zu Usratin Fa-naziratun illa Maisaratun*") (If the debtor is in difficulty, grant him time, till it is easy for him to repay.");

4) a person who misappropriates other's money and claims lack of it but did not show that he lost the money to thieves or inferno (fire disaster) shall be punished with imprisonment and beating/lashing continuously until he pays the money. Proof of poverty on his part is not acceptable. If he seeks for a guarantor and could not secure one he shall remain detained until he pays the money.

If the means of a debtor is not known or uncertain and there is the need for his examination so as to ascertain his means, he shall be detained for 15 days if the amount of the debt is not much or is scanty. But if the amount of the debt is of average he shall be detained for 4 months for his thorough examination. In any of these instances, however if he provides a guarantor he shall not be detained.

Garnishee proceeding

If a debtor has a property which is for sale his creditor may seek for it to be sold to pay him his debt.

If however the debtor objects to the sale of the property on a reasonable ground and seeks for a reprieve to a future time, the judge may detain the property as a pledge for the payment of the debt and give him time within which to pay, the judge shall take the interest of both the debtor and the creditor into consideration.

A debtor who refuses to pay his debt even though he is suspected to have the means to do so shall be detained until he pays up or alternatively judgment debt proceeding shall be taken against him after which he shall be required to swear on oath that at present he has no means of paying either known or unknown and that as soon as he becomes solvent he will pay and he shall be discharged.

If he declines to swear but seek to furnish a guarantor just to enable him prove his insolvency he shall not be granted in view of his being suspected of having the means he may therefore be detained to compel him to pay. But if he seeks to furnish a guarantor who will pay the debt on his behalf he shall be allowed adjournment to do so.

A debtor who is confirmed to be solvent but refused to pay his debt subject to the amount involved he shall be detained and may be allowed to remain in jail for live or until he pays.

A debtor who admits his indebtedness and seek for time to pay shall be granted time upon his furnishing a guarantor to pay the debt sum provided his means is not known. If however he fails to bring a guarantor he shall be detained.

But a debtor whose ability to pay his debt is known shall neither be allowed reprieve or time or allowed to furnish a guarantor he shall either pay the debt or be detained.

A debtor who is sued for the sums owed and he claims that he does not have the money at the moment whereas the creditor argues that he has the money to pay his debt, the Debtor shall prove his claim of lack of money by calling two credible witnesses. If the witnesses give evidence that they do not know whether he has hidden money or known money or give evidence that his business has run down and that they are unaware of any other thing he does which could fetch him money after *"Izar"* the debtor shall be required to swear that at the moment he does not have any means (public or hidden) with which he could settle his debt and in addition shall undertake that any moment he gets the money he will pay the debt. His oath shall conform with the statement of the witnesses. If he declines to swear he shall be detained until he pays the debt.

If upon investigation the court confirms that the debtor is bankrupt following interrogation of the witnesses and after *"Izar"* it was established that the debtor has nothing outwardly and inwardly, thereby confirming his insolvency, the court shall declare the debtor bankrupt and issue a declaration to that effect. After such declaration all creditors shall lose their claims against him until such a time his means improves, it is then they can make claim again. This is because the debtor in his oath had stated that he will pay when his means improves.

It shall be part of declaration of the court to order a public announcement on the debtor; that so-so person the son of such person of so-so area in so-so town is hereby declared bankrupt, and whoever transacts any business with him does so at his own risk. This type of declaration had its origin from *Sayyidina Umar Ibnul Khattab.*

The consequences of this declaration is that the state takes responsibility of his daily needs and that of his family.

A debtor whose means is confirmed to be below average shall pay his creditors according to his earning.

A debtor who issued before a court and the creditor alleges that he is capable of paying his indebtedness and the debtor maintains that he does not have but the creditor insisted on a search on his house, some jurists argue that the request for a search should not be entertained others argue that search should be conducted.

Chapter 19

Appeal

PART I
Introduction

Judgment of a judge does not make lawful an already lawful, nor does it prohibit what is already prohibited, this is predicated on the Hadith of the Prophet (PBUH) which says:

> "I am but a human, and you come before me for adjudication of your disputes, perhaps some of you are more eloquent with their argument than the other, if I adjudicate in favour of a person against his brother as a result of his eloquence while the later in reality has the right, then I would only be handing the former a piece of hell, let him not take it."

This Hadith, which was referred to by the Court of Appeal in *Biri* v. *Mairuwa*,[1] while making reference to the Hadith, clearly throws more light on the fallibility of human being to which a judge is no exception. A judge being human is therefore hardly perfect. He is susceptible to mistakes, misinformation and fraudulent misrepresentation, and likely to misapply the law in a matter before him. It is for this reason that Sharia permits a judge who delivers judgment but later discovers a manifestly clear error in his decision to revert to a better decision; in other words, set aside the wrong decision for a better one, so long as it is within his jurisdiction.

A judge is however not permitted to reverse his own final judgment where the error in the judgment does not result to miscarriage of justice, this is in view of the decision of Umar ben-Al-khatab in a case of *inheritance* involving a woman who died living her husband, mother, her parental brothers, her sister and her maternal brothers and Umar lumped them together on the share of one-third ($\frac{1}{3}$) thereupon a man reacting against the decision said to him. In your earlier decisions in so-so years you did not lump them together under one third. Then

---

[1] (1996) 8 NWLR (Pt.467) 425/ Fiqh Sunnah p. 356

Umar replied: "that remains of those judgments then, but this is our judgment today."[2]

This decision by *Umar Ben-Al-Khatab*, is suggestive of the fact that a Judge is not permitted to recall his earlier judgment for the purposes of its reversal even if he discovers that the decision was reached in error, except where miscarriage of justice is occasioned therefrom. He remains *functuo officio* to the decision to avoid setting in chains of reaction.

Umar Ben Al-Khatab, had measured both as the Supreme leader of the Muslim Umma as well as the Supreme Judge with only Quran and *Sunnah* as reference in addition to his application of "*Ijma'a* and exercise of *Ijtihad.* His position was superior to any other judge. The decision whether in error or not can only be reviewed by a team of jurists.

Historically, however, there was no regular court of appeal, but a board for the inspection of grievances. The *Nazrilul-Mazalim* effactually controlled the judiciary.[3] Its function was to set right cases of miscarriage of justice. In Nigerian context only an appellate court can upon a petition or application filed requesting for a review by a party against whom judgment was delivered. Under the Nigerian legal system no lower court is with powers to depart, reverse or review its earlier decision on any cause or matter except the Supreme Court of Nigeria. It is, the only court with such powers pursuant to Order 8 Rule 16 in exceptional circumstances.

Review of Judgment by Jurists
There are circumstances a reversion of judgment may be sought by a party who is not favoured from the authority in view of the fact that the judge is a *"Muqallid"* and not adequately endowed with knowledge of the Sharia his judgment may be subject to re-examination by team of jurists so as to reflect corrections where justice demands for it and same may be reversed.[4]

Ibn Farhun in Tabsiratul Hukkam gives details of the four instances an appeal can be made by a party aggrieved thus:

a. The judgment of a learned and upright judge, which should be dismissed;
b. That of a judge who is neither learned nor just which should be allowed;
c. Appeal grounded on incompetence of the judge for his possible bias for or against a party because of his relationship which should be allowed and finally;

---

[2] Fiqh Sunah, p. 359
[3] Century of the Othman Empire
[4] Tabsiratul Hukkam, Vol. 1, p. 70

d.   The aggrieved party having information, which he did not have during the trial.

Following the principles as stated by Abubakar B. Hassan Al-Katsinawy, in Ashalul Madarik, Kadi Wayya, in *Aisha Haruna* v. *Estate of Late Audu*,[5] held that;

> "If the court gives judgment based on what is not certain, the aggrieved party has the right to challenge it and ask that the verdict be annulled."

Thus where the decision of a court operating Islamic law principles was based on cogent, concrete and unimpeached evidence and the decision was based on known Sharia principles such decision has to be implemented. It is stated in the *Tuhfat*, page 23, thus: "Where (the judge) has arrived at a just decision, there shall be no doubt as to executing it." Ihkamul Ahkami, page 28, the commentary on Tuhfat, states the law further:

> "That a surviving serving judge's (writing) judgment to another judge must be implemented and executed there is no room for set aside."

In Ashalul Madarik vol. 3 p. 203, Al-Katsinawy stated: "It does not permit of a trial judge or any other one for that matter to annul a judgment unless it is clearly contrary or a direct opposite to the law."

In *Kausani & Others* v. *Kausani & 3 Others* (*supra*) per I. T. Muhammad, JSC. while referring to Tabsirat stated:

> "It is permitted for the jurists (appeal judges) to consider (a lower court's decision) where it is clear to them that it was wrongly based, they should reject it. But where it was based in accordance with the laid down procedures it should be affirmed and executed."

Where however the decision of a court operating Islamic law is not in accord with the principle of the law, it may be set aside under the following circumstances:

1.   where it is in conflict with the provision of the Quran
2.   where it is in conflict with the provisions of any authentic tradition of the prophet (PBUH)
3.   where it is in direct conflict with *Ijma'a*.
4.   where it conflicts with *Qiyas*

---

[5] SCA/CV/KN/186/2006

5. where it is against popular view of the official *mazhab* school applicable in the area of jurisdiction or against sound reasoning.
6. where the judge lacks jurisdiction.
7. where it was obtained under fraud, deceit, etc.[6]

Powers of Appellate Courts on Sharia Appeals

Under the Islamic law the trial and the Appellate courts are not restricted to the grounds or issues raised by a party before it. A trial Judge is required to apply whichever is the relevant law applicable to the case before him. On appeal the Appellate court can rehear or retry the case in whole or in part.[7]

> The Sharia court of appeal as an appeal court has the right to amend judgments or orders of the courts inferior to it on appeal, The court may rehear or retry the case in whole or in part and may, do or order to be done anything which the court below has power to do or order.

Ibn Farhun's Tabsiratul Hukkam vol. 1 page 80 says:

> "The fourth class of complainant against a decision from a court is that the aggrieved party comes up with evidence that had not been known (now available to the trial judge) there are three opinions. Ibn Qassim in Al-Mudawanah stated that we listen to his proof. If the evidence warrants nullification of the earlier decision we do."

There are two other opinions: Sahanun disapproved listening to such evidence, while Ibn Mawaz made it a condition that it should have been placed before the trial court to merit being entertained.

To the latter opinion, the Court of Appeal in *Yankatako* v. *Fatima Gwamaja*[8] had decided that according to the provisions of section 59 of Area Courts Edict 1968, the Sharia Court of Appeal has no power to call fresh witnesses who have not been called by the court of first instance. In his words, Maidama, JCA said:

> "Since the judgment of the Sharia Court is solely on the evidence of these two witnesses who were not called before the trial court the judgment of the Sharia Court cannot be allowed to stand."

---

[6] Ihkam Al-Ahkam p. 57
[7] *Ahmadu Sidi* v. *Sha'aban* (1992) 4 NWLR (Pt.113) 117; Rule 7 of Order 11 of the Sharia Court of Appeal, Rules 1960
[8] (1990) 1 ILR 44 at 49 Per Maidama, JCA.

PART II
Appellate Jurisdiction

The courts with jurisdiction to hear appeal on Sharia matters are Upper Area or Sharia Courts, Sharia court of Appeal of a state, Court of Appeal and Supreme Court. Upper Area/Sharia courts, in Nigeria have dual powers both as appellate and first instance courts.[9] Sharia court of Appeal on the other hand has its jurisdiction provided for under section 277 of the 1999 Constitution of the Federal Republic of Nigeria, in addition to such other jurisdiction as may be conferred upon it by the law of the state. Subsection 2 of the section gives to the Sharia court of Appeal jurisdiction and powers limited to issues relating to Islamic Personal Law namely: marriage, divorce, inheritance including matters concerning *waqf* (gift), will or succession, custody and guardianship of children.[10]

While the Upper Area and Sharia Court have jurisdiction to entertain any question of Islamic law, the Sharia Court of Appeal have their jurisdiction confined to the issues of Islamic personal law contained in section 277 (2) of the Constitution. What this connotes therefore is that it is not all Islamic matters determined by the Upper Area/Sharia courts that are subject of the jurisdiction of the Sharia Court of Appeal, the matter which is the subject of appeal must be among those enlisted under section 277(2) of the Constitution, thus once the issue of appeal is title to land *simplicita*, the jurisdiction of the Sharia Court of Appeal is ousted.[11]

The Court of Appeal is only constitutionally competent to hear appeals from the Sharia Court of Appeal with respect to matters involving Islamic personal law only.

PART III
Upper Area and Sharia Courts

Upper Area/Sharia Court of are created by state laws, sections 53(b) of the Area Courts Edict 1971 and section 3 of Sharia Laws of Kano, Sokoto and Zamfara states respectively created Upper Sharia Courts in the state and section 5 conferred on the courts appellate and supervisory jurisdiction over the lower sharia courts.

Upper Sharia Court of Appeal rules 2000 provides that an appeal to Upper Sharia Court shall be commenced by the initiation of appellant or by his authorized representative given the court from which the appeal is brought to the

---

[9] *Ige* v. *Dobi* (1999) 3 NWLR (Pt.596) 550
[10] *Alkali* v. *Alkali* (2002) 1 NWLR (Pt. 748) 543
[11] Ibid

Upper Sharia Court having jurisdiction in the Sharia in which such court is situated, oral notice of appeal or written notice of appeal. The mode of commencing appeal to Upper Sharia Court is different with that of Sharia Court of Appeal (see below). Under Area Court Edict, the Inspector of an Area Court has power to initiate an appeal at the Sharia Court of Appeal on his own motion or upon the application of any person concerned who in his opinion there has been a miscarriage of justice in a case before an Area Court to which he access.[12]

Oral notice of appeal shall be:

a. reduced to writing by the registrar or clerk of the court from which the appeal is brought or the registrar of the Upper Sharia court as the case may be; and

b. signed by the appellant or his authorized representative or if he is unable to write, thumb printed by him and counter signed by the registrar or clerk.

The appeal from the lower Sharia Court to Upper Sharia Court shall be made within 30 days of the decision appealed against. The court bellow and the Upper Sharia Court of Appeal may on sufficient course being shown extend the time.

A person who is not a party in the proceedings before a lower Sharia court may apply to the Upper Sharia Court sitting on appeal to be joined, upon satisfying the court that he has special interest in the matter. The Sharia court from which the appeal is brought shall, within two weeks upon receiving a notice of appeal, cause certified copy of the record of the proceedings to be made and served such notice to the Upper Sharia Court.

Upon receiving a notice of appeal the upper Sharia court may on application made by the appellant make any such order as it thinks fit upon the following:

(a) as to a respite of sentence or stay of   execution;

(b) for the release of the appellant on bail;

(c) for the appellant to file detailed grounds of appeal;

(d) as to a time within which an appellant shall comply with any such orders as may be made.[13]

The court may vary or rescind any such order by subsequent order if doing so is to ensure the justice of the case.

The Upper Sharia Court may allow the appellant to amend his grounds of the appeal at any stage before judgment upon such terms as it think just.

The court may, pursuant to its orders as provided by Order 8, if satisfied that the provisions have not been complied with by the appellant,

(a) extend the time for compliance with the order; or

---

[12] *Adamu* v. *Bashiru* (1997)10 NWLR (Pt.523) 81
[13] Order 8

(b) strike out the appeal and set aside any order as to bail, stay of execution or respite of the sentence.[14]

The court may upon application made within fourteen 14 days by the party against whom the order is made direct the appeal to be entered for hearing on such terms as the court may deem fit and just.

Upon receipt of the records of the proceeding of the lower Sharia court and after due compliance by the appellant with any order made by the court and payment by all appropriate fees the court shall:

a) fix a date for hearing of the appeal;

b) cause notice of the date of hearing and copies of the grounds of appeal to be served on the respondent or respondents; and

c) prepare such copies of the record of the proceedings in the court from which the appeal is brought as may be required by the parties to the appeal upon payment of them of the appropriate fees.

Hearing of Appeal

At the hearing of an appeal, the Upper Sharia Court shall peruse the record of the case in the court below, and begin with whosoever is identified as the appellant direct him to address the court either in person or through his representative in support of his respective case and in the course of any such address may read the whole or any part of the record of the court below and the respondent may reply to the address and submissions of the appellant. The court may where the need arises rehear or retry the case and such re-hearing and retrial shall be in accordance with the Islamic law procedure as is applicable to the court of the first instance. The court shall administer "*Izar*" on either party before proceeding to judgment.

PART IV
Sharia Court of Appeal

It was first established as a Northern regional court of appeal to determine appeals emanating from the decisions of area and upper area courts of appeal in questions of Islamic personal law. It was created by Laws of Northern Nigeria Cap 136; 1960. This creation was further confirmed subsequently by the Constitution of the Federal Republic of Nigeria 1979 and later the Constitution of the Federal republic of Nigeria 1999. Pursuant to section 6(6) of the 1999 Constitution of the F.R.N., the jurisdiction of the court is wholly appellate and all its jurisdiction is limited to issues relating to Islamic personal law namely; marriage, divorce,

---

[14] Order 9

inheritance including matters concerning *waqf*, gift, will or succession custody and guardianship of children.[15]

Commencement of Appeal in the Sharia
An appeal to Sharia Court of Appeal shall be entered within thirty (30) days from the date of the order or decision appealed against[16] when such appeal is brought against an order or decision of the court below, it shall be entered in the registry of the court and the Registrar of the court shall send notice of the appeal to the court below. Within one month of the date of receiving the notice of appeal, the court below shall forward to the Sharia Court of Appeal a certify true copy of the record of the case appealed against.[17]

Every appeal may be entered by either of the following:

a.   in the form of a petition in writing presented by the appellant or some person duly authorized to do so on his behalf, this will include a legal practitioner;
b.   the appellant shall enter his appeal by dictating his prayers to the Registrar or other officer of the court if the court so permits;
c.   the appellant may state his prayer orally to the court.

Every appellant shall when entering his appeal give to the Registrar a postal address to which notices may be sent to him, where however is unable to do so, he shall from time to time call at the registry or send his agents to the court to collect any notices awaiting him or any communication meant for him left at the court registry.[18]

PART V
Enlargement of Time
No appeal shall be brought after the expiration of the time limited by the rule. The prescribed period of appeal is one month calculated from the date of the decision appealed against. After the expiration of the one month limited for the entry of appeal no appeal shall be brought unless the court on the application of the party appealing enlarges the time. Every application for enlargement of time shall be supported by:

a.   An affidavit or affirmation or declaration having in law the effect of an oath setting forth good and substantial reasons for the application, and
b.   Grounds of appeal which *prima facie* shall give cause for leave to be granted.

---

[15] S. 277 Constitution 1999 /*Alkali* v. *Alkali* (*supra*)
[16] Order 111 R. 2
[17] Order 111 R. 4
[18] Order 111 R. 4.

Order VI of the Sharia Court of Appeal is similar to Or 3 R 4 (2) of the Court Appeal Rules. It is discretionary and not mandatory in nature and in considering any application for enlargement of time to appeal, the court should exercise its discretion judicially and judiciously.[19] This rule appears to be the only rule of the Sharia Court of Appeal requiring an affidavit, or affirmation or declaration in support of an application. The form such an affidavit, affirmation or declaration may take is not specified. But if it is an affidavit, it should be in line with the Evidence Act. Section 1 of the Act makes it applicable in Sharia courts.

The two conditions (a) and (b) must be satisfied together at the same time. If one fails, the entire application will fail. The affidavit in support of the application must state clearly the reasons for the delay in complying with the rules of court.

The length of time of delay is immaterial for the grant of an application for extension of time within which to appeal, provided the applicant is able to explain the delay and show good cause why the appeal should be heard. If there is no substantial reason for the delay the court may refuse the application.[20] For the reason adduced for failure to appeal within time to be acceptable as "good and substantial" must affect the applicant in relation to his effort to appeal against the judgment and the burden rests on the applicant to adduce it.[21]

Any application for enlargement of time may be made to the court and when time is enlarged, a copy of the order granting such enlargement shall be annexed to the notice of appeal.[22]

Immediately after the hearing of a successful application for leave to appeal out of time the court may, if it shall think fit and if the parties are ready, proceed at once to the hearing of the appeal.[23]

The appeal is heard at such time and at such place as the registrar of the court notifies the parties after he had caused the transmission of the copy of the record to all parties who shall apply for one, cause the appeal to be set down for hearing, and if the appellant is in custody require the officer in charge of the prison in which the appellant is in his custody to produce him before the court in the day fixed for the hearing.[24]

Non-Appearance of Parties

If the appellant or his representative does not appear on the day fixed for the hearing, the appeal shall be struck out on the application of the Respondent.[25] If

---

[19] *Ibodo* v. *Fnarofia* (1980) 5-7 SC 92
[20] *Ogundimu* v. *Kasunmu* (2006) All FWLR pt.326 209
[21] *Sam-Fam Financiers Ltd* v. *Aina* (2001) FWLR pt. 70 1601
[22] Order 111 R. 4
[23] Order 1V R. 4
[24] Or. viii R. 2
[25] Order 1V R. 1, 2 & 3

both parties or their representatives fail to appear on the day fixed for the hearing, the court may on being satisfied that the parties were duly served with hearing notice strike out the case on its own motion.[26] If the respondent or his representative applies for an adjournment or does not apply for the appeal to be struck out the court may grant an adjournment and if it does so shall give notice to the appellant of the date fixed for the resumption of hearing.[27] If the appellant or his representative fails to appear for the second time, and it is proved to the court that the summons was duly served in time, the court shall strike out the case.

If the appeal is struck out upon the application of the respondent or his representative or struck out for the non appearance of both parties or their representatives, the court may re-list the appeal if within a period not exceeding fifteen days from the date of the striking out on showing reasonable grounds for his non-appearance, the court may summon the respondent and proceed to hear the appeal.

If the respondent or his representative fails to appear on the day fixed for the hearing of the appeal and does not show reasonable grounds for his failure to appear, the court, may after satisfying itself that the summons has been duly served on him, hear the appeal and give judgment in his absence.

If the court is not satisfied that the summons has been duly served on the respondent or if the respondent or his representative satisfies the court that there were reasonable grounds for his failure to appear, the court shall fix another day and shall issue a fresh summons.

If the respondent and his representative in question of maintenance or divorce is absent or their where about are unknown or they are in a place where a summons cannot be served on either of them, the court after satisfying itself as to such facts shall hear the suit and give judgment accordingly.

PART VI
Hearing

At the hearing of the appeal, the court shall peruse the record of the case of the court below as transmitted to it.[28] The parties or their representatives may address the court in support of their respective cases and in the course of any such address may read the whole or any part of the record of the court below and may comment on it. The party who begins shall have a right to reply to the speech or submission of the party or parties opposing him.[29]

---

[26] Order 111 R. 6
[27] Order Viii R. 1, 111
[28] Order VIII R. 3
[29] Order III R. 2

The court shall not normally re-hear or retry the case but if it shall be necessary for the purposes of elucidating or amplifying the record of the court below and arriving at the true facts of the case the court may re-hear or retry the case in whole or in part. The re-hearing or the re-trial shall follow the same process as trial in the lower court shall be conducted. The court in the process may:

a.   allow or require, witnesses to be called whether or not they gave evidence before the court below;
b.   order any reference to be made;
c.   call any document or other exhibit;
d.   inspect any object or place;
e.   call for and examine all original records of the court below;
f.   adjourn the hearing from time to time and place to place;
g.   do or order to be done anything which the court below has power to do or order; and
h.   generally exercise any of the powers conferred upon it by Section 10 of the law.[30]

In the process of hearing an appeal before it, the Sharia Court of Appeal, shall be guided by the guideline the Supreme Court had given, that in claims before Native courts, Area courts or Customary courts, it is necessary to look at the substance, rather than at the form of the writ or claim. The appeal court must not be too strict in regard to matters of procedure. The court must look at the whole proceedings to understand what the parties were fighting for.[31] In the main, the appellate courts are mandated under Islamic Law to look into the whole gamut of a case and see where justice of the case lies irrespective of whatever technicalities that may be involved. It is, therefore, not mandatory nor is it necessary for the courts to rely solely on the grounds of appeal or issues raised therein. The court can go outside the grounds of appeal at any time and at any stage provided there are enough materials upon which a just decision can be reached. Thus, the procedure under Islamic Law is peculiar when compared with the Common Law.[32]

An appeal lies from decisions of the Sharia Court of Appeal to Court of Appeal as of right in accordance with the Acts of the National Assembly and Rules of court in any civil proceedings with respect to question of Islamic Personal Law.[33]

---

[30] Order III R. 3
[31] *Ben Ikpang & 1 Ors* v. *Chief Sam Edoho & 1 Ors* (1978) 6-7 SC. 221 at 238
[32] *Beli* v. *Umar* (2005)12 NWLR (Pt.983)325
[33] *Adamu* v. *Bashir* (1997)10 NWLR (Pt.523)81

The decisions of the Supreme Court and Court of Appeal by virtue of section 287(1) and (2) of the Constitution of the Federal Republic of Nigeria are to be enforced by all courts with subordinate jurisdiction to that of the courts including Sharia Court of Appeal. In the same vein, "where a decision of the Supreme Court or Court of Appeal is in consonance with Islamic Law particularly when it concerns the interpretation of a statutory provision it will be binding on the Sharia Court of Appeal, that court shall not only be guided by it..."[34]

---

[34] *Sa'adatu Mala Baba* v. *Mal. Baba Moh.* (2007) 3 SLR (Pt. iv) 184 at 201

Bibliography

Al-Quran AlKarrem

Al-Tashrihul Aljina'I Fil Islam

Ashahul Madarik by Abubakar Bin Hassan Al-Katsinawy, Darul Fikir.

Black's Laws Dictionary 8th Edition

El-Bahjah Fi Sharhil Tuhfah, by Bin Abdulsalam Al-Tasuli

Fathul aliyyi Al-Maliki

Figh Al-Sunnah, by Sayyid Sabiq

Ihkam Al-Ahkam, A short Commentary of Tuhfatul ahkam by Sheik Muhammad Bin yusuf Al-Kafey published by M. El-Husna - Cairo Egypt.

Jawahirul Ikleel, Sharhu Mukhtasar Sheick Khalil

Khashiyyal Al-Dasuki Alal Sharhul Kabir – by Shamsuddeen M.A. Al-Dasukey.

Law of Judgment, a treatise by Henry Campleel Black, 2nd Edition 1902.

Maliki Law, by F. H. Ruxton, El-Nahar Press, Cairo Egypt

Sirajul Salik, by Al-Sayyid uthman Al-Malakey Darul Fikir Lebanon

Strout's Judicial Dictionary Vol. 4.

Tabsiratul Hukkam – by Ibrahim Bin Muhammad Bin Farhoon Darul Kutub Al-Ilmiyah Beirut, Lebanon

Thamarad-dani Ala Sharhun Risalah of Imam Alkairawani

The Practice of Muslim Family Law in Nigeria by M.A. Ambali - the Grand Kadi of Kwara State.

Tuhfatu Al-Hukkam by Muhammad Bin Muhammad Bin Asimi

Bibliography

Index

www.ingramcontent.com/pod-product-compliance
Lightning Source LLC
Chambersburg PA
CBHW060256220326
41598CB00027B/4119